Emmanuel Jal is a rap artist who has won worldwide acclaim for his unique style of hip hop with its message of peace and reconciliation borne out of his experiences as a child soldier in Sudan. In 2005, he released his first album, *Gua* ('peace' in his native Nuer tongue), and his latest, *War Child*, was released in 2008 and is also the name of a documentary on his life, which won the 2008 Tribeca Film Festival Cadillac Audience Award.

Dedicated to charity work for Africa, he has established a trust, GUA Africa, to build a rehabilitation centre for child soldiers in Sudan. He is an ambassador for Oxfam and also undertakes work for Amnesty International, Save the Children, the Coalition to Stop the Use of Child Soldiers, UNICEF, World Food Programme and Christian Aid.

A boy soldier's story

EMMANUEL JAL

and

MEGAN LLOYD DAVIES

ABACUS

First published in Great Britain in 2009 by Abacus

Copyright © Emmanuel Jal and Megan Lloyd Davies

The moral right of the authors has been asserted.

Lyrics appear courtesy of Emmanuel Jal and C. Outten

A CIP catalogue record for this book
is available from the British Library.

ISBN 978-1-4087-0005-1

Typeset in Sabon by M Rules
Printed and bound in Great Britain by
Clays Ltd, St Ives plc

Papers used by Abacus are natural, renewable and
recyclable products sourced from well-managed forests and certified in
accordance with the rules of the Forest Stewardship Council.

Mixed Sources
Product group from well-managed
forests and other controlled sources
www.fsc.org Cert no. SGS-COC-004081
© 1996 Forest Stewardship Council
FSC

Abacus
An imprint of
Little, Brown Book Group
100 Victoria Embankment
London EC4Y 0DY

An Hachette UK Company
www.hachette.co.uk

www.littlebrown.co.uk

This book is dedicated
to the people of Sudan, and
the Lost Boys and the Lost Girls

Warchild

FOREWORD

I was a child of war, born in a land without books and writing, a land where history was carried on your mother's tongue and in the songs of your village, a land swallowed up by war even as I uttered my first cry. And so, even the date of my birth was lost when my world was lost to me, just as the names of some of the people whose lives were entwined with mine were. I have given them new ones.

Like other Lost Boys of Sudan, I took the birth date of 1 January 1980 as an adult and have used it for the ages contained in this book. I cannot be sure exactly how old I was nor for how long I was in certain places or exactly when. But I can remember pointers: I was so small, my gun was taller than me; I saw the wet and dry seasons many times when I lived in a refugee camp. The exact dates this book contains are those of events I saw written down in history books, but most of the everyday violence of war never makes it into books, and this one is not meant to be a history of a country to be read by scholars. It is the story of one boy, his memories, and what he witnessed.

PROLOGUE

The roar of the crowd fills my ears – like the roar of lions, the roar of a river you know you may plunge into and never escape, the roar of a gun as it sends bullets shrieking through the air. Blood leaps in my veins as I wait in the wings and look out at the audience. Far into the distance, faces are turned towards the stage, and beyond them I can see the hills of Cornwall.

'And now we are pleased to welcome Sudanese rap star Emmanuel Jal to the main stage at Live 8, Eden Project,' a voice booms out.

I step on to the stage and my legs begin to shake as excitement fills me. I can see faces smiling and hands waving in expectation. The crowd is waiting. Fear explodes inside me and my chest tightens just as it always does when my feelings run too strong. I feel sure I will not be able to sing a note. My breath is dying inside me as I stare ahead.

But suddenly time stands still. The lights, the noise, the colours, bleed into nothing and the faces melt away. I am a child again.

'God will look after us,' my mother is whispering as we lie under a bed.

She is holding on to my two brothers, two sisters, and me as we hide from a war being waged outside our hut. In the peaceful village we once knew, rockets blow apart houses with families inside, women are raped, and children are murdered. It is genocide and my people are its victims.

I cling to my mother as the sounds of bullets and screams fill my ears.

'Hush, little makuath,*' she says softly, and I breathe in the smell of milk, which clings to her skin. 'Hush, little darling.'*

I pull closer to her and listen as she speaks again. Beside me my brothers, Miri and Marna, and sisters, Nyakouth and Nyaruach, move closer too.

'One day we will be in a better place,' my mother tells us, and we believe her.

But soon I will come to learn that even a mother's fierce love will not protect me. War will rip her away, convince my father to give up his seven-year-old son, and pull me into its bloody heart as I am given a gun taller than I am and told to fight. I will not be alone. I will be one of thousands they come to call the Lost Boys of Sudan.

Yet I will also be lucky. I will escape hell, survive, and learn how to transform the war still raging inside me long after the battlefields have fallen silent.

Staring up, the stage lights blaze white into my eyes as I move towards the microphone. It is time for me to tell my story using the music and lyrics that are my weapons now I have laid down guns and machetes forever. The crowd calms as I stand still. I think of my mother and the songs we once sang in a village far away. For a moment I speak to her.

'Now we are in a better place,' I say silently.

I start to sing.

CHAPTER 1

My stomach felt empty as the truck crawled along. We'd been travelling since sunrise on a dusty road, and I wanted a taste of the *tahnia* hidden in a box beside me. The sugary paste made of sesame was my favourite to eat with *kisra* bread. I looked down.

'Jal,' my mother said with a smile. 'You must wait until we stop and then we will eat.'

'Yes, Mama,' I replied.

I looked up at the sky. I wished it were night again and the blackness was filled with fat silver stars and the shining moon. Each night when we lay down on the ground beside the truck to sleep, my older sister, Nyakouth, and I would search for pictures above or listen to the stories Mama told us as she fed our younger sister, Nyaruach, and baby brothers, Marna and Miri.

'Tonight we know the fox is on duty in the sky because there are so many stars,' Mama said. 'That's because the stars are like cows – the big fat ones are bulls and the smaller ones are their babies. They are safe when the fox is looking after them because he doesn't eat them.

'But on nights when there are fewer stars in the sky, then we know the hyena is on duty and he has eaten all the cows.'

I looked up at the sky again. I was glad the fox was on duty.

But today there was nothing to see except the sun above and the savanna grass rushing past. We'd left our home a few days before in a convoy of trucks and were going to stay with our grandmother in the south. My aunt Nyagai, who lived with us, was also on the truck, and my grandmother had sent our uncle

John to take us to her. I hadn't met him before but was happy when he told us that we'd soon see our father. I hadn't seen Baba for a long time.

'You'll grow big and strong with your grandmother,' Uncle John said. 'Maybe you'll even be able to wrestle lions and one day become a warrior.'

I shivered when he told me that. I longed to grow as big as my father.

I stared down again at the box beside me. How long would it be before we stopped to eat? Looking up, I saw staring at me the eyes of one of four men who'd also bought places on the truck. I felt strange. He and his friends were Arabs. I knew that because they looked different to us – their skin was lighter and they wore white scarves on their heads – and they were also Muslim, whereas we went to a Christian church. I also knew they didn't like being on the truck with us. The man looked at me angrily whenever my eyes met his, and his friends spoke softly to each other as they stared at us while the truck crawled along the roads to the south. We had to go slowly in case we were attacked by the Sudan People's Liberation Army – rebels who ate people and stole children. They had killed many Arabs and government troops.

The man's eyes slid from my face along the line of my family as he started talking to his friends about the war.

'The SPLA and their Christian followers will fail in their fight,' he said loudly. 'They will remain slaves beneath us just as they are meant to be.'

I felt Mama tense beside me.

'Their resistance is worth nothing,' the man continued. 'We will conquer them. It's Allah's will that they are slaves.'

Mama turned to Uncle John. 'The best way to fight is to keep quiet,' she said softly.

Uncle John said nothing as the men carried on talking, and I didn't listen either. The only thing that spoke to me was my stomach.

I looked down once more at the box that held our food. It was gone. I turned my head to see the Arabs eating *tahnia*.

'Is that ours, Mama?' I whispered.

Uncle John glanced up as Mama lowered her eyes to where the box had been sitting beside me, before lifting them to the men. She looked sad.

'We have to get it back,' Uncle John said. 'It's all we've got.'

Mama turned to him. 'No. There's no need to fight over food.'

But the men were glaring at her as she spoke.

'Keep quiet, woman,' one hissed.

Anger snapped sharp in the air. No one spoke.

'Give us our food back,' Uncle John said slowly. 'We have children to feed. You have more than enough.'

The men looked even angrier as he spoke.

'And who are you to talk to me?' one shouted.

Suddenly he got to his feet, and without a word his friends stood up beside him. Moving as one, they rushed at Uncle John and started beating him as I shrank back into my seat. I could hear Nyaruach crying as she held on to Nyakouth.

'Stop,' Mama cried as she stood up. 'We don't need the *tahnia*. It's yours. Leave him alone.'

But the men didn't listen and blood ran from Uncle John's nose as he was beaten. Again and again the fists flew into his face and body as Mama tried to pull him away. But she wasn't strong enough, and suddenly I saw a hand lift into the air and curl into a fist as it punched towards her mouth. My stomach twisted as she fell beside me. I felt sick.

I threw myself on a leg. I would bite it to the bone, anything to stop these men hurting Mama. But as I sank my teeth into the soft flesh, I felt a hand tighten around the back of my neck. I was dragged to my feet. The hand was so strong, so powerful. I couldn't move, couldn't hear. It felt as if a giant were swinging me through the air in his fingers. I wanted to breathe but my throat was too tight. I could not take in any air. Looking down,

I saw a wet stain spread across the front of my shorts as darkness exploded in my eyes. Everything went black.

Looking back, I can see that the seed of hate was sown inside me that day. Until then I hadn't understood what was happening around me – why the people called Arabs seemed to hate people like my family, why they were richer than us, why police beat men and women on the street, or why Mama was so silent and sad so much of the time. But the day an Arab raised his hand to my mother was the day that set me on a path to hatred. I was too young to give the feeling a name, but each time I thought of what the man and his kind had done, I felt my stomach twist and my heart beat faster.

There was peace in Sudan for the first three years of my life, but I cannot remember it. All I knew was a war that grew as I did. I was born in a village called Tonj in southern Sudan, but my parents moved farther north with my father's job as a policeman. The area where we lived was loyal to the Muslim government of the country and home to African Arabs descended from invaders from centuries before, their skin lighter than that of my parents, who, like most people from southern Sudan, were pure African. My father was a member of the proud Nuer tribe and my mother was half Dinka, half Nuer. War between the north and south, Islam and Christianity, had long been waged, and there were also conflicts between the hundreds of tribes who lived in Sudan. But when another civil war broke out in 1983, the Dinka and Nuer, who were traditional enemies, joined forces with other tribes such as the Shilluk, Murle, Nubians, and those from Equatoria. Their rebel movement was called the Sudan People's Liberation Army – the SPLA.

The war, which was to bleed the very heart of my country for decades, wasn't purely tribal or religious. At its heart was money – in particular the oil that lay hidden beneath the lands of the south and from which the northern government wanted to profit. Dollars were the prize, and the best way to get them was to drive those who claimed the land from their homes. Sharia law was introduced, and the government armed one tribe against another. Burning villages and dropping bombs from the sky, they would stop at nothing to get what they wanted as the displacement of a people became its destruction.

But I knew nothing of this as a child, and my first memories are of a happier time. My father, Simon, was a policeman and we lived in a house made of bricks, with bodyguards to protect it and a Land Rover parked outside. I remember staring up at Baba, in his green uniform with a gold eagle on his shoulder and red stripes below, as we walked to see his friends. I was wearing an army uniform he had bought me and felt so proud. Not only was he an important man, but the six scars running across his forehead told me he was a warrior who, like all Nuer boys, had become a man the moment the marks were cut bone deep into his skin. From then on he couldn't run for his life if war or a lion came to his village – attackers must kill every Nuer man before reaching their women and children.

My mother, Angelina, was beautiful with skin the colour of coffee beans, white teeth, and dimples in her cheeks. Trained as a nurse, she was a Christian and taught me right from wrong from the moment I was old enough to understand. My big sister, Nyakouth, and I never forgot the day when we took some sugar mixed with milk powder from the small tin box where Mama kept it.

'Did you eat some?' she asked.

We looked at her and remembered dipping our fingers into the magic whiteness and feeling its sweetness coat our teeth.

'No,' said Nyakouth.

'No,' I repeated.

But my mother stared at the ground beside my feet and I looked down to see sugar trickling out of a hole in my pocket.

'You must never lie,' she said sternly, and later that day Baba made us run around the outside of the house again and again in punishment.

Mama worked for a few hours a day but the rest of the time

was at home teaching Nyakouth and me some English, our ABCD, and Arabic. Soon our sister, Nyaruach, was born and later my brothers, Marna and Miri. Although Mama smiled, laughed, and cuddled us, I always felt she was sad, just as I sensed that the only day she was truly content was Sunday, because then she went to church.

Each week she would wake early and make us porridge made of sorghum grain before putting on our 'Sunday best'. Then we'd leave Baba sleeping and go to Mama's Protestant church, where she'd sit us down before walking up to take her place in the choir. I enjoyed going to church – the people, drumming, and prayers – but most of all I liked seeing my mother happy as she sang. Her face would light up as the music filled her, and I knew that for just a moment she had forgotten whatever made her sad. I learned to love the music because it made her happy and so it made me happy.

But the older I got, the sadder the weekdays became. I heard my parents talking more about war and the SPLA.

'Who are the SPLA?' I'd ask Baba.

'They are fighting for freedom,' he told me.

All Mama would say was that God loved everyone equally – all the Dinka, all the Nuer, all the Arabs – and had sent his son to die for them.

'One day we will live peacefully together in heaven,' she told Nyakouth and me.

We both knew there was no crying in heaven because angels protected you. I'd see them in my mind – some light brown, some dark black, and all with white or brown wings.

But as time went on and my parents got sadder, my father started to drink more. Where once he'd shared traditional alcohol with his friends on our veranda, he now drank alone as one by one they were arrested. Southerners were hated by the police, and the only thing that saved my father from arrest was his important job. Baba seemed more and more angry, and I would hear Mama crying. It made me feel strange but I soon forgot about it when she laughed and smiled as on any other day, singing hymns as she walked through the house.

Jesus loves me this I know
For the Bible tells me so
Little ones to Him belong
They are weak but He is strong.

As refugees started arriving in our town and our house filled up with aunties and uncles I'd never before met, my mother couldn't hide her tears anymore. I felt more and more scared. Aunt Nyagai was arrested and beaten by the police, and it seemed as if Mama had to go to a funeral almost every day. When we woke up one morning to find Baba had gone, I was sure he was dead.

'He's had to go to another place to work,' Mama told us.

But I did not believe her, and when a policeman came a few days later to tell us that we had to leave our house, I was sure I was right.

We left our home that night with clothes and bedsheets stuffed into plastic bags and stayed with friends in their *tukul*. It was so different from our home – no electricity, just paraffin lamps, no cement on the floor, just earth and made out of mud and grass – and I felt scared without Baba to look after us. Here all the adults spoke in whispers and we lived by a curfew. My mother had to wear a scarf to cover her head, was sometimes beaten when she tried to get to her church, and at night, when we lay on the floor as police raided *tukul*s nearby, she would soothe away the screams by cuddling us. Even the singing that I loved so much and accompanied every kind of celebration went silent. In Sudan there is music for everything – cultivation, harvesting, when the sky is clear at night, for sorrow, marriage, and birth. But soon the only song permitted was the Muslim call to prayers. I wondered why we weren't allowed to sing any more. Some people still did, but they got into trouble if they were caught – grown-ups spoke of a marriage at which police opened fire and killed the bride and groom.

It was then that my uncle John arrived and told us we were going south – a place of safety where he promised I'd grow big and strong, see elephants, and drink as much milk as I wanted. We were going to stay with my grandmother in the southern town of Bantiu before moving on to a village nearby.

'It will be beautiful and green there,' he told Nyakouth and me. 'The trees are filled with fruit, the river is full of fish, and you'll be able to dance and sing whenever you want. Your father is there too and you will be able to see him.'

I was so excited. I wanted to see lions and tall green grass, but most of all I wanted to see Baba.

CHAPTER 2

My grandmother was famous in Bantiu. Short, with smiles in her eyes, she made the best illegal alcohol in town and produced three types – one for the poor, one for the middle class, and one for the rich. She was also clever and gave it free to musicians, who made up songs about her in thanks, which people would hear and then search out Nyapan Deng and her famous *kong*. In fact she was so well known for it that my mother was named Nyakong – meaning 'daughter of alcohol' – before she became a Christian and changed her name.

My grandmother lived with Uncle John, two of my aunts, and their husbands and children in a compound filled with *tukul*s. It was even more crowded when we arrived because my grandmother, like many others, had taken in children orphaned by the war. So each night we would all eat from a huge metal bowl, and sometimes there were fights if one of us took too much. Then we would settle down to sleep on the dirt floor. Around us were windows covered with wire mesh to allow smoke from the cooking fire to escape, and outside was a mango tree, goats, sheep, chickens, and a donkey for carrying things.

The area of Bantiu where alcohol was usually made had been shut down because it was strictly forbidden under sharia law. But my grandmother carried on making it secretly in her *tukul* because it earned her precious money to buy food and put Uncle John through school. So three times a week she would send my aunts off to collect wood, build a big fire, boil up crushed sorghum or simsim in a huge tank, and carefully collect the steam in a tube that ran into a gourd surrounded by cool water. *waragi* was the highest-quality alcohol, and Grandmother Nyapan Deng made the best in Bantiu, which kept us well fed because of its high price. Even the top government commanders wanted only her *Waragi* and closed their eyes to what she did as they sipped it.

Bantiu was controlled by troops employed by the Muslim government in Khartoum. But the SPLA were in charge in the villages outside, and the government used another force as well as their army to fight there – armed Arab militias known as *murahaleen*. When we first arrived, though, all this was far away, and Bantiu was peaceful just as Uncle John had promised. When the moon came out, we would sit and watch the older children play *nurei* – singing and dancing in front of each other to try to prove who was best. We also swam in the huge river beside the town and fished with hooks in its clear water or hunted for mangoes in the trees and filled ourselves with the juicy flesh.

But soon the war started to come closer.

'T-t-t-t-t-t' went the guns in the distance.

'Boooooom' went the big bombs.

'Grrrrrrrrrrr' went the tanks as they circled the horizon.

What scared me most were the rumours of war. People talked about it all the time – the SPLA were coming to get us, they'd captured a village nearby, they would kill us all. It was the same whenever a radio was switched on, and we were also called to meetings where the government troops warned us that the SPLA were our enemies.

'They eat people, teach children to fight, and will destroy your homes,' they told us. 'But we will beat them and peace will come to our country once again.'

I didn't understand. Baba had told me the SPLA were good, and my uncle John had said they were fighting to keep us safe from the Arabs. But so many people said they were evil, and I was scared when I finally discovered that Baba had joined them.

'He is training to become a commander,' Mama told me.

'But the rebels are bad,' I whispered.

'No *makuath*,' Mama replied. 'They're fighting for our freedom to worship, to have our own culture. But you must be sure never to tell anyone what I have told you, otherwise we will be in trouble. It is a secret that your father is fighting.'

Soon I felt more fearful than ever before. Every day the war seemed to get closer, and it wasn't long before it finally burst into our world. I was outside the *tukul* one morning when a boom so deep and loud filled my chest that I thought my ears would burst. Suddenly the air was filled with screams as chickens started squawking, dogs howled, and the donkey broke its rope and ran. I looked up to see people running from where the big bomb had hit. Women and children rushed past the grass fence around our compound in every direction. I could see flames leaping into the sky as *tukul*s burned, and the sharp crack of fire filled my ears. Everything was roaring. The world was ending. I was finally going to heaven. My stomach felt liquid inside me.

'Jal,' my mother screamed as she ran outside.

Taking my arm, she dragged me into the *tukul*. Nyakouth and Nyaruach were crying hard as we threw ourselves on to the ground beside them, but no one spoke while the battle raged outside. All we could do was hope it did not eat us up in its hungry jaws.

For three days we lay on the floor, only getting up when darkness fell and we hurriedly ate *kisra* sprinkled with sugar before lying back down again to sleep. Outside bullets left slashes of red fire in the air as they flew through it, and the orange glow of flames lit up the distance. War had finally arrived in Bantiu, and it would be longer than I could ever imagine before I would finally escape it.

*

It was a hot morning and I was walking along a dusty road with my aunt Sarah and one of the girl orphans who lived with us. We had been sent to buy sugar and I was glad we had a job to do. I hadn't left the compound for a long time because I'd been injured during the war. It happened when I was playing with a bicycle and the sound of bullets and big bombs suddenly filled Bantiu once again. The town was under attack from the SPLA, and my heart thudded into my mouth just as it always did when the day was split open.

Once again people screamed as they ran to flee the explosions, and I too turned to run. But I crashed into the bike as I did so and it fell on top of me, pinning me to the ground as feet raced past my head. My heart hammered. Everyone had forgotten me. I would be left and a bomb would blow me up. Kicking out, I tried to throw the bike off me but forgot a pot of *kong* that was boiling nearby. My foot went into the fire and flames licked the bottom of my leg. I thrashed my foot again and again to try to escape, but each time I could feel the fire eating me up.

A stranger's hands finally carried me home, where I was thrown into water. My mother cried as she tried to stop the pain, but while I screamed, I didn't shed a tear. It was the first time I had known pain so bad that even your tears cannot fall. Later, after Mama and Grandmother had gently put sugar on to the burn, I was treated like a king as my leg went pink and white and my mother massaged the huge blisters that grew where the burn had been. I couldn't walk for a long time and shivered every time I thought about the fire, but slowly I got better.

'Do you think Grandmother will give us a taste of the sugar when we get it home?' I asked Aunt Sarah excitedly.

Even though she was a woman now that she was a teenager, I was sure she loved sugar just as much as I did.

'I don't know, Jal,' Aunt Sarah said with a smile.

I turned my head to see a government soldier standing in

front of us. I did not know where he had come from. One minute the dusty road was empty except for a *tukul* ahead and the next he was standing there. Fear rippled down my back. The soldier was carrying a G3 gun and wearing combat trousers. He was Muslim. He hated our kind.

'You go home,' he said as he looked at me and the orphan girl.

He moved a step closer and grabbed her arm. I could see that she was scared too.

'We can't go home,' I said. 'We don't know the way alone.'

But the man started shouting as he pulled her with him towards the *tukul*'s grey metal door.

'Just go,' he screamed. 'Do as I say. Get away.'

Aunt Sarah didn't make a sound, but I could see tears on her face as the man dragged her.

'Leave her alone,' I screamed as I ran forward.

The soldier slammed the door shut. My heart started racing. The soldier was going to kill her. I was sure of it. He had a big gun.

I ran around the side of the *tukul* to the mesh-covered window and pressed my face against it. Beside me the orphan girl stared inside too. I had to help Aunt Sarah, save her, but how? No one else was on this deserted road and the soldier had a gun. Mama had always told me to be quiet around anyone with a gun.

'You are like a chattering bird,' she would tell me. 'You must learn to hold your tongue and hide yourself in silence.'

But now I watched without a sound as the soldier pushed Sarah to the ground and hit her before taking off his belt and one of his boots. Without a word, he pulled down his army trousers as he stood above her.

'Open up,' he screamed as she covered herself with her hands.

Aunt Sarah didn't move and the soldier raised his belt above her. I heard the sharp crack of leather against soft skin as the belt sliced through the air to whip her. It was like watching a hyena snapping at a baby antelope. She looked so afraid. But she was quiet when the soldier knelt down and pulled up the skirt she was wearing before pushing the long material over her face.

I couldn't breathe as I watched. He was going to kill her. He was going to shoot her with his gun.

Turning around, I started running. I had to get away, get back to the compound and find someone to help. But in the next second I turned back. Something drove me back and I pressed my face once more to the mesh to look inside the darkness. Beside me the orphan girl was still as she too stared.

I didn't understand.

The soldier hadn't killed her. He was cuddling her as he lay on top of her.

The orphan girl laughed. 'They're doing grown-up things.' My parents played that game.'

I didn't know what she meant. Why had the soldier beaten Aunt Sarah but not shot her?

'Leave her alone,' I cried out.

But the man didn't hear me, and as he carried on holding on to Aunt Sarah, I felt my cheeks go hot. I didn't want to see any more. It didn't seem right. I turned once again and ran towards some nearby bushes. I just wanted to hide until whatever was happening in that dark hut had finished. Somehow I knew Aunt Sarah wouldn't want me to see it as I crouched down to wait.

A few minutes later the door of the *tukul* finally opened and the soldier stepped outside. He started walking down the road away from us. I waited until he had disappeared before going to the door of the *tukul* and opening it.

Inside Aunt Sarah was still on the ground. I walked up to her and crouched down. She said nothing as she stared at me. But her eyes looked strange. They were empty but full at the same time.

'Aunt Sarah?' I asked.

She was silent as she slowly got to her feet, walked out of the hut, and turned towards home. No one spoke during the journey, and when we got back to the compound, she didn't tell anyone that we had met the soldier. I never spoke of that day either. Somehow I knew it was a secret to be kept between us, that something very wrong had happened. But I felt confused. Wasn't it nice if the soldier cuddled Sarah instead of shooting her? And why did I feel so sick inside when my auntie didn't even cry about what had happened?

Slowly I began to learn more about what I had seen that day as people talked about soldiers who stole young girls or families who gave their daughters to the militia in return for protection. Again and again I heard a phrase I never had before – *kun ke bom* or 'sex by force'. I wanted to understand what it was, but no one would tell me more than I knew from hearing them talk – that girl after girl was taken and never seen again. Boys were taken too, captured and stolen to be carried north to work as slaves.

But it meant little to me as a child because the world was falling apart each day in a hundred different ways. Men kept disappearing as they were accused of spying for the SPLA, and soon Bantiu was under almost constant attack. Soldiers who knew my father had disappeared from the police force would come to our compound and beat my mother. Even my grandmother was arrested and beaten by junior soldiers, who didn't understand how important she was until the officers told them to release her. Mama just kept telling us how careful we had to be, and even the bush where the mango trees grew was forbidden because SPLA hid in them. Other areas had been mined, but all we knew was that something had been planted in the ground that blew up cows, goats, and sometimes people who walked on it. We also heard stories that streams and rivers had been poisoned by the army, making people sick when they drank there. Two of my aunts who lived outside Bantiu died that way.

I was like water – flowing around whatever dropped into my path because children adapt easily to change, whether good or bad. But two things I could not get used to. The first was waiting for war. At least when it came, you had something to run from as your heart hammered, but waiting was like having the breath slowly squeezed out of you. The other thing was death. The dead were everywhere – skeletons no one buried, people with bullet marks in them and burned bodies lying amid the ruins of a *tukul*. I knew how painful it was to be burned and turned my eyes away whenever we saw a ruined house. But I still couldn't stop the pictures in my head. I knew what lay inside the *tukul*s – people with blackened skin and shining white bones. Death was coming closer and closer to my family every day, and I was sure it would soon touch us.

Bullets were being fired in the distance, but the only sound on Death Route was the flapping of birds' wings. We were in a group of people trying to escape Bantiu, and as we walked along the road out of town, vultures flew into the air as we approached. The whoosh of wings filled my ears and I held tightly on to Nyakouth's hand as we moved forward.

Mama had told us we would be leaving a few days before.

'Baba will be able to visit us in the villages,' she said. 'It will be safer for us there because the SPLA are in charge. The war will be far away and you can learn to look after cows, Jal.' I felt excited when she said that. Cows are the most valuable thing to the Nuer. Offer a Nuer man money or a cow, a car or a cow, he will always take the cow. A cow can keep a family in milk, hide, and meat, and a man is measured by the number he owns. The Nuer even believe that every cow in the world belongs to them and will take them from other tribes who have them. Learning to look after cows would make me a man.

But I also knew the main road out of Bantiu had been nicknamed Death Route because it was so dangerous to try to escape. The road led to the river and was the most direct way to cross into the villages on the other side. Many people had been shot in the crossfire as government troops and the SPLA battled each other. It didn't matter who you were when a bullet found you – the bodies of women and children, old and young, lay there.

Now I stared at the road in front of me. Ahead I could see a burned tank and the bleached bones of cows lying scattered. But the smell scared me most, so strong that I could feel it curling thickly down my throat and into my lungs. I tried not to breathe. I didn't want to taste it. But I could not escape it. I could feel it filling my nose and mouth, clinging to my skin and smothering me. It was unlike anything I'd ever smelled before – human flesh turned grey as it rotted on corpses.

The angry beating of wings filled the air again as more vultures took flight now that we'd interrupted their feast. They rose to reveal a naked woman lying on the ground next to a baby. There were holes where her eyes were meant to be.

'Don't look,' Mama said sharply to Nyakouth and me. 'Turn your heads away.'

But it was too late. My sister and I had seen the woman and would never forget. Her memory was carved into us. The stench of this place was inside us. Death was part of us now.

CHAPTER 3

The villagers' voices rose louder and louder as they sang. Drums thudded to greet us: the family of Simon Jok, the SPLA commander who protected this village and the ones around it. Everyone seemed so happy and I was too as I stood next to Baba – taller than I remembered, with a bigger belly now. He'd been treated like a king after arriving earlier in the day, and he had shown us to the *tukul* we'd been given as a home. We even had cows now, just as Mama had said we would. They were black-and-white with big, curled horns. An elder, naked except for beads around his waist and a necklace of ostrich eggs around his neck, stood in front of my family. Next to him was a *riek* – the altar found in every home to make sacrifices to gods. Like many in the south, these villagers were animists who believed in many gods and made sure a cow's blood touched the *riek* whenever one was slaughtered to please them. The singing got louder as an old woman tried to sprinkle water on us.

'Please no, we are Christian,' Mama said.

'Jeeeeesus,' the woman crooned as she carried on sprinkling water.

A bull tied with a leather rope stood in front of the *riek*. Its eyes rolled as the old man took a spear and stood in front of it. It knew what was going to happen as well as I did and moved restlessly. The elder lifted his spear and in one fast move sliced into the bull's heart. I watched as it fell on its left side and blood spread slowly across the earth. It was a blessing. Later the elder would cut off the bull's head and skin before handing me one of the testicles. It was burned on the fire and I had to eat it, but while the village boys loved the taste, I did not.

'Come, Jal,' my father said after we had finished.

We left Mama, my sisters, and my brothers behind as we started walking through the village with some soldiers. They were big and strong too, but I knew my father was the most important one. He had just come from Ethiopia, where he'd learned to be a lieutenant commander.

'I am happy you are here where I can visit you,' Baba said as we walked.

So was I. It had taken so long to escape Bantiu. We'd had to turn back that day on death route because a village was burning in the distance, and after that it was always the same until Mama made a new plan. The only people the troops sometimes allowed to move in and out of the town were villagers from outside Bantiu who came in to sell milk to the soldiers. It was dangerous but Mama told us we were going to pretend to be with them. I thought of the naked children and women who wore just a skin around their middle. I didn't want to be bare. But of course I had no choice, and soon Mama, Aunt Nyagai, Nyakouth, Nyaruach, Miri, Marna, and I had melted into the group.

My brothers, sisters, and I hated being without clothes and shoes, and Mama looked strange too. The sun was so hot as we walked that the earth burned us and we had to take turns standing on her feet. The moment our turn came to an end, we'd step back on to the ground, and thorns would dig into our soft skin as the village children laughed. I turned my back on them. All I cared was that I was leaving Bantiu – and the war – behind.

I looked up now at Baba as he spoke to me.

'This is our land,' he said as he swung his arm in the air around him. 'This is what we are fighting to protect because this is what the Arabs are trying to take from us.

'They want to change us, our way of life, and make us like them. But I will never let them do that.'

Bending down, Baba put his arms around mine and lifted me into the air. Higher and higher I went until I could finally twist my legs around his shoulders. I felt his hands holding firmly on to my legs as he stopped to speak to a man.

'This is my son,' Baba said as I sat silently looking down.

I knew he would never let me fall.

Baba left soon after to go back to the war, and I cried when he told me he was going. He saw my tears and told me I was a man, a soldier, a warrior now.

The village was as beautiful as I'd been told so long ago it would be. *Tukul*s lay in long lines near ours, and there were also bigger *luak*s, where the men slept with cows after the fire-red sun had sunk into the night. The villagers also had many sheep and goats, and the thing I liked most was that I could walk wherever I liked because it was safe.

Soon I had learned not to wear clothes as I made friends with some of the village children who I entertained with stories of the city. I liked making them laugh as I told them about the black-and-white television we'd had – they didn't understand that a box could show moving pictures. But there were also many things for me to learn. Village life in Sudan is traditional, and girls and boys have different jobs to do. While Nyakouth was taught how to help in the kitchen and milk the cows, I learned how to dry dung, which was then burned on fires to chase mosquitoes away. Nyaruach tried to help us, but she mostly made more trouble than she solved. Her name meant 'talkative', and she loved the sound of her voice even more than I did my own. Somehow Mama always found out whenever I did anything wrong, and I was sure it was because of Nyaruach and her big mouth. I was glad that Nyakouth was quieter.

Miri and Marna were still too young to work, and we, the older children, helped look after them. Of course, there was still time to play, and the game I liked most was with a baby sheep I had made friends with. Staring at it seriously, I would drop to my knees and throw myself forward as it butted its head against mine.

'You will break your bones one day,' Nyakouth used to scold me when she heard the crack of our heads colliding.

I didn't listen because the sheep made me laugh too much to stop.

Mama was also busy. As well as feeding Miri and Marna her milk, she looked after the many people who came to see her. Injured soldiers who needed their wounds dressed with old pieces of bedsheets, and Mama also had some needles for stitching, which she boiled again and again, to look after them. Villagers also arrived at our *tukul* – some wanting the fruit of the neem tree, which Mama boiled to treat malaria, while others asked for the salt-and-sugar drink she made for those weak with diarrhoea.

Although the war was far from us now, we still had to learn to follow rules. Soon after we arrived, Mama was beaten with a stick by angry SPLA soldiers. Villagers were supposed to leave out food and milk to feed the rebels, and she hadn't known. What they didn't realise was that when government soldiers came to watch the bush with binoculars, the villagers also gave them milk. But Mama quickly learned what she had to do, and Baba sent us a soldier called Gatluak to look after us so we were safe again.

I loved life in the village. Watching the ostriches and buffalo in the bush, learning to use the ashes of cow dung and sticks to brush my teeth, and dyeing my hair red using the bark of the *luor* tree. I also liked having Gatluak with us because he played with me often. But most of all I was glad to have left the war behind.

One morning, we were all outside. Nyakouth was milking a cow and I was bringing the others outside so I could sweep up the dung in the *luak*. But really I just wanted to keep laughing at what I'd seen earlier. There is an animal in Sudan called a *jeer*, which is about the size of a large cat. Earlier one had come out of the bush and fallen asleep in the grass near our house – or so we'd thought. The *jeer* lay still as the minutes passed and flies collected on its huge bottom. But a passing chicken could not resist such good pickings and pecked along the trail of flies until it reached the *jeer*'s backside. As its beak pecked, the *jeer* woke up, sucked the chicken's head inside, and ran away. Nyakouth and I had laughed and laughed as we watched. Now I giggled to myself again as I led a cow out of the *luak* into the daylight. I hoped that we would see another *jeer* soon.

I froze as I saw an Arab standing in front of me. He was wearing a long, black jellabiya and holding a gun. Everyone had stopped moving. The morning was silent. He said nothing as he walked towards the *tukul* and came out with Gatluak.

'Put your hands up,' the Arab shouted as he pressed his gun into Gatluak's back. 'Turn around, move over there.'

Gatluak stepped forward and lowered his hands as he turned around. The two men stared at each other for a second before the sharp crack of bullets sliced open the silence. Gatluak dropped on to the ground and the Arab started running away. My eyes did not follow him. All I could do was stare at Gatluak as he lay on the ground. I knew the sound of a gun well and how people looked after they'd been shot, but had never seen the moment when bullet met flesh.

I couldn't breathe. Gatluak's stomach had been ripped apart and his intestines spilled out of the wound. The smell of shit filled the air. Steam rose from his body as he lay on the ground, body jerking and eyes empty. I watched as Mama sank to her knees beside him. Tears ran down her face as her hands closed around Gatluak's stomach. They were bright with blood as she tried to hold the skin together.

'Get some rags,' she shouted.

I couldn't move, couldn't take my eyes away from the sight of Gatluak's guts – grey like a goat's – mixing with a sea of red. I watched as he twisted in the dirt, his breath coming in gasps as he choked for air. Then a low moan escaped his lips and he

went silent. Mama bent her head towards him and cried. Still I
did not move.

Days later a witch doctor arrived at our home wearing a leopard skin and carrying a big spear. He was tall and wore many
beads and bangles, which rattled as he told Mama he wanted us
to sacrifice a black goat for his gods so that he could tell us our
future.

'He is a devil trying to trap us,' Mama said as we stared at
him. 'We will not give him a sacrifice.'

But the man didn't listen as he started banging a drum in
front of our *tukul*.

'You will be punished,' he said in a suddenly deep voice. 'Our
god is the one who protects you, and you must listen to him. He
is telling me that your village will be burned. You must listen.
You will soon all die.'

'Leave us in Jesus' name!' Mama shrieked at him.

Soon he left, but the fear that had wrapped itself around my
stomach the day Gatluak died now pulled even tighter. I knew I
shouldn't listen to a man who worshipped gods that were not
ours, but I couldn't forget his words. I wondered what it all
meant for us.

It was afternoon and I had left the village with my friend Biel to
go fishing. We were walking back home when we heard the deep
blast of a big bomb. It was close. We looked at each other quickly
before running to the top of a hill. Below us was our village.
There was smoke and fire, people running in different directions
like frightened chickens. Government soldiers were attacking.

The savanna grass crunched beneath our feet as we started
running down. As we neared the road into the village, we saw
two SPLA soldiers lying on the ground ahead and stopped. Hiding
ourselves in the long grass, we poked our heads high enough
to see about twenty villagers gathered by the side of the road
surrounded by soldiers pointing guns at them. Other troops were
beating a family.

'You're keeping rebels here, aren't you?' they screamed. 'You're giving them food.'

Children cried as they watched while the rest of the crowd – men and women, babies strapped to their mothers' backs, and elders – looked on with fear in their eyes.

'We've found these rebels here,' a soldier shouted as he pointed to the dead SPLA. 'Where are the others? Where are the rest of your men?'

Suddenly the soldiers rushed at the people and started pushing them with their guns towards a *luak* nearby. The villagers cried as they were herded back, and a man ran at a soldier. A bullet rang out, then he dropped to the ground.

'Get inside,' the soldier hissed as he fired at two other men in the crowd.

Beside me Biel was breathing hard. I looked at him. Tears were on his face. I turned my head again to see troops hitting women with their guns as they pushed the villagers inside the *luak*. Bullets cracked in the distance and screams echoed above us as the soldiers closed the wooden door. I could hear people crying, and I thought of them trapped in the darkness as I watched a soldier throw gasoline from a can on to the *luak*'s straw roof.

I saw the light before I heard the noise. Something bright burned in front of my eyes, and a huge boom roared in my chest as the *luak* exploded into flames. Biel jumped up and started running to the fire. I knew I should not follow. Death was trying to trap me in his jaws once again, and I had to move faster than him. I turned and started running back into the savanna. Deeper and deeper I went into the long grass as my heart pounded in my mouth. My stomach felt liquid. I wanted to empty myself. Suddenly a hand closed around my neck and I screamed as it pulled me to the ground. I saw a man's face. I was dead.

'Don't move,' a voice said. 'You must stay with us, keep hidden.'

Looking around, I saw a small group of villagers. They were

trying to escape death too. I turned on to my stomach as bitter smoke filled my lungs and sounds washed over me – screams and the k-k-k-k-k-k-k of gunfire. Where was Mama? Where were Nyagai, my brothers and sisters? When would Baba arrive to save the village?

I don't know how long it was before I felt the man's hand take hold of me once again and pull me to my feet. We started walking through the grass and soon reached the river, which we crossed before making our way to another village where Mama found me.

'We should have listened to the witch doctor,' I said to her.

I couldn't stop thinking about the people in the *luak*. I could see their faces, the hate in the soldiers' eyes as they looked at them.

'Are they dead, Mama? Have they gone to heaven?'

'Hush, *makuath*,' she replied. 'They are sleeping, and if they are in heaven now, they are safe. All the pain they have suffered will have ended, their bodies will be whole again. God is watching over all of us and He will look after them.'

'But when will we go to heaven?'

'I cannot tell you, Jal. Only God knows when each of us will join Him.'

I looked up at Mama. I hadn't known before that the people I saw were just asleep. I felt happier now.

Pain returned to our lives once again. Our village had been burned to the ground and we couldn't return. Many others did, though, and I soon learned that people go back to the place of their birth just as birds return to their nests. Even if nothing was left, they would still go back and rebuild on the place their ancestors knew. Mama, Aunt Nyagai, my brothers, sisters, and I had no such place, and we ran and ran as village after village was attacked. People were generous with what little they had, and we were given a place to rest and food to eat as we moved across the south with other refugees.

'God will protect us,' Mama told us night after night, and cuddled us to her.

But even she was different now – her smell had changed. In the city the scent of perfume and incense had clung to her skin, whereas now the smell of milk mixed with the sharpness of fear lingered on her.

I knew why. The soldiers came in jeeps and trucks to attack, or sometimes we would hear tanks in the distance and escape the low growl. But on other days they arrived as light was breaking and took us by surprise. The dry season was the worst because they could move more easily. Burning and looting crops, they destroyed anything that might feed us or the SPLA. They wanted us to starve and set village after village afire as the lucky ones escaped to the rivers or the forest, while their friends and family perished. *Murahaleen* also came, and they were the ones I was most afraid of as they shouted, '*Allahu Akbar*', and shot. The village men would try to fight them with spears, but they were no match against the guns, and the *murahaleen* would kill everyone they could.

I remember walking into one village where bones covered the ground. Some were small and some were large, and Mama couldn't cover our eyes that day – there was too much to see. Tears ran down people's faces as they cried without sound, and I had many bad dreams afterward. Sometimes Mama would sing me a song to go back to sleep, but the only time I felt really protected was lying beside her or Nyagai. I had to make room for the younger children, though, so I never really did feel safe.

Sometimes we saw helicopters in the distance – gunships that hovered in the air before firing – and I learned that people running for their lives never go in one direction. Instead they scatter like ants and flee wherever instinct takes them. With the smell of burning flesh in the air and the memories of bodies lying still on the ground, I'd run as if the devil were chasing me. I became good at war. Soon I knew the different sounds of explosions –

the boom of big bombs, the smaller one of grenades thrown from the hands of soldiers, the hiss of a rocket from an RPG. There were also different guns – the AK-47s carried by the SPLA, the Mack 4s the *murahaleen* used, and the G3s of the government soldiers. I learned how to run until I felt my feet would touch the back of my head even as my stomach twisted and tumbled inside me. Often I fell down and each time prayed that I would disappear into the ground. But of course I had to get up and start running again. I wondered if I would ever stop.

Stories woven tight with threads become simple ones in the mind of a child, and the war in Sudan was less distinct than a fight between black and Arab, Christian and Muslim. Centuries of marriage had blurred our tribes, age-old rivalries were used by the Northern government to pit one against the other, and black Muslims from Darfur fought alongside Arab Muslim troops in the belief that they were taking part in a holy war against the infidels from the South. Even black African Christians joined the government forces to earn money.

But I forgot about the African faces I saw among the enemy as I thought of the Arabs who attacked us and hate grew inside me. Arabs and *murahaleen* became one in my mind – *jallabas* – whom I hated more and more. In the north I'd wondered why they had better clothes than we did, why they were allowed to go to mosques while Mama got beaten for going to a church. But now I saw for myself what they could do. The answer was always the same when anyone asked who'd done something: '*Jallabas* – Arabs.' The *jallabas* were to blame for all I had seen; they were the reason my family had been tossed on to the wind as our world disappeared.

'I don't like them,' I'd tell Mama. 'They should go to hell. They are bad people.'

'No,' she would reply. 'Heaven is for everyone and God is for all people.'

Sometimes I wondered how God could let them into heaven when they killed everyone, and secretly I told myself I would

attack the Arabs with my father when I grew up. All I wanted to
do was stop them from hurting us any more.

But at times I could forget the hatred I felt for *jallabas*. The
moment the battle was behind us, we would start playing again
and laugh as we remembered how funny people looked as they
ran. It was only at night that you couldn't forget, but in the
day we would always find a game to play in the dust or a joke
to tell.

My family and I were separated many times as war snaked
around us. Sometimes I was alone, sometimes with Aunt Nyagai
or Nyakouth, but I quickly realised that wherever I found
myself, I had only to mention my father's name and Mama
would find me. I hated being apart from her, and in the days
without her I would be restless and crying as I waited. Yet even
when Mama came back, I would be ready to run again, and if
we ever came to a stop in one place, I would feel my stomach
trembling as it waited for the next battle.

'We are safe now,' Mama would tell us.

But the war was never far away, and even when we did stop,
people were forced to help the SPLA on the front lines by carrying food and ammunition there. Aunt Nyagai had to go once
and was silent when she returned. She'd seen many dead people
and heard of families crying for boys who'd been taken as slaves
on sugar plantations and girls who would be used by the militia-
men for *kun ke bom*. She refused to eat when she came back and
couldn't taste meat. I knew what she was remembering – the
smell of the burned people.

'It was so terrible,' I heard her say one night to Mama.

I'd been woken up by the sound of Aunt Nyagai being sick,
and now she spoke to my mother in a low voice.

'Angelina, there were children and babies, a pregnant woman
lying burned on the ground with her child inside her.'

'Hush, Nyagai,' Mama said. 'You're safe now.'

I was scared by what I'd heard. It put pictures in my mind – I
could smell the air and hear the cries. I kept telling myself what

Mama had told me – the people were asleep and would wake up later, and if they didn't, then God would make them whole again in heaven.

It felt as if we'd been running forever until we finally found a village that wasn't attacked for many weeks.

'The SPLA are protecting us now,' Mama told us one night. 'The war is distant. We can stay here and rest.'

I almost dared to believe her. Baba had brought us some cows, his soldiers had built us a *tukul*, and Mama's belly had swollen with another brother or sister for me.

'Tell us a story,' Nyaruach said.

'Will you ever be happy to listen to the silence?' Mama laughed as she sat down beside us. 'I will tell you one story and then you must sleep.'

We looked at her as she sat down.

'Did you know that the fox and the dog were once cousins who played happily together?' she asked. 'But one day the dog went to visit the fox and told him, "It is hard to live in the bush, but in the village all you have to do is warn people when the hyena is coming. You should come and live with me."

'So the fox decided to go to the village, but got there to find the dog hadn't been given any food that night. Silently he watched as the dog went to his master's house to ask. But he was kicked and given only bones to chew on.

'The fox told him, "In the village you are humiliated. All you get is bones. In the bush I kill my own meat and eat what I want."

'"Just wait and see," the dog told the fox. "My master looks after me well."

'And so the fox stayed, but the next day the dog and the fox killed an animal, took it to the master, and were given only bones to eat once again.

'"I must go back to the bush," the fox told the dog. "I will never be happy here."

'And so the fox returned to the bush and the dog stayed loyal to his master, and the two became enemies, which is why they fight today.'

Mama kissed the younger children as I turned on to my side to sleep. I was seven – too old for kisses. I felt her hand touch my shoulder as I closed my eyes.

The boom in my belly told me that war had come again. I opened my eyes. I could hear guns spitting bullets and the low *tuk-tuk-tuk* of helicopters throbbing overhead. I jumped to my feet. Everyone else was up. Miri was crying, scared by the loud noises. Running to the door of the *tukul*, we plunged into the daylight. My heart was beating fast and my legs felt weak. Would I be able to run fast enough this time?

Aunt Nyagai's hand took mine as Mama held on to the babies and we all started running. All around us people were screaming. Dust and smoke filled the air; I could smell fire.

'Wait,' Mama shouted as she turned back.

I knew what she wanted – her medical box. It was the one thing she always ran with during war.

'Don't go,' Nyagai screamed. 'There's no time.'

Mama stopped for a moment, unsure of what to do. She turned to us again. 'Run for the river,' she screamed.

I could see government soldiers in the distance and told my legs they must be strong as I gripped Nyagai's hand. I didn't look behind at Mama and the others. I knew they were there.

Suddenly the little boom of an exploding grenade came from near us and I heard cries.

'Quick,' Nyagai screamed, and we turned towards the forest that lay on the outskirts of the village. We'd be safer among the trees there.

My feet flew through the air as I forced myself to go quicker. The battle screamed in my ears, and all I could feel was Nyagai's hand in mine. Thorns dug deep into my legs but I didn't feel them. Fear will always win against pain, and all I had to do was run. Run and run, keep going, never stop until I'd left the guns behind. I wanted to silence the crack and roar and hiss and screech of war forever.

When the world was finally quiet again, I realised that I had lost Nyagai. I was alone but knew what to do. I joined a crowd of refugees to start walking. I didn't know where they were going, just that when they finally stopped, Mama would find me. She, my brothers, and my sisters had to be somewhere close by, and until I met them again, someone would look after me as always.

'Mama will find you,' I told myself again and again. 'God will look after her.'

CHAPTER 4

'Bring me a bowl half-filled with water,' the witch doctor said as he stood outside our *tukul*.

I stared at the man. I knew what he wanted – to use his gods to speak to us of things we didn't yet know.

'Let's hear what he has to say,' Aunt Nyagai said as she stood beside me.

I looked at her. Mama would not want us to help this man. Beside me Nyakouth, Nyaruach, Miri, and Marna were silent as they waited. People like this witch doctor came often to Luaal, the village where my father was born and we were now waiting for Mama. It was a four-hour walk from Leer, a town south of Bantiu, where I'd walked with other refugees before being taken to the SPLA headquarters.

'I am the son of Simon Jok,' I told them, and they stood me in front of a radio to speak to my father.

I had never used one before and the soldier used a special language as he spoke into it. 'Whiskey, tango,' he'd said as he pushed the buttons for me to speak.

I could hear the boom of explosions in the background as I spoke to Baba.

'We will find everyone else – you must wait,' he said.

I was sent to stay with an aunt in a village near Leer, but soon war broke out again and we had to run – this time to Luaal, which was where Nyagai, Nyakouth, Nyaruach, Miri, and Marna had joined me. But Mama was not with them.

'Where is she?' I'd anxiously asked.

'With your father,' Nyagai told me. 'She will join us soon. But for now we must stay here, where it is safe.'

'But Mama might not find us.'

'She will.'

I had to do as Nyagai said, and Baba was right – Luaal was safe. Surrounded by swamps and rivers, it had not been attacked during the war. But with each day that passed without Mama, my stomach knotted tighter and tighter inside me. Nyagai looked after us, and Grandmother Nyaduaf, my father's mother, often came to visit the *tukul* and *luak* Baba had given us. But it wasn't the same. I just wanted Mama back.

Nyagai turned inside the hut before stepping out into the sunshine again carrying the bowl of water the witch-doctor had asked for. He stirred it and put three sticks in as he started speaking in a language we didn't understand.

'I can see that somebody close to your family is dead,' he finally said in Nuer.

Nyagai gasped as she looked at the man, and Nyakouth and Nyaruach started crying. But I didn't listen anymore. I would stop my ears from drinking in a single word of what he said.

The man stared once more into the water. 'It is your mother.'

Anger burned hot and bright inside me. He was a liar.

'Stop crying!' I shouted at my sisters. 'Why are you listening to him? We are Christians. We mustn't believe him.'

Mama was right. This man was a devil sent to hurt us. But a few days later one of my uncles arrived, who was well known in the village for performing magic. He too wore a leopard skin and held a long pipe as he talked while smoke puffed out of his nose – once again telling us that our mother was not coming back.

I knew in my heart it wasn't true, but no one would listen to me, and within days our *tukul* was full of relatives. The women held their stomachs as they cried, Nyagai screamed, and my sisters shed tear after tear. They even killed a cow in celebration of my mother's life, but I told myself Mama had always found us before and she would do so again. I knew that I would soon smell her and hear her soft voice as she laughed: 'Hush now, *makuath*, you must learn to keep quiet while I tell you a story.' Mama would never leave us. If she was asleep, then she would wake up. God wouldn't want her with Him in heaven when we were waiting for her.

It took several weeks for something to change inside me.

'It has been so long,' my mind kept whispering. 'Mama would have returned by now if she could.'

Suddenly I felt cold and shaky and soon stopped eating. At night as I lay down, pictures of all the hurt people I'd seen played in my head, and sometimes in dreams my mother's face would be among them. But I didn't cry. Boys didn't cry.

They say there is a season for everything, and in Africa there is one for hunger. For four months of every year when food stocks run low and new crops are not yet harvested, villagers struggle to find food. Soon the emptiness in my heart was mirrored in my body as hunger season took hold of Luaal. War made it worse than ever because refugees and relatives flooded into Luaal and shared our food. Nyagai did her best to look after us, but I would look each day at the three *guey* we had in our *tukul* – huge pots in which we kept sorghum. I knew the food should last us until the rainy season, but soon one of the pots was just half-full and the others were empty.

My family was lucky, though, because we could at least still eat once a day. We sat down together at nighttime so that we wouldn't sleep hungry, but the days were long and I ached for food. I was tired, my stomach burned, and I felt dizzy sometimes. I tried to pass time by sleeping, waiting for the evening to come, and trying to forget Miri's and Marna's cries for food. But others in the village weren't so lucky, and soon there were stories that old people and the very young were dying.

I was lucky because I could look for food in the bush. For instance there was *wur*, the leaves of a beautiful plant, or *shia*, a baby palm tree. But competition between hungry children was fierce and I had to search long and hard for precious food. Soon I watched as villagers were forced to bleed their cows: men tied them down, cut a vein in their neck with a spear, and filled a bowl with blood, which Nyagai then cooked into a broth for us.

'It will make you strong again,' she said as we ate.

The villagers were careful not to kill their cows. It might have been accepted as part of a sacrificial celebration, but at any other time it was a desperate act that would kill hope in all but the strongest.

The hungrier I got, the more I missed my mother. I was sure that if she was with us, we wouldn't have struggled so, and I longed for her touch, her smell, her sound. But most of all I missed her presence – fixed and reassuring in all the chaos. Without her I feared the war would suck me into its dark heart at any second and my chest felt hollow with longing.

'I miss her,' Nyakouth told me one day. 'Sometimes she comes to see me at night and tells me we will be safe.'

I didn't understand what Nyakouth meant and it scared me. But her name meant 'daughter of God' and so maybe she knew things I didn't. I wished I could see Mama too, but however hard I tried, her face only came to me in my dreams of war and then the only thing I felt was fear. On the few occasions I cried for her I hid myself up a tree before allowing the tears to fall hotly down my cheeks.

Finally the hunger season ended and the heart of the village began beating again as people started to sing. When the moon and the stars were bright, for a wedding or a harvest, they found a reason to celebrate, and the voices that rose together told me the worst was over. Whenever a drum was placed outside a *tukul* with oil on it, then word would go around and people would listen for its beat later that afternoon. Then they would gather around a fire to dance, sing, and recite poetry. The music made me happy as well as sad. Some moments I could close my eyes, imagine myself back in church watching my mother, and feel close to her. But then the music came to an end and she would die with it once again.

Life in the village was very different from that where we'd grown up, and as a 'city boy' it was important for me to prove myself. The best way to do that was in the many games the children played against each other. But unlike them I had not learned the skills needed from the moment I could walk and was poor at most of them. The others could easily beat each other with sticks when their hands were tied together, but I found it too difficult, or they could wrestle each other and I didn't understand the rules.

Another favourite was the dissing competitions, in which children threw insults at each other to make others laugh.

'Your grandmother is so fat that God won't let her into heaven,' one boy would shout at another as the crowd laughed.

'And your sister's breasts are so large that when she is milking the cow, she has to tie them around her back,' another replied.

In the beginning I'd fall silent when it was my turn. I'd been taught not to be rude about someone else's family, and the children looked at me in disgust when my usual stream of chatter failed me.

'Jal, you talk too much all day and then you say nothing when you really need to,' Nyakouth would tell me.

But I started improving when Nyagai offered to help me write lyrics. As well as the insults, we also had to rap for the older boys – tell stories in chanting rhythms to entertain them – and I found that I enjoyed entertaining people. But while I became a little more accepted the better I got, I knew I would never really be one of the village boys.

Maybe that was why the highlight of life in the village for me was *gaar* – the ceremony in which strokes were cut into the skin of boys to make them men. Seeing it for the first time taught me how Baba had got his scars, and I longed to have them too. Then I would be accepted. The SPLA had tried to ban *gaar* because they didn't want to encourage tribal divisions – while a Nuer man had six cuts across his forehead, a Dinka had a series of short ones that together looked like a chicken's footprint. Although the SPLA started confiscating cows if people allowed their sons to be marked, the villagers didn't care, and *gaar* continued to be performed on fourteen-year-old boys.

It was an important day – with dancing, singing, and eating – but the high point came when an elder walked up to each boy carrying a *ngope*. Holding the small, sharp knife in his hand, he cut six lines bone deep into the boy's forehead as his blood ran into holes dug in the ground on either side of him. I never saw a boy cry or move when it was being done. If he did, the lines would be crooked and people would know for ever that he was a coward, and if he cried, then everyone watching would know he felt pain and wasn't a proper man. Either way he would shame himself and his family. The boys remained silent and were taken away to a *tukul* after the ceremony to be cared for by women while the rest of the village celebrated. Several weeks later they'd go down to the river, where the men of their family would welcome them as one.

Gaar meant so many things – you were ready for war, able to tell younger boys like me what to do, and forbidden from going into a kitchen again or crying. But the most important change it heralded was the start of romance. It made me laugh to see older boys sitting in front of a girl's home singing as they waited for her to come out and hand them a cup of water or milk to show she liked the attention. If she did not, then her father or brothers would come and tell the boy to leave. My friends and I never stopped laughing at how strange it all was.

I longed to ask Baba about it but knew that he would simply say *gaar* for me was many years away. He came to the village whenever he could, and I was always happy when he did. Since coming to Luaal, I'd learned that he had four other wives, and when my many uncles boasted about how many they had, I realised it was the Nuer way. I never asked Baba about it, and instead he spoke of the future, of the day the SPLA would win the war and bring peace to our lands once again.

'You have to be strong,' he'd tell me as we walked around the village. 'I know the life you are living now is not the same as it was in the city with sweets, sugar, and biscuits. But you have to understand that this is a struggle and you are a big boy now. You must not complain or cry. You are my soldier and must show your brothers and sisters what it is like to be a man.'

I could feel my head growing bigger as he talked and told myself that while I might not be the best boy in the village, I would one day show Baba I was brave.

'We've been sent to collect you,' the SPLA soldier said as he looked at me.

I was standing at the door of our *tukul* days after returning from the bush. I'd been there with other boys from the village to feed our cows on the rich grass and to spear fish. I'd also watched the bigger boys hunt buffalo and seen hyenas, elephants, giraffes, rhinos, and eagles. Now I'd returned to the village fat and proud of what I'd done.

'What do you mean?' I asked.

Two soldiers were standing in front of me.

'Your father sent us,' one replied. 'He wants you to come with us. You're going to school.'

I stared at him. School? It had been so long since the days when we had a home and Mama had taught us our lessons. But she'd always promised that one day I would go to a proper school.

'You must learn your ABC,' Mama would tell Nyakouth and me as we recited the English letters. 'Education is how you earn respect and a place in the world.'

I felt Aunt Nyagai's hand take mine tightly as she came to stand next to me.

'He's not coming with you,' she said softly.

'But he has to,' the soldier replied. 'Don't you want to learn, Jal?'

I stared up at the man. Part of me felt excited, but I didn't want to leave my sisters and brothers. I had to look after them.

'Where will you take me?' I asked.

'To school in Ethiopia.'

Nyagai sucked in her breath beside me.

'Ethiopia?' Nyakouth squealed. 'Can I come too? Can I learn with Jal?'

The men stared down at her.

'No, not this time,' one said. 'This time it's just boys who are going to school.'

'Do you know the *nyanking*, Jal?' the other soldier asked as he dropped down on to one knee in front of me.

Of course I did. I loved the white planes that left smoke in the sky when they flew above us. Their name meant 'daughter of the king' and we were told she was flying above us when we saw them. Sometimes I'd stand staring after they'd disappeared, watching the smoke thin to a wisp in the endless blue.

'Yes,' I whispered.

'Well, the *nyanking* are made by people who've gone to school,' the soldier said.

'And do you see this gun?' the other continued as he touched the AK-47 at his side. 'Well, that is made by people who've gone to school too. And so are cars and biscuits and all the things we need more of. They've all been made by people who go to school.'

Excitement bubbled up inside me as they talked. I wanted to fly a plane and know how it felt to be a bird. I wanted to soar in the blue sky and look down on the world below me. I also wanted to help Baba fight the Arabs and punish them for taking Mama from me.

'I will come with you,' I said finally.

'You're a good boy,' the soldiers replied as they turned to leave. 'We'll be back to collect you tomorrow morning.'

Nyagai looked sad when she turned to me after they'd gone. 'You cannot go, Jal. I've heard about these places. You won't go to school. Instead the SPLA will sell you for guns.'

I breathed in as I looked at her. I would not listen to her sobs. I was going to school to learn how to fly *nyanking*, and Mama would be proud of me.

'But I have to,' I said.

Tears fell down Nyagai's cheeks as she looked at me.

'There is nothing to be afraid of,' I told her. 'Baba would never let anything bad happen to me.'

CHAPTER 5

We are going to school
We are going to school
Sudan our country
Sudan our country
We are going to school
To learn to read and write.

The voices of the boys from my village rose around me. The soldiers had taught us the song earlier that morning after we'd left Luaal. Other parents had done as Baba had and sent their sons to school. They knew we would be safe from the war in Ethiopia and hidden from the *jallabas* who might take us as slaves. Mothers cried and fathers waved as we left, but they knew it was right to let us go. Some battles cannot be won simply with guns.

Now we were nearing the centre of Leer. There were so many people, so many children, who all wanted to go to school. Adults were shouting, others were singing, drums and cow horns were being played, and some people were holding up huge crosses to bless us on our way to a new life. Excitement danced in the air and hovered above us like a bee over a flower.

'I have come to wish you well,' a voice suddenly shouted above the noise.

A shiver ran through me. Baba.

'I am Commander Simon Jok and I am pleased that you have decided to take the great opportunity the SPLA is giving your children.

'We have all heard the stories of children being sold for guns or made into soldiers, but they are not true. My own son is with yours. Would I send him to school if there was any danger?

'Ethiopia is a good place. There is food, no war, and your sons will have shoes and education. They will return to you educated and strong – ready to rebuild our country when we have won it back for ever.'

The crowd screamed and my chest puffed up as I stared at Baba. He was such an important man and I must honour him by doing well in school. Every child in southern Sudan dreamed of being educated.

Later I was taken to see Baba at his barracks, where he introduced me to a boy who looked a little older than me.

'This is Madit and he will be your brother from now on,' Baba said. 'You must look after each other.'

Madit smiled as Baba handed me some clothes and shoes made from tyres for the journey. My feet were too small for them. I would have to go barefoot.

'You must be strong now,' Baba told me as his eyes dug deep into mine. 'You're my first son. I'm proud of you and know you will make me even more so.'

My throat tightened. Suddenly I felt scared about going – leaving my village, Nyagai, my brothers and sisters, everything that I knew, for a place so far away.

'Work hard,' I heard Baba say. 'You're the person the whole family is looking up to now and must be brave.'

'Yes,' I said as I stared at the ground.

Baba's hand shimmered in a thousand parts as he held it in front of me. I took it and squeezed my eyes tightly.

'*Wakemale*,' Baba said to me. 'Go in peace.'

I knew I must not shame my father by showing him my tears and held my head up straight when Madit and I left him to go back and join the crowd. Slowly my fear disappeared as we left Leer amid shouts, screams, and cries of good luck. Big SPLA soldiers were coming with us on the journey to Ethiopia to protect us from the war, and I would then learn how to fly *nyanking*.

A few hours later we reached the town of Adok, where we boarded a boat to take us south down the Nile. The captain argued with the soldiers that there were too many people on board, but he could not do anything to stop the SPLA, and so by the time we set sail we were crushed against each other. I was pleased when I met a woman who'd known Grandmother Nyapan Deng and Mama. Her name was Fathna, and because her husband was an important soldier, she was sitting behind a rope with her children – a girl of about three and two babies. When she realised who I was, she invited me to sit with her and gave me a biscuit. But as I handed half to Madit, he looked at me and I could see he was afraid.

'There is something I must tell you,' he said. 'When we got on to the boat, I saw a snake in the Nile looking at us. It's called a *lou*, and if you see it before it sees you, then it is good luck. But if it sees you before you see it, then it is bad luck, and that is what happened today.'

'What do you mean?' I laughed. 'I don't believe in such stories.'

'But you have to,' Madit insisted. 'We have to be ready.'

Fathna leaned towards us. 'Stop it, boy,' she snapped. 'Don't scare people.'

Madit turned away and I put the last bite of my biscuit into my mouth. Soon I would go to sleep, and tonight I would dream of school instead of war.

A low roar woke me. I opened my eyes and felt the deck tip. I heard the rushing sound of water as people screamed.

'Quick,' Fathna shouted.

Water spilled on to the deck, and all around us, people tried to escape it. Fathna started moving with them as she clung to her children.

'Stay still,' a voice shouted. 'Spread out.'

But nobody listened as the overcrowded boat tipped again to

the other side and people once more rushed in the opposite direction.

'Water's coming in,' a voice screamed.

I knew I had to get through the knot of people, but feet kicked me and hands knocked my head as I pushed against them. I couldn't see Fathna or Madit anymore. Once more the deck rolled, and people screamed even louder as they tried to outrun the water as it crashed around us. I had to get to the other side. Jump the way the soldiers were doing to escape the water and swim as I used to in the river in Bantiu.

But suddenly the world turned upside down.

Everything went black.

I was underwater.

Legs thrashed around me as my hands pushed above my head. My lungs were empty. Something huge and round was in front of me. A light shone somewhere near. All I could think of was God as I closed my eyes and kicked.

Cold air hit my face as my head broke through the water and I gasped. I looked into the darkness. The boat was in front of me, upside down. Half of it was in the river and half out. The water felt hot around me, and I kicked my legs to escape it, but something pulled me down. I turned to see Fathna's daughter clinging to me. I grabbed her.

I kicked again and swam to the upended boat. It was hard pulling myself and the little girl and I had to use all my strength. I felt weak and sick. The air around me was so quiet. The river was silent. I couldn't hear any voices.

'Help,' I screamed.

But no one was near. We were all alone. Madit had been right to warn me.

'We're here,' a voice shouted. 'Jump. Jump to me and I'll catch you.'

I looked towards the riverbank. The voice was part of the darkness. How could I jump? Crocodiles and hippos were in the water – things that could eat us in one bite. But as I leaned forward to hear the voice again, I felt my legs slip from beneath me and we plunged into the water. Swimming hard, I tried to get to the riverbank as the little girl's hands dug into me. She was so strong. But the river was carrying me. I didn't know how long I could fight it. Reaching up, I hoped the voice would find me.

A hand gripped mine as the little girl's fingers dug into my leg, and we were pulled on to the bank. My head went dizzy as I felt the hard ground beneath me. I breathed in. The smell of fuel filled my nose. Suddenly I felt cold. It was as if something were crawling inside my brain. Everything was fuzzy.

'Are you okay?' a voice asked, but I couldn't speak.

'Take her,' it said, and I felt the little girl's hands slowly prized from my leg. 'They're the only ones I could find.'

I lay on the bank trying to breathe down the sickness rushing over me but couldn't stop it. I turned on to my side and the taste of engine oil filled my mouth as I was sick. I closed my eyes when it finally stopped, but it was as if I were back in the water. I could feel it close cold around me.

I do not know how long it was before I felt strong enough to get up and walk to the edge of the bank. Below me in the water a body floated still and face up with a baby in its arms. The child was crying. Its screams felt like knives in my head and I lay back down again. But still I could not close my eyes. I knew that to forget I would have to keep them open.

Many children did not survive that night. Some like me were dragged out of the water and on to the riverbank, but most were gone, including Madit. The soldiers lost only guns, but children too weak to fight the current were sucked into the blackness. Some were trapped in an air pocket underneath the overcrowded boat as it capsized and managed to escape, but many were not strong enough and slipped away. As morning came, Fathna found me lying on the riverbank. She was alone, but when she saw her little girl, she hugged me. All I could hear were her sobs as she thanked God that he had spared one of her children.

The next morning the adults told us we had to start walking back to Adok. But they soon realised it was impossible because snakes hid in the muddy ground at the edge of the river and we went slowly. Time and time again I dropped to my knees to vomit.

Soon the men realised we couldn't walk any more and made rafts from the *orr* plant. Several children were clustered on to each raft with an adult to guide it, but I was hardly able to keep my eyes open as mine slid into the water. All I can remember of that journey are flashes – the gleaming grey skin of a hippo emerging from the water and a boy being clamped into its jaws in one bite, people throwing themselves off the raft in terror and being pulled into the shallows by crocodiles. I prayed to God to keep me safe, but my head felt so heavy I could hardly lift it as the oil I'd swallowed pumped through my veins. Many times I was woken by cold water touching my face as my head fell forward into the river, and jerking awake, I'd tell myself to stay strong. But as the *orr* got soaked in water and the raft began to sink, I wondered how long I would be able to hold on. Maybe God wanted me now.

We were finally rescued when people in boats arrived from Adok. I was lifted into one and taken back to the port to find hundreds of parents waiting on the riverbank. They had heard about the accident and were crying and screaming as we arrived, desperate to see if their children were among the survivors. Only about forty children had lived, and each parent hoped to welcome his or hers back from the dead.

But the soldiers refused to let them snatch back their children and forced a path between the crowd to take us to a huge boat shed where our names were put on a long list. One by one the names were called out and boys were reunited with their families. Some took their children home, determined to forget about school and willing to pay a fine of two cows just to have them back, but others simply wanted to see if their child was safe before the journey to Ethiopia started again. As the hours passed, the boat shed slowly filled with boys being comforted by mothers unwrapping food and fathers talking in low, steady voices.

But no one came for me.

I kept telling myself that Baba would soon arrive. I knew he would have heard about what had happened. But, as the day grew long and my nausea was replaced by hunger, he didn't arrive. My clothes smelled of oil and my stomach growled as the smell of food filled the boat shed. I had not eaten for nearly two days, and when someone threw meat bones and small pieces of *kisra* on to the floor near me, I crawled over and stuffed them into my mouth. As evening came, Fathna found me again and said she would send word to my father. I was sure that if he couldn't come, then he would send someone – Nyakouth or Nyagai maybe.

But the next day came and still no one arrived. The emptiness I'd felt during hunger season filled me once more as I thought of Mama. It had been a long time since I'd felt like that. But in those hours as I watched the other boys being reunited with their families, my wounds were reopened. I felt my father had succeeded where war had not – his decision to give me up had separated me from the people I loved. I hated him in that moment and wondered if I should run away back to Leer to find him. But I knew I shouldn't. He was a commander and I would shame him if I ran. I just had to wait patiently and he would come as all the other parents had. As the second day drew to a close, I told myself that he would soon arrive.

The soldier's boots were big and black as they appeared in front of me. I was lying on the floor of the boat shed, trying to sleep and forget how empty my stomach was.

'Are you Jal Jok?' a voice asked.

'Yes.' I sat up as the soldier bent down.

'Your father sent me.'

A flame of happiness leaped up inside me. Finally Baba wanted me. The soldier had come to take me to him.

'Your father asked me to give you a message. He said that you must carry on with your journey.'

I looked at the man silently.

'Commander Jok said you must go to school and be brave like a soldier. You must wait until another boat is ready to take you to Ethiopia.'

'What do you mean? Where is my father? When can I see him?'

'You can't. He's busy. I have only come to give you his message.'

I didn't move as the soldier walked away. Why hadn't Baba come himself? Why hadn't he sent food and clothes? Why didn't he want to see with his own eyes that I was safe? I knew I must have done something wrong and felt scared as I wondered what it was. I must be a bad son if no one came for me, no one wanted me.

I could feel tears burning bright behind my eyes. They felt so hot. But as I looked down at the ground, a voice inside told me to listen to the message that Baba had sent. He'd said I should be brave like a soldier, so that is what I had to be – a warrior who feared nothing. First I had to find food and water, then I would wait for the journey to begin again and Baba would know I was a brave son.

CHAPTER 6

I stared down at the grass. Flies were buzzing around something hidden in it. A boy next to me waved his hands, and for a moment the black, buzzing veil rose up.

'It's a hand – a child's hand,' the boy screamed.

I looked down at the ground again and my stomach clenched for a moment. I didn't know what was there, but it wasn't the first time I'd heard of such a thing since leaving Adok. War was everywhere, and there were stories of boys disappearing as we walked. Some said they had been taken by villagers who had lost their children in war, others claimed it was the *murahaleen*, but some believed something else was stalking us.

'You should all keep close to me,' said Bol, the elder who was looking after my group of boys. 'Otherwise a *nyakuthunj* might eat you just as he ate that child.'

I shivered as I thought of the monsters. Grandmother Nyapan Deng had told me about them long ago, and I knew they were huge and hairy with big teeth and four legs.

'You will have to be careful all the way to Ethiopia,' Bol continued. 'And even when we arrive, you'll have to stay close to me.'

Some boys had already tried to run away and I knew why. We had only eaten maize as we marched south to board another boat to take us some of the way to Ethiopia along a big river, and they were hungry. They also thought that being educated would mean they wouldn't be at home in their village any more. But I knew differently. I couldn't stop thinking of school and what I would learn there. Soon I would be flying through the sky and helping fight the Arabs.

I was happy we were on our way. I'd done what Baba had wanted when his soldier gave me his message and made friends with an old man who'd given me a hook so that I could catch fish for him, his friends, and myself. I'd fed myself that way and slept in the boat shed each night to keep safe. But I was glad to be with people now and forget the loneliness that had made my stomach ache as I thought about my brothers, sisters, and Nyagai.

'Tell us some more about Ethiopia,' I pleaded with Bol. 'How far is it? What does it look like? What will we eat? What will we learn?'

He smiled at me. I had been asking many questions today.

'It is the land of milk and honey and biscuits,' he told me. 'There are schools there, no bombs, food and drink.'

I looked at him excitedly.

'And there are even *khawaja*s.'

I sucked in my breath. 'White people?'

'Yes.'

I'd never seen one. I was sure I'd be scared if I did. I knew they'd come to our land long ago to try to take it, but our ancestors had fought and won. They'd also brought Christianity and even visited my village once. The people there thought they were beautiful albinos, and some boys had followed one of the women into the bush to see if she did the same as we did there each morning. She did.

We walked for a long time to reach the boat, and our group grew bigger as villagers we met along the way sent their sons with us to school. One was a chief called Malual Wun, who had ninety-nine wives. He was the fattest man I'd ever seen, and I understood why when his wives cooked food for us. When we got to the place from where we'd take the boat, our numbers grew even bigger as hundreds of Dinka boys joined us.

We left the next day and I had to be beaten on to the boat. I couldn't stop thinking of what had happened before – the blackness with hippos and crocodiles waiting in it. When the journey ended several days later, I, like many boys, felt weak as our final march started to the *khawaja*s, their food, and our schools.

'If any of you try to escape on this journey, then you will be eaten by wild animals,' an SPLA commander said as we gathered together.

'You must not try to run,' the commander continued. 'Just remember that school will be waiting for you at the end of your journey.'

We were driven in trucks on to the plains to start walking, and I'd never seen a land like it – huge cracks split open the earth and only the small thornbushes broke the flat horizon. The sun hit the centre of my forehead as I filed into a long line of boys, which grew as the hours passed until it snaked away far behind me. In front the dry earth stretched into the distance, and I knew Ethiopia must be far away. We started to sing and the sound echoed along the line as the melodies of those at the front were taken up farther back. The noise moved over me like a wave as it travelled up and down.

After walking for many hours, we finally stopped as the sun started to go down. We'd been given some boiled maize and a small gourd of water before setting off, and I was longing to drink. I took a sip and felt it slide coolly down my dry throat. I took another gulp. And another. And another. Soon I had finished it all.

The next day we started walking again but were so thirsty we couldn't sing anymore. It was the dry season and the streams and pools that ran through this desert when it was raining had dried up. My mouth felt drier and drier and my feet swelled in the heat. I watched as older boys peed on theirs to cool them and did the same. But I felt scared as I looked at the land running away ahead of me. I had heard stories about people dying in such places, but Bol kept reassuring us that we would soon find water.

'You will drink and you will be strong again,' he said. 'And then we will walk even faster and arrive at school and you will have all you want to eat.'

School, school, school – it was all I thought of as those hazy hours became days and I put one heavy foot in front of the other. I was lucky because I had eaten well in Luaal and become strong, but other boys were not so fortunate. We'd been divided into groups with older boys mixed in with younger ones and an elder to guide us. I was among the smallest, and many of us found it hard to keep walking as the third day without food and water began. Silence fell among the children until someone cried out that a silver line was shimmering on the horizon, and I asked an older boy to lift me up to see it. My eyes showed the water to me, but some boys simply sat down on the dry earth and stopped moving. They said they would catch up to us, but I didn't see them again, and slowly the long, straight line we'd walked in broke up as groups straggled behind.

School, school, school – I asked myself why it couldn't come to my village as I walked. Why did we have to travel all this way? As well as the elders, some families were with us, including a mother who marched with her two children nearby. I was sure that if Mama were alive, she too would have come on this journey with me. This woman was Dinka and her soldier husband had died. Now she wanted her children to have the life we were walking towards, and she gave them all her food to keep them strong. Later on the journey she disappeared just as the other boys had done, but her children stayed with us.

On the third day we finally reached water, and I remember it looked like a huge river but cannot be sure if that is what it was.

'Don't drink too much,' the elders warned as we made our way. 'Lie down, let your body cool, and then drink slowly.'

I tried to listen as I lay on my stomach and held on to a stone so the river didn't wash me away. But I couldn't as I opened my mouth and felt the water embrace me. Each drop felt like the first and I drank greedily. I finally pulled myself out when my belly started hurting and crawled up the riverbank to lie down. Children moaned all around me. Would our journey ever end?

Animals, just like people, are drawn to the places where water flows, and we stayed at the river for several days because the elders were finally able to feed us. They killed whatever came to drink at the waterside and cooked the meat over fires. Slowly I got stronger again, but death remained close to many as some children sickened with diarrhoea or were just too weak to survive. Others took off their clothes and walked naked because even a T-shirt was too heavy to carry.

As we prepared to start walking again, we were told we must sometimes march at night when government planes would be less likely to see us and shoot. We started off, and soon it was clear that the river was a divide between the dry desert and a greener stretch of land where trees and plants grew. Now we were able to survive more easily – drinking from streams or digging our way into *beras*. We knew when such an oasis was near because birds gathered on the horizon, and my heart would beat when I saw the black shapes circling. We continued to eat what animals we could find or roots we clawed out of the earth, but food was still not plentiful and I would often be given just a tiny cube of meat. My mouth watered as I chewed, but all too soon it had gone and I didn't know when I would next eat. All the boys got thinner as the march continued, and we learned to press our hands into our stomachs when they burned like fire inside us. Only the thought of *nyanking* drove me on, and I asked Bol many questions about Ethiopia. Once you plant a seed of belief and excitement into a child's heart, he will patiently wait for a thing to arrive – just as children in the West wait for Father Christmas. Bol's answers pushed me forward.

Going to sleep at night always made me afraid because children were often taken then. A single cry and rustling in the bush would pierce the darkness before silence swallowed up the noise again. The elders tried to shoot at whatever was taking boys, but

I knew their guns were no match for a *nyakuthunj*. Other people said wild animals were following us or the Anyuak tribe, which lived in the region, was stealing children, but all I could think of were monsters as I lay in a long line of boys at night. No one wanted to be on the edge, and we would often fight as we tried to hide ourselves among each other. If I was ever on the edge of the group, I'd wait until everyone was asleep before crawling into the middle of the line. Finally the day came when we reached a huge river.

'This is Ethiopia,' we were told, and I stared at the water rushing ahead of me.

The elders fired bullets into the river to scare the hippos and crocodiles away, but the water still looked so strong. I shivered as I watched it but knew I had to cross. *Nyanking* and school were on the other side. In the end I walked far upstream with a group of boys and we let the river carry us down as we crossed. It took several hours for us all to do it, and as we started walking again, I felt very tired. My hungry belly was now rounded as I looked down and my shorts were torn. Just one thing helped me move forward. School, school, school.

The trucks sent clouds of dust spiralling into the air as they drove towards us. I held my breath as they stopped just ahead and the doors opened. *Khawaja*s.

White men and women got out, some carrying cameras, others pointing bigger black boxes at us. We stood still as we watched them. I'd never seen women like this before. They were wearing trousers, carrying pencils, and telling the men what to do. But they were indeed beautiful albinos in their clothes and leather boots.

The *khawaja*s started speaking in a strange language to some black people with them. They sounded funny and we laughed as we listened. One of the women walked by me and touched my shoulder. Her eyes were blue and I thought of a fish I had once seen with eyes the same colour. She started to write something on a piece of paper.

'What's she doing?' one of the boys asked.

'Writing our names down,' I told him. 'This is what we'll soon be learning to do. Our ABC.'

'And what is the small black box they are pointing at us?'

'A camera.'

'And the bigger one?'

'I don't know.'

Suddenly a camera flash exploded bright white and the boys got scared.

'It's lightning,' one said.

'No – it's the camera,' I told them, and felt proud that I could explain *khawaja* things to them.

The white people looked at us closely as the elders told the Ethiopians with them that we had arrived to go to school. Excitement filled me once more as they talked. We were so near – perhaps we would be given books tomorrow to start our classes. *Nyanking* flew around my head as I waited.

We started walking again. We were in Ethiopia, we were going to a place called Pinyudu, and soon we could see white tents in the distance with huge blue letters on them. Were they our classrooms? Would the *khawaja*s be teaching us or just feeding us? How long would it take to learn how to fly *nyanking*? My heart felt as if it would burst as we walked, and I thought of Mama, Baba, Nyagai, my brothers and sisters – they would all be so proud if they could see what I was seeing.

I took a sharp breath as I looked around. Stretching into the distance were people so thin and sickly that I wondered if they would ever be able to get up from where they sat on the ground. Children with big bellies and empty eyes lay next to their mothers and did not move as flies landed on them. The air buzzed with a noise like birds chattering, and the smell of death hung in it.

Nearby I could see a man whose bones stuck out of him. He kept coughing and his skin was dry and grey. The chicken's footprint of the Dinka was scarred on his forehead and his face scared me – his eyes too big for his shrunken cheeks, his bones like knives as they jutted out. To cover his nakedness, he had tied a blanket around his shoulder as he leaned on a stick where he sat. He was motionless, eyes blank, as he stared ahead waiting. But for what?

The silence among the boys in my group seemed to stretch for ever as we stood looking at Ethiopia. Even after the long march, we could see that we were stronger than many of these people.

'What is this?' one of the boys asked an elder, who had, like the others, hidden his gun now that we had reached Pinyudu.

'The food is finished for the time being,' he replied. 'The white people will soon bring more.'

'But where are the schools?'

'They are here somewhere. We just need to find them.'

I did not speak as we were guided into a line and I sat down to wait. All I could see were thousands of people waiting. Why were they here? Did they want to go to school too?

The *khawaja*s seemed to be in charge here, and I could read letters on tents and trucks spelling out UNHCR thanks to the ABC that Mama had taught me. We were told to stand in long lines so our names could be written down, and when I got to the front, I saw a *khawaja* man sitting on a chair. I can't remember if I spoke Nuer or Arabic to the black man standing with him, but I do remember one thing.

'My village has been burned,' I said. 'I have come to go to school.'

The *khawaja* looked at me with blank eyes. He didn't know what had brought me hundreds of miles across the desert to a place where hope had died.

CHAPTER 7

The boy was lying curled up on a dusty blanket. His hands were in front of his face, but I could see his mouth twisted to one side in a painful smile.

'You four will have to carry him,' said an older boy. 'Tie the ends of the blanket together to make a sling, then you'll be able to lift him.'

We said nothing as we moved the boy. He was one of the thousands like me who'd come to Pinyudu to go to school. The boy was about my age and his skin felt cold as I touched it. He was one of three in my group who'd died that day, and now we were going to bury him in the forest just as others had been before. My heart beat hard. I didn't understand why we were dying when *khawaja*s were all around us at Pinyudu.

School had become a distant dream as we grew hungrier. At first we were given chicken or beef in metal boxes that I used a knife and a stone to open. But soon we were given only maize, and hunger gripped us all again. I quickly learned how to use one of the tin cans to cook for myself. Stealing some maize from one of the big sacks the *khawaja*s gave us, I'd build a small fire under a tree. Singing softly, I'd put the maize into the empty tin with some water and watch it smoke and bubble as it cooked. It was hard because I had no energy, but I made myself stir my food just as I had once seen Mama do. Many other younger boys didn't know how to cook, and they were thin and weak – coughing and staring into the distance just like the children I'd seen on the first day at Pinyudu.

I had made a friend because I could cook. His name was Deng Deng and he liked me because I knew how to make something like popcorn using the maize. He was a Dinka from Bahr al-Ghazal, and although we didn't speak the same tribal language, we talked using Arabic and sign language. I quickly learned at Pinyudu that many boys had seen a war far worse than mine, and Deng Deng was one. He told me his people had once traded salt and milk with the Arabs, but they burned their village when they became enemies. Deng Deng's father was a brave man who'd tried to use his spear against the *murahaleen* on horseback.

'Run to the bush and I'll catch you up,' he'd shouted at his son, but Deng Deng was the only one of his family to escape.

Then he'd heard about Ethiopia and joined a group of other boys walking to Pinyudu to escape the war. Stories like Deng Deng's made me hate the Arabs even more than I already did.

Life was harder than I'd ever known before. Where once I'd been able to run from death when it came hidden in tanks and guns, there was nowhere to escape any more. Death was all around me as disease spread quickly through the camp and boys died day after day. Everything stank as we relieved ourselves in the river where we collected water and the forest where we lived. Terrible diarrhoea made us bleed and grow thin; measles, whooping cough, and chickenpox were also common. Even our skin crawled with lice, and the worst were chiggers – mites that burrowed into our skin and laid their eggs. It hurt a lot to remove a chigger, and another would soon bury itself inside you if you did. It was easy to see who had them because they walked with their feet stiff like wood. Some boys even lost chunks of skin and had to push themselves along the ground with their hands. But they'd get chiggers there too and their nails would drop off as their hands swelled. Sometimes we used car fuel to kill the chiggers, but it didn't always work.

The *khawaja*s came often to take whoever was sick to the hospital tents, and I was taken there as well. I'd thought God wanted me to join him soon after arriving in Pinyudu when blood poured out of me as I squatted on the ground. But I was made better at the hospital – a long tent with beds down either side just like the one I'd slept in when I lived with Baba and Mama. I loved the hospital. The *khawaja*s were kind – the women especially, who would take me on to their lap some-times – and I was sure it was like heaven. There were food and biscuits, tea with milk, latrines, and people to clean you. When I left, I was even given a box of special biscuits that I was told would give me energy. I hoped that I would be sick again very soon so that I could get another. But I soon forgot the *khawaja*s and their kindness when I got back to camp and found that Deng Deng had gone. Death had taken him.

We lifted the boy and started walking into the forest. Looking up at the sky, I could see that darkness was coming. We had to hurry, otherwise Nyanajuan might get us. The elders were still with us now that we had arrived at Pinyudu and had told us about the two-legged monster who lived in the forest after boys kept disappearing. He was even stronger than the *nyakuthunj* who'd lived in the desert, and we were all so afraid of him that we'd even made up songs warning people about him.

Le le le Nyanajuan
A shamran
Le le le Nyanajuan
Eats men.

We'd sing it over and over until we screamed, but now I couldn't shout to make my fear go away. I was silent as we walked into the dark forest, the blanket making my hands sore. The boy was small but felt so heavy now that we were carrying him.

'There it is,' someone said, and I looked to see a pit dug in the earth.

Those who died of hunger were buried on the way to the river, but those that had been sick like this boy were taken to the forest and buried in holes dug with sticks. Soon we would say prayers to God as we put the boy in the ground, and as I looked into the dark pit, I wondered when it would be my turn to die.

Pinyudu was one of three huge refugee camps just over the Ethiopian border where almost 400,000 Sudanese refugees fled. Among them were around 17,000 children and we came to be known as the Lost Boys of Sudan. Some 80,000 people lived at Pinyudu and more than 10,000 of these were Lost Boys, who lived in their own section of the camp. Some, like me, had been told they would go to school and been guided to Ethiopia by the SPLA, others had simply run away from war and joined the line of children streaming towards the refugee camps. Only a few Lost Girls reached Ethiopia because villagers who found them wandering on the journey through Sudan kept them as adopted daughters knowing that one day the girls would marry and earn them a dowry. It is not known just how many died on the march to Ethiopia but it was said the paths of the refugees could be traced by following the bones which lay scattered in our wake.

Human misery knew no bounds in Pinyudu. It was like a huge prison where birth, death, and every shade of life in between unfolded each hour. I was too young to understand what cholera or polio were and learned new words such as *kwashiorkor* without understanding their meaning. The protein-deficiency disease is what made our stomachs swell, and that, combined with illness, killed many boys. I was used to seeing death, but Deng Deng's made me think of other things. I missed my friend, and sadness filled me when I thought of my father. Why had he sent me to a place with no school and where children buried their friends? Then I'd watch the *khawaja*s as we lined up for food and feel angry at them too. Why weren't they helping us and teaching us? Why were they nowhere to be found except in food lines or the hospital?

I thought of my family more and more, and pain gripped my

heart as I remembered Luaal – the rapping competitions, the cows, the sheep, the music, the drums, the games, and the cream my grandmother Nyaduaf made by shaking milk in a gourd and skimming off the thick, white paste. Luaal was the one place I could remember being happy, and when my stomach did not ache for food, it ached for all that I'd lost. Sometimes I'd wake in the night and feel tears wet on my cheeks; at others I'd walk down to the river and cry alone.

Where once memories of Mama had comforted me, now only pictures of war filled my head whenever I remembered her. *Tukul*s burning, children crying, Mama's sad eyes – I knew my feelings could weaken me as I watched boys cover themselves in shit as their memories haunted them and they screamed. A few were even found hanging from trees. I told myself that at least in Pinyudu I didn't have to run from war any more. I made myself forget about school and home. I pushed memories to the back of my head. I did not want to feel so sad and cry each day. But it hurt even more when I thought of Baba. I decided that it was better to forget him than feel this pain

Slowly I forgot everything except my hatred for the Arabs. Night after night I'd listen to tales of mothers being raped, sisters taken, and villages destroyed, feeling my anger harden even more inside me. It felt like a spear twisting in my chest whenever I thought of the *jallabas*.

Nyuol was beside me as we hurried to the meeting ground. He was my new friend, and even though he was Dinka, we could talk. I had learned many languages in the months since arriving at Pinyudu because of all the different tribes living there. I'd first seen Nyuol as he kicked a ball made of socks stuffed with paper bags and tissues that we used for football games, and he was so good that I knew I wanted to be his friend.

He was taller than me and suffered from swollen gums. Sometimes when he smiled, blood would stain his teeth, and whenever I wasn't doing jobs in camp such as collecting firewood and water, sweeping or cooking, I would search him out and we'd play football or go to the river to swim. Now we were on our way to a meeting where SPLA soldiers would tell us what had happened in the war – which towns had been captured, how many Arabs had been killed, as we cheered at the news.

'Look,' I said suddenly, and pointed ahead in the crowd.

In front of us was an SPLA soldier wearing a khaki uniform and boots with an AK-47 hanging low at his side. But he was different from the soldiers we were used to seeing – he was a boy.

Nyuol and I ran ahead to catch up with him and his friends, who were marching together, all dressed as soldiers.

'Have you killed any Arabs?' I asked the boy excitedly.

His eyes glittered. 'Shut up,' he shouted.

But I couldn't be stopped. 'Where did you get your gun?'

'We don't talk to civilians.'

'How about your boots?'

'Leave me alone.'

'What is your name?'

'I said leave me alone.'

'But we want to talk to you.'

The boy turned towards me. 'You don't want to go?' he shouted, and his hand cracked across my face.

I saw stars as I stared at him.

'Now do as I say and leave us alone.'

I stared at the soldier's back as he walked on. My face burned where he had hit it.

'Jal's mouth,' a boy said, laughing, as he moved past us. 'It always gets him into trouble. You can't play with soldiers like that.'

But Nyuol and I couldn't stop staring at the small soldiers when we went to the meeting. They were so clean with smart boots and they marched and saluted like the big SPLA. Stamping their feet on the ground, they stared fiercely ahead as they stood with their guns. Today we didn't listen as an officer spoke. All we could think of were the soldiers just like us.

'Who are they?' we asked an elder as we walked back to camp.

'*Jesh a mer*,' he said. 'Red Army.'

'Who?'

We knew older soldiers were called *jesh a suad*, or Black Army, but we hadn't heard of this.

'*Jesh a mer* are young people who are trained to fight in war,' the elder told us. 'The gun does not know who is old or young.'

Nyuol and I were silent as our eyes opened wide as an owl's.

'We will never get our land back without blood being shed,' the elder continued. 'The Red Army is our future.'

'But how have they become soldiers?'

'They are lucky,' the elder said solemnly. 'They have been chosen because they are so brave. There is nothing braver than a *jenajesh*. They never run from a battle, they would fight a lion if they had to.'

Nyuol and I fell silent as we walked. In that moment I had forgotten everything but the *jesh a mer*. How lucky they were to have guns and boots while we scratched in the dust.

CHAPTER 8

Slowly more *khawaja*s arrived at Pinyudu, with words such as World Food Programme, Save the Children, UNICEF, Red Cross, and Médecins sans Frontières written on their tents and trucks. Soon the hospital was replaced with a brick building with a metal roof, food stores were built, and a black market thrived far from the centre of the camp, where you could trade UN food in return for other goods or birr – the Ethiopian currency. You could buy everything there from clothes and boots to slippers and goats – there were even restaurants for tea. But, however much I wanted to see the market, I knew I would be badly beaten if a *shurta* caught me. They were the boys the SPLA had put in charge of us like policemen and were always quick to use their whips if we did some thing wrong.

When we'd first arrived in Pinyudu, we'd been divided into groups with older boys overseeing the younger ones as we fought for food, wood, and water. At the top of us all were the elders and the SPLA, and we all knew that while the *khawaja*s thought they ran the camp, it was the SPLA who were really in charge. They controlled many things and had an important friend in Ethiopia – the ruler Mengistu Haile Mariam, who was also fighting a war against rebels. The SPLA grew strong with his help, and they were always on the watch for Khartoum spies among us or sending out troops to fight battles in my country.

Over time, the SPLA took tighter charge of us. We were divided into groups of a thousand boys, which were then split into smaller units of thirty-three. Elders were put at the head of each unit, and the boys who made up yours were your family. After sleeping under the trees when we first arrived, we now built our own *tukul*s – younger boys helping with cutting and carrying grass while the older ones chopped wood. More *khawaja* food also arrived in camp, and our hunger eased when we were given beans and oil as well as maize – eventually we would even receive sugar. It was never enough though, and we soon learned ways to get more food from the *khawaja*s.

Eventually, several months after arriving in Pinyudu, we started going to school. At first we had sat under trees while Uncle Sam, the elder in charge of my group, taught us from a blackboard. It made me laugh as we repeated the words he said.

'One, two, three,' Uncle Sam would shout.

'Waaal, tuuu, treeee,' said the Dinka boys.

'Wang, tung, tring,' said the Nuer.

It was difficult at first to learn because we didn't have enough paper or pencils and had to write in the dust using sticks. But I knew that English was the language spoken by the people who flew *nyanking*, and thanks to the ABC my mother had taught me, I was a quick learner. We also started going to church every Sunday, and I was baptised many times. All the Lost Boys were, and most of us answered to several names. I was baptised in the church and the river, and each time I was given a different name. John, Michael, and Emmanuel were three of them. Whoever inspired me with their preaching, I took their name. One boy even asked to be baptised as Mary after hearing the story of God's mother.

We were told at church that when the world ended, Satan would take people who didn't believe, and I would see him in my mind with a big spear, ready to slash me into two. But deep down I didn't really believe in God any more. I had when I was with Mama and we'd run to a village during war where I'd seen a *riek* shaking when Christians came with their drums. But now I asked myself, if He was real, then why couldn't He fight the

Muslim God? Why had we lost everything and He didn't care enough to help us?

When school started, we went every day from Monday to Friday. We'd been taught the days of the week in class, and my favourite was Saturday, when we played soccer and wrestled. The Nubian boys were the best because they were so big and fat. They ate anything to make them strong – snakes from the bush, frogs, and leaves on trees – and never got sick. Then on Sundays we would go to church before all the different tribes gathered to dance and learn each other's songs.

The SPLA made sure that discipline was strict. If you fought with another boy, you were beaten on the buttocks by members of your group; if you stole something, you were beaten again. I was often punished for forgetting to do jobs such as collecting firewood and water, sweeping and cooking, because I was too interested in trying to find fun. When trouble broke out between groups, we could go to a court where elders listened to disputes. If you had done something wrong, you could be put into jail – a deep hole with thorns around it – for one or two days. But we were most afraid of the *shurta*s. The SPLA chose only the cruellest boys to be *shurta*s.

Life always settles into its familiar patterns – the weak and the strong, the hunters and the hunted – even in a city such as Pinyudu, which has sprung up out of nothing, ready to be blown away on the wind.

I smiled at the boy sitting beside me as we sat on the mud benches. The teacher had left the *tukul* for something and I was bursting to speak. The boy was silent. I wished Nyuol were next to me, but we were in different groups and so did not go to school together. Nyuol would be as excited as I was by what we'd heard the night before. We went to many meetings now where soldiers told us about the war as SPLA and Ethiopian flags hung in the air and we sang songs to welcome whoever had come to see us.

The pencil is my home
My home is my pencil
My future, my mother and my father.

I knew more than ever now that the SPLA would one day save
me. Baba had sent me away, Nyagai, my brothers, and my sisters
must have forgotten me, but the SPLA were still looking after me
and would one day win back my country. The previous night an
important commander had come to speak to us and described
the towns and villages the army had captured from the government. We cheered as he described the Arabs who had been
beaten, and I felt the spear of anger and hatred rising in my chest
as I listened.

'Many of you were disappointed to find there were no
schools when you first came here,' the commander said as we
fell quiet. 'But if we hadn't told you about the schools, then you
would not have wanted to make the journey here, and the
*khawaja*s did not keep the promises they made us. Now you are
starting to learn at school and must do the best you can so that
when we recapture Sudan, you are ready to return and run our
country.'

My stomach turned over as I listened. Might I one day finally
fly a *nyanking* and help fight the Arabs? That night I could
hardly sleep as I thought of being in the plane and flying high
over the earth.

I looked once more at the door to the *tukul* to be sure our
new teacher was still outside. Uncle Sam had stopped teaching
us when we built ourselves a schoolhouse with mud benches to
sit on. Now we even had chalk, pencils, and books – the older
boys had one called *Brighter Grammar* in English, and we had
ones with cartoons and words inside. We also had a new teacher,
and when I was sure I was safe, I started laughing as I looked at
the boy beside me.

'Did you see the commander's belly last night?' I said with a
laugh. 'It was so big he must have eaten a whole goat.'

The boy said nothing.

'Didn't you see?' I insisted. 'He was huge and fat. He could be a champion wrestler.'

I felt a sharp point in my back.

'Jal Jok,' the teacher hissed as he poked a stick into my back. 'Once again I am going to have to punish you. When will you ever learn to be quiet?'

I kicked the ball as hard as I could at Nyuol. We were so close to scoring a goal. But suddenly out of the corner of my eye, I saw a group of white people had stopped to watch us playing.

'*Khawaja*s, *khawaja*s,' I shouted as I ran towards them. 'How are you?'

I always wanted to practice my *nyanking* language with them but couldn't do it that often because *shurta* beat us if we were seen talking to *khawaja*s. Today though we had finished our classes early and no one was around.

They smiled as we ran up to them. We always liked to look at them, touch their hair if we could, and smell them.

'My name is Jal, and this is Nyuol,' I said to a woman in the group. She was tall with blue eyes and blond hair.

'You speak English?' she said.

'Small, small.' I laughed.

'My name is Mary.' The woman leaned closer to me and started speaking. It sounded as if she was hissing.

I couldn't understand what she was saying. My English had run out, and someone called over a passing elder to translate. He stared as he stood next to me.

'What are you doing?' he asked angrily.

I looked at the stick in his hand as I wondered what to say, but the woman started speaking before I could answer and the SPLA had to tell me her words.

'Where did you come from?' she asked. 'Why are you here?'

She wrote notes as I told her my story – the villages that had been burned, losing my mother and family. The woman's eyes were kind as she looked at me, and I spoke more and more as the time went on.

When I'd finished, the elder told us Mary wanted to see more of the camp, and Nyuol and I took her to see the river before going to visit other children. The elder didn't look so angry now that he had realised we were talking about the past instead of the present. He knew more food would come when the *khawaja*s heard our stories.

'Where you from?' I asked Mary.

'The USA.'

I didn't know that place. Mary opened her bag and took a tin out of it. On the side, painted in red, white, and blue, was the flag I'd seen many times.

'This is my country,' Mary said, and I knew she would be near whenever I saw that sign from now on.

Mary touched my cheek as she bent down and looked into my eyes. Hers looked sad.

'I want to be a bird,' I told her. 'Fly a plane.'

Later Mary took us to the market. It was the first time Nyuol and I had been, and we were so excited to be free. There were mangoes, bananas, and clothes, and the sharp smell of *anjera*, our favourite Ethiopian bread, hung in the air. I thought I would burst when Mary handed us a real soccer ball. I had only ever touched one before when I lived in the north, and now we had one of our own. She also bought us soda, food, clothes, and a pair of slippers each.

'I'll come again tomorrow,' Mary told us as we left her.

Softness surrounded me as she bent down to hug me. It was the first time anyone had touched me like that since the *khawaja*s had taken me on to their laps in the hospital and looked at me with sad eyes. For a moment I thought of Mama, but pushed her face out of my mind. I did not want to feel sad today. It was the best day I could remember since leaving Luaal.

*

My belly felt full as I left Dr Kong Tut's. He was just one of the new friends I'd made since meeting Mary. She'd come back to see Nyuol and me the day after we first met and taken us to the *khawaja* compound wearing our new clothes. Our eyes were big as we looked around – there were drinks and biscuits and more white people together than we'd ever seen before. But soon Mary had told us she was leaving.

'My work is finished,' she said as an elder translated her words.

'Can I marry you?' I asked.

'Why don't we see next time I come?' She laughed.

'I'll get many cows and then we can marry and go to your country,' I insisted.

I felt sad when Mary left but was soon happy when I realised that now the *khawaja*s knew who I was. Sometimes they visited me with sweets and biscuits and asked for more stories about the war. I'd find boys to tell them, and as time passed, I became well known among doctors and people with cameras who wanted to know more about Pinyudu. They came because my English was better than that of most and I was always happy to talk. But I was also pleased to see them for other reasons.

'Pick someone and see how hungry he is,' I'd say after gathering together all the boys I knew could eat more than anyone else.

Then the *khawaja*s would watch with their mouths open as the boys ate and ate and ate. Soon more food arrived for us, and even the SPLA were happy with me for what I'd done and told the *shurta* to leave me alone.

But sometimes the *khawaja*s didn't come and I missed the biscuits they'd once brought. So then my friends and I made the plan that brought me to Dr Kong Tut. We decided to steal into the one place we knew was full of biscuits, the hospital, and soon we were visiting the sick sometimes twice a week.

'Hello, my cousin,' I'd say as I sat down beside a boy so weak that he wouldn't know me or be able to speak. Then I would talk and talk to him until his biscuits arrived.

'Are you hungry?' I'd ask as I took them, and if he groaned, I'd give him a taste before eating the rest.

Some boys wanted biscuits so much that they got into beds left empty because someone had just died – however much they stank – but I never did. I was just happy that our plan was working, and the biscuits made us popular as we shared them around or traded them. I'd even stopped getting beaten by *shurtas* because I used the biscuits to bribe them.

But then came the day when I met Dr Kong Tut and my luck finished. He knew me from when I'd been sick myself and now came up to me just as I'd slipped some biscuits into my pocket while sitting next to a bed.

'Hello,' he said.

'Hello.' I smiled.

'It's Jal?'

'Yes, sir.'

'But what are you doing here? I thought you were well now.'

'I am.' I looked at the sick boy lying silent beside me. 'But this is my cousin and I've come to visit him.'

The doctor stared at me.

'He's been very ill but I hope that soon he will come home to us. I am sure my visits make him stronger as I tell him about all the things we are learning at school.'

The boy gave a soft moan and I put my hand on his arm. 'See? He knows I am here and likes me to come and see him.'

But the doctor took one look at my pocketful of biscuits and knew I was lying. 'Get out,' he shouted. 'You are a bad boy to steal from the sick.'

I was whipped long and hard by the *shurta,* and after that Dr Kong Tut wanted to punish me even more for what I had done. He ordered that I be locked in the biscuit store until I had eaten up everything inside, but I knew that even I would not be able to do that. Dr Kong Tut knew I wasn't a bad boy though – the biscuits had made me so – and soon let me out.

'I will give you biscuits each week to keep you good,' he told me, and we became friends.

Now I was on my way back to camp after going to see him, my belly full and my heart light because I knew my stomach would not roar like a lion at school tomorrow. It is hard to study when you are empty inside. But as I neared our *tukul*, I saw boys gathering at the meeting ground.

'It's the commanders,' one shouted to me. 'They've come to speak to us.'

The top SPLA were in Pinyudu, and it meant something special was happening. I quickly found Nyuol and started running with him to the meeting ground, two among hundreds of boys who wanted to hear what they had to say.

'Do you think they've killed all the Arabs in Khartoum?' Nyuol said in a rush.

'Or maybe the SPLA have won the city and taken over the government,' I replied.

The crowd hushed as an officer stood up.

'This war is a long and bloody one,' he said. 'But we will fight it to the death and we will win.'

A cheer went up as we all stared at him.

'For many months now you have been hearing news of our struggle and the battles we have won,' he shouted. 'But now is the time when you too must start to learn about discipline and the sacrifice needed to win a war. To win back Sudan will require much from each of us, and all of you have a part to play.'

There was silence as he stepped back and another SPLA officer stood up. I stared at the *jesh a mer* surrounding him. My heart beat as I looked at the little soldiers. They looked so fierce and strong.

The officer lifted his AK-47 into the air above his head. 'We will not win freedom for this country of ours the easy way,' he cried. 'Much blood will have to be shed. But is there anyone here tonight who can say they have not already seen it spilled? Who can raise their hand and say they haven't seen their house burned, their sisters raped, their mothers beaten?'

The officer stared down at us, his eyes black like charcoal as he waited to see if anyone would move. No one did.

'The Arabs have shown no mercy,' he roared. 'They are to blame for every drop of blood spilled, for every child left lying in the dust, for every boy stolen as a slave, for every girl taken. They have destroyed our people, our homes, our land, and our religion. They have starved and murdered us, and now it is time for us to fight.

'Remember what they have done to each of you, think of what you have heard here in Pinyudu, never forget why you had to leave your homes to come here.'

Pictures danced in my mind as I listened to the words – villages burning, my brothers and sisters running, bones lying on a dusty road, my aunt's empty eyes and the government soldier. Anger pricked hot and sharp inside me. Bitterness enveloped my body.

I closed my eyes . . . Nyagai's face wet with tears after she'd returned from the front line, Biel's eyes burning as we watched villagers being crowded into a *luak*, a mother lying still on the ground with a baby in her arms as vultures pecked, Mama's mouth twisting in fear as she screamed at me to run.

'Think of everything you have lost,' the officer screamed. 'Think of all that has been crushed and destroyed by the *jallabas*. Remember the life you once had, the peace you once knew, and be sure that the only way you will get it back is if this war is won.'

Helicopters, *jallabas* shooting guns, troops in lorries, fire and bullets – the past ran through me like a river.

I looked around me. Thousands of boys were here tonight, and I knew each was remembering his war just as I was.

'Children of Pinyudu,' the officer screamed. 'You must never forget what you once had and what you could still win back. With your help we will win this war, and you will return to the land of your birth, your country, your homes. You too could be *jesh a mer* – brave young men who are fighting alongside us for victory.'

My heart hammered as I listened, my throat felt dry, and my head hurt. I stared at the Red Army. They looked so proud and tall. They would fight like men.

'This gun is my mother and father now,' the officer screamed as he raised the Kalashnikov above his head. 'How many of you are willing to say the same? All of you are alone here – you have left your families far behind, and now is your chance to have a new one with the SPLA.

'But how many of you are brave enough to fight? How many of you are ready to be soldiers?'

Time stood still for a second. I felt dizzy and breathless.

Noise exploded all around me as I punched my hand into the air. Beside me, Nyuol also lifted his arm. We were not alone. Every boy in the crowd had raised his hand.

Excitement flooded through me as my body shook. At last I was going to leave Pinyudu, at last I was going to fight to get back home, at last I would be able to do to the *jallabas* what had been done to me and my family.

I lifted my head to look at the *jenajesh* standing in front of me. Holding their guns, they stared ahead. I was going to be like them. I was going to be a soldier.

CHAPTER 9

Time is like sand running through my fingers as I look back on my childhood, but I think it was almost two years after arriving in Pinyudu that I finally left for training. I was nine years old.

The camp was a day's march away in the bush close to a river, and on my first morning I woke to see damaged *tukuls* grouped around a huge parade ground. Just as we had been in Pinyudu, we were divided into groups as we were told to repair the *tukuls*. But now, instead of an elder in charge of us, there was an army trainer called the *talemgi*. Ours was huge with scars on his face and big red eyes. I was sure he could eat a lion if he wanted to. Other *jenajesh* who'd already been trained also told us what to do and laughed at us – particularly the small boys of seven or eight who found it hard to keep up.

We worked hard in those first few days cutting wood for the *tukuls* and learning to be soldiers. Nyuol had been trained without me and was now back at Pinyudu, so I was glad when I made a new friend, Malual. We worked together as we built beds out of wood for our *tukul*. I had lost my blanket after being beaten by a *shurta* on the march to the camp, and Malual told me I could share his.

Soon our days settled into a routine. We woke up when it was still dark and the birds were asleep, went jogging, then drank tea made from roasted maize. As the sun rose higher in the sky, we went to the training ground to start learning. We were taught to hold our hands behind our back with our feet apart 'at ease' or be straight like a spear as we stood to 'attention'. We repeated the moves for hours and hours until it was time to go back to our *tukul*s to eat maize porridge served on the lids of empty bullet boxes. I felt a rush of excitement as I looked at the lids. I would soon be using bullets in the kind of gun I had seen so many SPLA soldiers carrying.

Then we went back to the training ground for several more hours and were taught how to about-turn and march. Afterward we had duties such as cleaning soldiers' boots, fetching water for the women who lived in the officers' area, and washing their clothes or watering their gardens. Then we went for another jog and my stomach would grumble until finally, just as darkness started to creep into the sky, we would eat maize and beans before our curfew at 6 p.m. Night after night I fell into a sleep from which only dreams of war could wake me. Fires burning, guns firing, people screaming, soldiers laughing, lorries rumbling, helicopters whirring . . . All I had once seen haunted me now that I was in the place where I would learn to fight it.

'Get up.'

The *talemgi*'s voice rattled in my head as I opened my eyes in the darkness. My hand rushed to my side. My gun had gone.

'Get up now,' the trainer shouted again. 'Outside. All of you.'

My chest felt tight as I jumped out of bed. We'd been told to always keep our guns by our side even when we were sleeping, and mine had disappeared. I knew the *talemgi* would be angry. I ran outside with the rest of my group and stood silently waiting for him. Soon his boots crunched on the dusty earth and he stood in front of us.

'Call yourself soldiers?' the *talemgi* barked. 'So where are your weapons?'

We'd all carved rough wooden 'guns' for ourselves after being taken to the parade ground and shown AK-47 and RPK guns as well as a rocket-propelled grenade launcher, or RPG. Each looked bigger than the last as they were held above our heads and excitement rushed into our veins. The training was over. We were soldiers. It was time to go to war.

But instead we were told we would have to practise with a pretend gun and were taken into the bush to cut wood to make it. I wanted an AK-47 and spent days making one as splinters bit into my hands. Bigger boys made RPGs and RPKs, but even the AK-47 was too big for me, so I had to make mine smaller before tying a rope to each end to carry it. Soon I would have a real one.

But now my heart felt light with fear as the *talemgi* stared at us. I didn't understand where my gun had gone. I hadn't let go of it since I'd finished making it.

'Anyone who has his gun can leave,' he growled, his voice soft and dangerous.

No one moved. I looked around. All of us were empty-handed.

'I have your weapons,' the *talemgi* shouted. 'And it was like stealing from sleeping babies. It's time for you to learn what it really means to be a soldier – to sleep with one eye open, to never rest, to always be ready for your enemy. Now get on the ground and do a hundred push-ups.'

I threw myself down. Looking around, I saw older boys lying flat and pushing their bodies into the air with their arms. I tried to do the same but couldn't. I pushed myself up once again, locked my arms straight, and started moving my hips up and down as fast as I could.

Black boots appeared in front of my face. 'What's that?' the *talemgi*'s voice screamed above me.

My breath disappeared as his foot flew into my stomach.

'Do it properly,' he shouted.

I pushed myself up and down even faster. I couldn't do what the older boys did. My arms would break.

'No,' the *talemgi* roared. 'I said do it properly.'

Again he kicked me. Again I tried to lower my arms. Again they buckled under me and I fell.

'Do it,' the *talemgi* screamed. 'Do it, I say. Do you think I was born yesterday? What kind of soldier will you ever be?'

His boot buried itself in my stomach. I couldn't breathe and I gasped as sickness rose in the back of my throat. Pain filled me.

'Do it properly,' the *talemgi* screamed. 'And if you can't, then keep trying until you can.'

I pushed myself up and down – arms burning, stomach twisting in pain. A whip singed across my buttocks.

'Call yourself a soldier?' the *talemgi* screamed. 'You're a joke.'

Finally his foot stopped kicking me and I fell into the dust. Grit filled my mouth as I lay there.

'Just remember,' the *talemgi* said in a low voice as he bent down to me, 'I haven't even started with you yet.'

From that day on, I was beaten almost every day. Anything was reason enough for the *talemgi* – not training hard enough, not saluting straight enough, not doing my duties well enough, trying to tell him jokes. He'd beat me and other small boys until we almost screamed, then start again the moment he found another reason to. Night after night, he woke us up as we slept and we'd run into the darkness, where he'd shout that we had taken too long. My head ached, my back hurt, and as soon as we got back into bed, he'd wake us again and we'd have to start jogging. I felt as if I never slept.

There were many different punishments for all the mistakes I made – sometimes my feet and hands were tied up and I was beaten as I lay on the ground; or I was chased to the banks of the river and whipped in the mud until I thought I would drown; or I was made to hop on one spot until my leg felt as if it would break. I didn't want to be a soldier any more. I was too small to be one, not strong enough. I understood now why the *jenajesh* I'd once spoken to was so angry. Just as I had

learned to do with sadness at Pinyudu, I now wrapped up my
rage deep inside me.

About two weeks after we arrived, the whistle went off while
we were eating our morning porridge. I wanted to eat as much
as I could because otherwise I felt dizzy and weak during the
long, hard days. But the single burst of the whistle told us to
gather at the training ground, and I got up to start running.

The training ground was empty when I arrived and joined the
other boys. Time ticked slowly by as we sat and waited. The sky
got lighter, the birds louder, and boys started complaining that
their porridge was getting cold nearby. I sat silently. I didn't
want the *talemgi* to beat me today.

'What kind of soldiers are you?' an officer shouted as he
walked on to the training ground. 'Why are you sitting around?
You need to sing when you wait for your leader and build
morale.'

We were silent as the soldier stood looking down at us.

'*SPLA wea yea*,' he suddenly sang.

We looked at him, unsure of what to do.

'*SPLA wea yea*,' he repeated.

No one moved.

The officer gestured to some soldiers nearby who marched to
stand beside him.

'*SPLA wea yea*,' he sang once more.

'*SPLA wea yea*,' replied the troops in strong voices as they
punched the air.

The officer turned to us. '*SPLA wea yea*,' he shouted.

'*SPLA wea yea*,' I shouted back as I remembered the singing
in Luaal.

Other boys sang too but many were unsure, and our sound
was thin in the air.

'You have to learn,' the officer shouted, and looked at his
troops. 'Now show them how to do it properly.'

The soldiers' eyes were like arrows as they looked straight
ahead. No one moved as a high scream echoed in the air.

'*U-lu-lu-lu-lu-lu-lu-lu,*' a soldier roared, and the others started to sing.

We are commandos
Yes
There are no sick
Yes
We are all young
Yes
All of us are youth
Yes
Fire, fire,
Burn it
Fire, fire
Shoot it
Madingbor
Madingbor is burning.

The soldiers screamed and their hands beat against their guns as their boots stamped on the ground. The deep voices made my chest shudder, and I shivered as memories rose inside me. The words were different but the singing made my blood dance just as it always had in my village. I knew the other boys felt the same as we listened to the soldiers' chants. Burning towns, using guns and rocket launchers, this was why we were here. The kicks, the punches, the aching belly and sleepless nights – it was all worth it because soon we'd destroy the *jallaba* army. I longed to learn the words the soldiers knew and be ready to fight just like them, but now I knew that training would take much longer than I'd expected. The *talemgi* had told me we'd only just started, and I wondered how long it would be before we were ready.

When the officer had finished with us, we went back to the *tukul*s to find our porridge gone. 'You must learn to eat more quickly,' the *talemgi* told us. 'The enemy could come at any minute.'

From that day on we had only minutes to get the burning porridge into our stomachs before the whistle shrieked at us. To
save food, boys began filling their cupped hands and taking it
with them, but the porridge was too hot and they had to find a
way to cool it down to eat it quickly. Soon they had learned to
smear it on the backs of smaller boys, who screamed as the
burning porridge cooled on their skin before the bigger ones
picked it off in sticky chunks, leaving red burns behind. Many
boys were hurt like that – one so badly he had a scar on his head
where his hair never grew back – but I was too quick.

Instead I shoved the food into the pockets of my shorts, but
was beaten when the *talemgi* discovered it. Then I learned how
to fill my mouth with saliva and gulp down lumps of steaming
porridge in seconds. My chest felt tight but at least my stomach
was full. Later I taught myself to smear a thin layer of porridge
on my palm to cool it. Then I'd roll the layer into a big ball
and eat it as I smeared my other hand with more food. I was
becoming clever in ways I'd never even known I could be.

The SPLA told us that while the Dinka and Nuer had once
fought for cows, we were now fighting for our land and must do
it side by side. If boys ever got into fights, they were punished
badly.

'You cannot hurt your own brother, you must be loyal to him
because when you go to war, you will be his keeper,' the *talemgi*
told us.

Although we weren't allowed to fight, we weren't allowed to
be friends either. Boys were punished if they seemed to be, and
so Malual and I knew we must keep our friendship hidden. At
night as we lay in the bed we shared, he told me his father was
a fisherman. Malual had been taken from his family when the
SPLA said he would be going to school. He hadn't really seen
war, and so I told him my stories. I could see he was impressed
when he heard them.

'This is why we must work hard here,' he told me. 'Because

we're learning the skills to fight the *jallabas* and win back our land. You must try even harder, Jal.'

I didn't mind that Malual told me what to do. He was older than me and I liked having a friend. But we were soon discovered sleeping together one night and the *talemgi* was angry.

'If I ever find you doing it again, then I will beat you harder than you've ever been beaten before,' he shouted. 'You are soldiers, not babies.'

Malual and I were sent to sweep the commander's compound, but I didn't like my job. I was too clumsy, it was too boring, and I just wanted to get back to our *tukul* and practise the war songs we were learning. Malual helped me, but when we got back to the group, the *talemgi* punished us once again for the bad work we had done.

'It's because of you that we have been beaten tonight,' Malual said later.

'But I did my best,' I said with a laugh.

'No, you didn't,' he snapped.

'I did,' I shouted.

'No, you didn't,' he screamed back. 'You're lazy and ungrateful.'

Suddenly Malual pushed me. Anger spurted up in an instant, and I slapped his face. Boys watched as we fought – pulling and slapping, we rolled on the ground as we tried to beat each other.

'Stop,' a voice shouted as rough hands pulled us apart.

We looked up. The *talemgi* was staring down at us.

'Why are you fighting?' he asked.

'Because—,' I started to say.

'Shut up,' he boomed. 'We did not bring you here to fight each other. You must save your energy to fight the Arabs.'

'But—,' I tried to reply.

'Shut up,' he screamed again.

I stopped myself from crying out the words bubbling up inside me. The *talemgi* stared at us quietly as we stood in the dirt.

'It seems to me that you two friends are going to have to learn,' he said quietly. 'So if you want to fight that much, then why don't we let you finish?'

Looking around, the *talemgi* called over some nearby *shurta* and asked for their whips. I knew all too well how the long, thin branches bent and cracked before they sliced into skin.

The trainer stared at me. 'Give him twenty.'

I glanced at Malual. I didn't want to fight any more. He said nothing as he lay down on the ground to wait.

'I said give him twenty,' the *talemgi* said quietly. 'Do as I say now.'

I couldn't whip Malual. He was my friend. Standing still, I raised my hand, but my arm felt weak as I tried to push the whip down.

'You're not doing it right,' the *talemgi* screamed. 'You're sparing him. Use all your strength, soldier.'

His whip cut into my stomach, and anger rushed into me again. Malual was my friend, my brother. Jumping up, I raised my hand again and pushed the whip with all my force through the air. Groaning, I wanted the *talemgi* to hear the effort I was making to beat my friend, but in the split second before the whip struck Malual, I slowed my hand down. I didn't care if the *talemgi* was clever enough to see what I was doing. I couldn't hurt Malual.

Jumping and grunting, I played a good performance for the *talemgi*, and so did Malual as he writhed and screamed on the ground. Our faces were hard to each other as he stood up, but smiles were in my eyes as I looked at him. He knew what I'd done, known the game we were playing right under the nose of the *talemgi*. I smiled to myself as I lay down in the dust. I would cry and scream even as the whip landed softly on my arse.

I heard the sharp slicing of air before pain exploded white in front of my eyes. The breath was knocked out of me as the whip came down again and again – each time harder than the last. I felt as if I would be cut in two as I moaned and cried in the dirt. Above me I could hear Malual panting with effort as he beat me.

'Well done,' the *talemgi* said softly when I finally stood up.

Now he was the one with smiles in his eyes. 'You two friends are finally becoming soldiers.' He laughed.

I could not speak to Malual that night or for many days after. My anger felt as fresh as the welts across my buttocks, but when I finally asked him why he had beaten me so hard, he looked at me strangely.

'Because I was ordered to.' Malual's eyes were empty as he stared at me. 'You have to learn to follow orders, Jal, or you will never become a soldier.'

I looked back at him.

I was a soldier. I was in training. I would soon go to war.

CHAPTER 10

Everything you have is a weapon,' the *talemgi* would tell us day after day. 'Your gun, your feet, your hands, your teeth – you must use each of these to kill *jallabas*.'

Burying machetes into the trunks of trees, watching big SPLA plunge their knives into bags stuffed with rags and painted the light brown colour of Arab skin, learning how to bite someone on the throat and dig my fingers into his eye sockets . . . as the days turned into months, the child inside me hardened into a soldier.

Week after week, we were taken into the bush and drilled. Pulling ourselves on bleeding elbows along the ground as bullets were fired into the air above us to make sure we kept low, gulping down pain as we crouched for hours at a time learning how to stay still, or being kicked in the head by the *talemgi* if we raised our legs too high as we crawled along the ground – every lesson in being a soldier hurt. If boys bled, vomited, fainted, or fell, they were left behind.

'The weak don't survive,' the *talemgi* told us. 'Your pain will teach you how to be strong, keep your tears on the inside like men. If you can't carry the wounded, then shoot them, but never leave their gun behind.'

After marching and saluting, we were taught how to handle our 'guns' and the twelve different styles of attacking a town – 'leopard' meant crawling on our elbows into battle, while a night attack would see us holding our gun in one hand and feeling through the darkness with the other.

'You must get used to the voice of the gun,' the *talemgi* told us.

Shaking with excitement, I listened to the click and crack hissing in the air above me.

I and the other younger boys were too small and clumsy for many important jobs. While we were shown how to bury mines, how to walk and run in areas where they had been put, we were too small to learn how to fix them. In war we wouldn't be allowed to throw grenades either because our hands were not strong enough – instead we used stones to practise with.

But in all other ways we were drilled as hard as any of the teenagers at training camp.

'Stand straight,' the *talemgi* would say as I stood to attention and he stamped on my feet or slapped my face.

'Yes, sir,' I'd shout back at him.

On one occasion I was marched back to Pinyudu with hundreds of boys because the UN wanted to count people. The *khawaja*s still asked to see me because I had become well known among them since I'd met Mary, and I was taken to tell them we needed more food, which I knew would later be shared with the SPLA.

'How are you?' a white man asked me.

'I am a soldier,' I replied excitedly.

The elder translating for me stamped on my foot, and the white man never knew what I said. But the story got back to camp, and everyone laughed as I was punished.

'Why can't you shut your mouth when the *khawaja*s are near?' boys spat as they turned their backs. 'You have betrayed us and the SPLA.'

The other thing I hated was guarding at night because I was sure Nyanajuan would eat me as I stood alone in the dark. We talked all the time about the monster and knew he had followed us to training camp. Standing alone outside the *tukul*s beyond the ditches we had dug to jump into if war came, I would watch the trees and shadows for any sign of him. At my side was my wooden gun, but in my hand was a machete to use if Nyanajuan came for me. When I eventually went back to bed, pain would fill my head as I lay down. I got many headaches now as the memories of war kept me awake and I waited for the *talemgi* to surprise us in the night. In the darkness, I would listen to the other boys telling their stories, and my heart would quicken as they did.

'You cannot afford to feel now,' the officers would tell us as we gathered in the training ground. 'Love, friendship, pity . . . all these will weaken you in war. Instead, remember what the *jallabas* have done to you, your family, and your land. You are Red Army now and soon your time will come.

'The Arabs have taken everything we own for the oil buried beneath our ground. They have turned our fellow Africans against us in the name of Islam and tried to destroy us. But you will fight to take our land back just as our forefathers fought, and if every last one of the Black Army dies, then you, the Red Army, will carry on.'

I didn't understand what oil meant – the black gold my land was being torn apart for – but still my heart thudded as the screams of our voices joined together when the officers fell silent.

'*U-lu-lu-lu-lu-lu-lu-lu-lu-lu,*' we screamed as my blood leaped and my head felt dizzy.

Every moment made me stronger. I had learned from the day Malual beat me that I wouldn't have friends again. I would laugh and joke with other boys, tell them stories and entertain them, but inside I was becoming hard as stone. I smiled to myself as I thought of Luaal, where children were trained how to throw dung in a fight with the Dinka over cattle. Now I was being trained for a real enemy, and as my muscles developed, I knew I would be strong enough to fight people far bigger than myself. I forgot about fun and friends; now all I thought of was what had been done to my people and how I would pay back the *jallabas*.

I worked harder and harder as I watched the *jenajesh* in

camp whenever they passed. Looking at them, my mouth would dry a little. All I could think was that I would soon be one of them, and if thoughts of home ever came into my mind, I pushed them out. Mama wasn't here to see what I was doing, and if God cared so much, then why were my people being fed by *khawaja*s? Why were we refugees in a country where no one wanted us, forced out by a government that hated us? Why did the villagers in Luaal and Pinyudu beat drums for God on Christmas Day when He wasn't anywhere to be found?

I stared at the river and the big SPLA waiting on the other side. Clusters of boys were lined all along it, and the *talemgi* stood in front of our group.

'Your gun and your bullets are the most important things in war,' he said. 'If you are walking across a desert, throw your food away but keep your gun and bullets. If you are crossing a river, let the water pull you down, but keep your gun and bullets.'

Fear pricked inside me as I looked at the water rushing past. The river was full, the water quick, and I could see big boys being pushed downstream as they swam. They were strong and heavy, I was small and light. Memories of the night on the boat flickered in my mind.

'Get in,' the trainer commanded, and I walked slowly to the river's edge.

I pushed my fear down. The trainer would smell it if it bubbled up too high.

The water was cold as I walked in, the river bottom uneven as my feet slipped. I threw myself forward, my gun over my shoulder, and started to swim. But the wooden gun floated and pulled me up as I tried to move. I dived under the surface like a frog and kicked hard, but still the gun dragged me back up. I had to show the *talemgi* I was swimming like a good soldier. I held the gun even tighter as I started making my way across the river.

Holding on to it, never letting it go as I fought the current that pulled me downstream, I kicked and used one hand to swim until I reached the other side and pulled myself out.

'Some of you have lost your guns,' the *talemgi* said quietly as we gathered around him. 'How will you fight the Arabs' G3s without a weapon? Do you think your hands will be enough to stop their bullets?'

I looked around and saw Malual standing at the side of the group. He was not carrying his gun.

'Those of you who have lost your weapons will be punished,' the trainer said. 'You will be whipped by the soldiers who kept hold of theirs.'

Something flickered inside me.

'You,' an older boy said as he looked at me. 'Take him.'

He pointed his finger and I followed it. My eyes locked with Malual's.

I smiled inside.

He was silent as he lay on the ground and I stood over him. Raising the whip in my hand, I brought it down using all my strength. Malual gasped as the whip cut into his back, and each scream he gave made my heart beat a little faster. Now he'd feel as I had when he beat me. I had to obey the command I'd been given.

My arm was numb when Malual finally stood up, and I could see he was crying without tears. The worst kind of pain. I was glad.

I gazed at the AK-47 standing by my side. Looking up, I could see the long, black barrel pointing into the sky. I laid the gun gently on the ground and wondered how I would ever clean it. The metal was rusting and dirty, but nearby a big barrel of red grease waited for it. This was the day when I finally became a real soldier.

I'd first held a Kalashnikov a few weeks before when the *talemgi* had called us to a clearing in the bush and told us we would each have seven minutes to dismantle one. I felt nervous as I stepped up to take my turn. I'd only ever watched a soldier do this before – now I had the chance for myself. The metal felt cold in my hand as I lifted the gun. It was heavier than I'd imagined, hard and straight. I breathed in as I tried to remember all I'd been taught.

'At ease,' the *talemgi* said as I saluted him.

I knelt on the ground and lowered the gun down beside me. Easing off the magazine, I took out each bullet from inside and shined them slowly with a cloth. My breath was steady as the *talemgi* watched me. One by one I put the bullets back into the magazine before the *talemgi* took it and handed me an empty one. I slid it back on to the gun and cocked it. Stretching out my fingers, I felt for the trigger. I could not reach. I stretched my fingers as much as I could and felt the trigger at their tips. I held the gun up to my shoulder.

'Now you aim and fire,' he said.

I stiffened my shoulder and lowered my cheek near the barrel. I knew I would fail the test if I shook or breathed too hard. I had to be still.

Everything slowed down around me.

I squeezed the trigger.

A hollow pop.

I felt as if I were falling.

Silently, I put the gun down and eased it apart piece by piece to clean it. When it was put back together, I once again raised it to my shoulder. If the gun didn't fire, then I would fail the test. It fired. Happiness flared inside me.

'Next,' the *talemgi* said.

I knew I had passed the test when I wasn't punished the next day and the *talemgi* gave out promotions and rankings to the best boys. I was among them. I had the highest rank among the small boys like me, and I felt proud. It meant I could tell older boys to fetch me water and they had to do it. But later that day I walked up to a group who stayed still as I looked at them.

I was angry. I had earned my rank, done well at training. I was a good soldier. I went to see the *talemgi*.

'It's nothing to do with size,' he said as the boys were beaten. 'It's his rank you must obey.'

After that the big boys stood and saluted me. It made me feel happy every time they did.

Now I just had to clean my gun before the parade that would make us real soldiers. *Jesh a mer* at last. I wished I were wearing a uniform, but there were none for us. Only the older boys who were going to fight had them. I would be going back to Pinyudu to wait with other boys to be called to battle.

Slowly, I cleaned the AK-47 before putting it on the floor and kicking the lever to cock it. This gun was old and stiff. I wasn't strong enough to do it with my arms alone. Once again, we hadn't been given ammunition. There were stories of boys who'd fired at the *talemgi*s, and we couldn't be trusted not to do the same.

Soon I marched on to the training ground. I had been chosen to parade in front of the top commander who was overseeing the ceremony, and long lines of *jenajesh* snaked ahead of me. I stood alone behind them. My back was as straight as a spear as I marched up to the platform where the commander stood. Eyes staring ahead, my gun at my side, I flicked my head to the right as I walked past him. I wanted to look as brave as the *jenajesh* had once seemed to me.

'This is a proud day,' the commander told us. 'You are now all ready to fight for your country, your land, your freedom.

'Together you will claim victory over Khartoum, the *jallabas*, the African Muslims who have betrayed you.

'Together you will take back the blood of your mothers and fathers, sisters and brothers, uncles and aunts, cousins and grandparents, which was spilled on the earth of Sudan.

'Together you will win this war with the guns that you are now holding. With an AK-47 in your hand you are equal to anybody.'

The commander stared out at us. 'Always remember: the gun is your mother and father now.'

I looked at him. I had a family, a home again.

The training was over. I was a soldier. I was going to war.

The sharp crack of bullets filled the air as guns were fired in celebration, and I lifted my head to stare into the endless desert sky stretching above me. I never wanted the sound to stop. Dancing in front of my eyes, I saw the *jallabas* I'd soon kill.

CHAPTER 11

Usually you could hear men shouting and dogs howling as darkness fell across Pinyudu and the horizon was swallowed by the night. But now we were silent as we waited for Dr John Garang. The leader of the SPLA. The man we'd heard about so much during all the long months of training.

'Do you think Nyanajuan has really been killed?' Nyuol asked.

Fear snapped up inside me like a snake until I crushed it again.

'Yes,' I told him. 'The elders killed him. He's been defeated. Nothing can harm us now.'

I listened as the sound of singing filled the night air.

The children of southern Sudan
Are not scared
Yes, yes, we are all men
So what if we die?
I swear, I swear
That even if I do
I'll fuck your mother and your father too.

Excitement rushed into my veins as I sang. I was a soldier now. I could sleep with one eye open and stop myself from crying out even when I was beaten until piss and shit ran out of me. I knew there were eleven ways to attack a town; how to open, fuse, and throw a grenade; how to load and fire an AK-47; how to raise a machete and hack at an enemy or use stones as a weapon when my bullets ran out. There was nothing to be afraid of.

The singing grew louder and a shiver ran through me. As always, the music made me feel brave. Invincible.

The land of Deng Nhial
We are not going to let it go
The land of Dr John Garang
We'll not let it disappear
We'll take Sudan back by force
We have Kalashnikovs
And with those we'll shoot you
We have AK-46s
And we'll shoot you again
RPG is the artillery of SPLA
And we'll use it against you
46 and the RPG
Boom!

Looking down, I felt anger flash inside me. Our guns had been taken away from us at training camp, and we were told they would be returned when we went to war. I missed the feel of the cold metal in my hands, the moment of stillness before pulling the trigger.

'Soldiers. I am here to talk to you about our war.'

My body tingled. Garang.

'We are going to win the struggle, we will never lose,' he shouted.

Even without a microphone his voice was loud and strong.

'The SPLA are winning towns, we will take Khartoum and soon we will take all of Sudan. We will not fail in our struggle, and each of you will help us to victory.'

My ears opened wide as an elephant's to catch every word. Excitement filled the crowd. I could smell it in the air, taste it on my tongue. This was what we'd been waiting for all these months. We were going to fight.

'Always remember that the gun is your father and your mother now,' Garang continued. 'You are on the side of justice, and any person who opposes the movement of SPLA is your enemy. If your mother is against us, you kill her; if your father is against us, you kill him. The SPLA is your family now. Together we will take revenge for all the wrongs done to us and win this war.'

A roar of shouting exploded. Stamping and clapping, boys made the cry of war to fill their hearts with bravery.

'U-*lu-lu-lu-lu-lu-lu-lu-lu-lu-lu*,' we screamed into the night.

Beside me a boy fainted as the sound of the chant cut into the deepest place in our hearts. I'd heard that a pregnant woman had once even died after a speech because Garang had made her so happy. I understood why. The skin on my neck shivered as I stared at him and pictures filled my mind – the bruises on my mother's body after she was beaten by government soldiers, the tears on Nyagai's face as I was taken to join the SPLA. Now I'd have revenge.

We were told we'd be called to battle soon after that night and did not like waiting as the days slipped into weeks. Life in Pinyudu was the same as ever. But now as well as going to school, we also practised the new skills we had learned in training, such as digging holes to hide in during an attack and guarding the boundaries of the SPLA section of the camp. *Khawaja*s were not allowed in after dark.

Some days I felt bored. I wanted to be a real soldier, not a pretend one, but I enjoyed going to see the wounded in camp with Nyuol and another boy we'd met, Machar. Some of the wounded had no eyes, and others had lost their legs, but they all told us their stories. One man said he'd gone to the fields and returned to find war had started in his village. He was lying on the floor as he spoke, his legs deeply gashed from thorns as he'd run into the bush. As he hid from the government forces, he could see his sister being raped, his house being bombed, and his brother taken by the militias to the north.

'When I can walk again, I'll kill my enemies,' he told us. 'I don't care if it's a baby, I'll blow its head off. I'll kill them in the same way they killed my people.'

Nyuol and I looked at each other.

'I want to kill five soldiers,' he would tell me.

'I want to kill ten,' I'd boast.

When we weren't with the wounded, we still spent hours lining up for food distribution. Sometimes it took days to get to the front of the line, and the *khawaja*s only brought us maize, wheat, lentils, or beans – never bananas or fruits. My mouth watered when I thought of the mango trees I'd once known in Bantiu. I longed to taste such juicy sweetness again.

'We should just go to the Anyuak villages and take what we want,' a boy said one day as we all talked about it.

The Anyuak lived in mud houses with grass roofs in a string of villages along the river near Pinyudu. Instead of the cows prized by the Dinka and the Nuer, the Anyuak lived off fish from the river, goats, sheep, and chickens, as well as fruit that grew on trees planted in the rich soil near the water.

'They have more than they need and we know how to get it,' the boy continued. 'We're fighters now.'

Everyone agreed to the plan. We could climb trees to get to the mangoes and kill animals quickly before burying them in sand to hide them just as the *talemgi* had taught us.

Soon we'd started stealing whatever we could, and although I was too small to take animals, I climbed trees to get fruit. But the Anyuak quickly realised what we were doing, and a few boys were caught. We knew they'd been punished for stealing, some even disappeared, but it didn't stop us. We were practising for war.

Things changed one afternoon about a month later when we all went to the river – some to search for firewood or to wash clothes, others to swim or play games at the water's edge. In the days before, some boys had disappeared after going swimming – eaten by crocodiles or hippos probably – but no one showed he was scared of the water. Machar, Nyuol, and I were playing our favourite game of making hard balls of sand that we'd throw at each other to see whose cracked first. Soon we'd play hand slaps.

'*Aeeeeeeeee*,' a voice cried, and I looked up to see a boy crawling out of the water, which was stained red behind him.

Blood poured from him and his creamy pink intestines poked through a hole in his stomach. They shone against the ebony of his skin. Machar, Nyuol, and I ran to where the boy was lying.

'Get back,' an elder shouted at us as he knelt down to him.

'There's something sharp in the river,' the boy whispered.

He was bleeding badly and soon he was lifted up and taken back to camp.

'What's down there?' boys started asking each other. 'Is it a crocodile?'

But we soon knew it wasn't when someone dived into the river and found spears stuck to the bottom. The Anyuak must have put them there to punish us for stealing.

Word spread quickly. Who were they to attack us? Didn't they know we were soldiers? We could fight and kill these villagers if we wanted to. But it was not until a few hours later that something snapped in the air like a scorpion. Hundreds of us were chattering on the riverbank when we heard that a group of boys had been shot by the Anyuak after going into the village to beat a family in revenge for our friend. Suddenly a high, thin whistle sounded in short, quick blasts.

'Listen,' Machar said excitedly.

It was a noise we knew. The whistle said, 'Run, get your weapon, and assemble.' It was calling us to war.

We surged back to the camp like an army of ants. Machar was beside me, but Nyuol had disappeared and I didn't have time to look around for him. I felt light inside as I fell down repeatedly before getting up and running on. I hardly knew what I was doing. My body was tight, my heart hammered in my chest, and my head felt as if there were only air inside it.

This was what we'd spent all those months training for.

We were going to war. We were going to fight.

A familiar smell filled the air as a brown stain spread across the shorts of a boy running in front of me. Others were running naked after jumping out of the water. Fear and excitement danced in the air.

'The villagers are coming,' voices shouted. 'They're going to kill us. The Arabs have paid them to attack us.'

'We've been trained for this,' another boy screamed. 'It's a practice for a war.'

But I knew it wasn't, as Machar started screaming beside me, '*U-lu-lulu-lu-lu.*'

The *talemgi*'s face flashed in front of my eyes. Finally it was time for war, to prove myself a real soldier.

Reaching camp, I could hear older boys shouting instructions as they tried to get us into our divisions, but no one listened as we collected our weapons. Hurriedly, I grabbed my fishing spear. Others carried stones or pangas and a few had guns as we turned back towards the river and the Anyuak villages.

My chest tightened even more as I started running again. Machar and I said nothing. All I could see were faces floating in the air in front of me – my mother and sisters, my grandmother and aunt. Rage filled my heart as my breath came in gasps.

When we got to the river, I could see some boys crossing it to attack a village on the other side, but I stayed with a group heading down the riverbank. As we neared the huts, shots started to ring out in the air, and I saw smoke in the distance. Nearby a soldier boy sat on the ground as blood ran from his head. Beside him, an Anyuak man lay still on the ground staring vacantly into the air.

My stomach swooped as the sharp sound of bullets hissed through the air. Urine ran warm down my leg as I threw myself to the ground, and Machar fell on the hard earth beside me. I looked at him. I had to be brave.

'U-*lu-lu-lu-lu-lu-lu-lu-lu-lu*,' I screamed as I stood up. I was a soldier, not a boy. 'U-*lu-lu-lu-lu-lu-lu-lu-lu-lu*,' I screamed again, letting the sound fill my head and the blood pump into my veins.

I was a man, not a coward.

We had AK-47s. We were brave and strong. We were trained fighters who would win this war. Screams tumbled in the air around me as boys shouted, their faces twisting into the mask of battle as they bared their teeth.

We flooded into the village where the Anyuak were waiting for us. All around me I could see boys practising the attacks we'd been taught. Running and diving into a crawl like a leopard, crouching on their heels and moving forward in a group to take cover from the bullets. As I ran forward, I saw a man holding a gun about thirty feet in front of me. He pointed it at me and I raised my arm to throw my fishing spear. Pushing with all my strength, I flung it. But the spear missed him and the man raised his gun once more. I couldn't stop running. It was like being caught in a river current and being pushed downstream. My feet just kept moving as I stared at the gun and ran straight at it.

A shot rang out and a big SPLA soldier lurched in front of me. His body jerked to the side as the bullet hit him and he fell. I could see a hole in the back of his head. His brains were oozing from his skull – white jelly mixed with red blood. Suddenly my legs felt heavy. I couldn't run any more. I stopped as boys rushed by on either side of me desperate to get to war. Looking ahead, I saw Machar disappear. I didn't want him to leave me.

I stared at the big SPLA lying in front of me. Pictures of Mama holding Gatluak on the ground flashed into my mind. I couldn't take my eyes away from the dead man as screams echoed in my head. They felt like knives, no longer carrying me forward into battle but stopping me from moving. When would this man wake up? When would he look at me, smile, and jump up laughing at the joke? But the man didn't move and I looked up to see the Anyuak who'd shot at me being attacked by five boys. They jabbed with spears and cut him with pangas while he screamed.

'*Aaaaaaah*,' he cried.

The world fell silent around me.

I was afraid.

The bitter smell of smoke filled my nostrils and jerked me awake. Looking down at my still feet, I knew I had to keep moving and attack as I'd been taught to. I would be known as a coward for ever if I ran away. I had to speed up and get to the front to show how much I wanted war. But the older boys were so fast. I had to carry on – make my legs go quicker and be brave.

'Be a man,' I told myself sternly as I started running again.

The voice in my head sounded like the *talemgi*'s. I had to listen to the voice.

I ran into the village and saw bodies of Anyuak men lying all over the ground as women and children rushed towards huts. Ahead, a group of three boys were running after a woman wearing a loincloth. She was trying to reach a hut with an older woman, and both were screaming as they held on to babies. I ran to join the group as the women disappeared inside the hut, and we stopped at the door. We knew there could be a man inside who might chop us if we followed.

'Get out,' I screamed.

'But there's no one here,' a woman's voice cried.

'We don't care. Just get out. We're setting the house on fire.'

The women started wailing and the sound made me feel braver.

'Come on,' a boy screamed as he snatched up a piece of dried grass from the floor and lit it on a nearby fire.

He flung it on to the roof and the women ran out. Fear glittered in their eyes as they looked at us – four boys who were men now with machetes and spears in their hands.

'Sit down,' I shouted. 'Don't move.'

The women did as I said. I was a soldier, not a child. They must listen to me.

'Quiet,' I screamed at a pregnant woman who sat moaning on the ground nearby.

She was silent but I could still hear crying. I hated the sound. Who was making it? Looking around, I saw babies wailing as they smelled our revenge being lifted on to the breeze. Nearby a little girl ran up to a soldier and start hitting him. Her face was twisted in pain, but the boy pushed her back and she fell on the ground. I remembered my village – the people who had come to take it from us.

I looked around and saw an SPLA boy lying on the ground as blood slowly soaked out of him. He'd been cut with a machete. How red the earth was. My head felt light as hunting cries filled the air. I had to be a good soldier.

'Lie down or I'll cut your head,' I said as I turned once again to the women in front of me. 'Don't make noise. Lie down.'

Lifting a stick in the air, I started hitting the old woman. Again and again I beat her until my arm hurt.

'Please, please, stop,' she cried.

But I was still thinking of my village. Memories of all that I had seen writhed like ghosts in the air around me. The little Anyuak girl's face hovered in front of me.

Anger burst hot in my stomach. 'Shut up,' I screamed at the old woman.

She looked up at me – her eyes dark in her velvet skin.

Grandmother.

Something else stirred inside me. Pity.

I screamed again. '*U-lu-lu-lu-lu-lu-lu-lu-lu*.' The cry of war, the cry of bravery, the cry of revenge.

The air roared with sound: the crackle of huts burning and goats bleating. In the distance I could see big SPLA soldiers dragging a girl into the bush. *Kun ke bom*. Her screams cut into me as a memory of Aunt Sarah flickered inside .

As I stared at the girl being taken by the SPLA, the old woman followed my gaze. 'Leave her alone,' she screamed as she started to get up.

'Down,' I shouted, and the old woman was silent once again.

I was in charge now. We were beating the Anyuak. What had happened to my people was happening to these. Now, it was their men who were dead, their women who were afraid, their children who were crying.

The boy next to me raised his panga. I stared at him as the old woman began to cry. His eyes were empty as he looked at her.

Finish her, a voice screamed in my head. I looked at the boy.

'*Stop*,' a voice behind us screamed.

We turned to see a big SPLA soldier.

'You know the rules,' he told us. 'We have beaten this village, captured its people. You cannot attack its women and children.'

I did not understand what he meant. Had we really won? No one spoke as we looked around. I could see women and children crying on the ground as *jesh a mer* looked down at them. A baby bleeding. It had been beaten. Bodies lay everywhere – some were our soldiers but most were Anyuak. They'd been shot and stabbed with spears, cut with pangas and beaten with stones until their skulls cracked. We'd won the village. Boys danced as they celebrated.

Suddenly my legs started shaking. I tried to stiffen them, hold them still, as I saw boys entering the huts that hadn't been burned, grabbing goats, eggs, chickens, and blankets – whatever they could take before more big SPLA arrived. We could have what we wanted. Sickness made the back of my throat water as I looked back at the two women I was guarding. Then I turned away and ran to join the looting.

The big SPLA arrived soon afterward and ordered us to carry our injured soldiers back to Pinyudu. Our commanders had known nothing of our attack, and clearly we'd angered them.

'Peace must be made between us and the Anyuak,' an officer told us the next day at a meeting. 'These people are not our enemies. They are our friends.'

Our attack had caused a lot of trouble between the SPLA and

the Ethiopians. But we did not understand this as we sang freedom songs while nine men were brought on to the parade
ground with hands tied behind their backs.

'You know our laws,' the commander shouted as we watched.
'These men have raped women and must be punished.'

A few of the prisoners lost control of themselves as we fell
silent. I knew they'd be standing there with the smell of their
own shit filling their noses. Cowards.

The big SPLA cocked their guns to the right, then on to the
other shoulder, and stepped forward.

'*Aaiiiiiiiiim,*' a voice shouted as the guns lifted.

'Fire.'

Bullets rang out and the nine men dropped to the ground. I
stared at them as the warm, earthy smell of their blood was
lifted on to the wind. I'd always thought those who fell in war
would get up again in time. But now I knew the people I'd seen
weren't sleeping. They had gone for ever.

CHAPTER 12

Everyone was quiet in the first few days after the war, but soon boys started telling stories of bravery. Machar had fought well and was admired for it, but others had not. I joined in the laughter at a boy who hadn't even got to the battle because he'd been injured on the way to the village as he dived to the ground.

Mostly, however, I kept silent as a voice inside me whispered, 'You're as bad as the *jallabas*. You did to the Anyuak village what was once done to yours. You stole from them and attacked them, but they're not your enemy. It is the *jallabas* you want to fight – not these people.'

In dreams I saw shadowed men coming to cut my head with a machete or fire bullets into me. Waking up in the darkness, my skin damp with sweat, I thought again and again of Mama. I remembered the faces of the women and children we'd attacked – their eyes begging for mercy, their cries of pain. Mama had told me that doing wrong was a gift to Satan, and we would all be judged when the world ended.

I knew I had to stop the doubts inside me just as a leaking gourd must be stopped. I was old enough to fight, old enough not to feel. Day after day I tried to remember all the *talemgi* had taught me.

'You can't be weak, a woman,' I told myself. 'You're a soldier. Other people did it to your village, and what did they think? The battle only made you stronger.'

It took many months for my guilt to disappear, but slowly it

was replaced by rage. Why had the soldiers been shot after the
battle when they had fought and won? Why weren't our commanders happy that we had proved ourselves so well against the
Anyuak? Bigger boys were being marched out at night as they
were called up to fight, but the rest of us waited idly. At least
I was lucky because I still had a job to do when the *khawaja*s
wanted to speak to a Lost Boy – if journalists or aid workers
wanted information, I would talk to them, show them round
the camp, and make them laugh. But mostly I was bored. We
went back to school as the SPLA told us, but the teachers
weren't skilled and I longed to speak English – the language of
nyanking – instead of Arabic. Food was still rationed; Pinyudu
was getting more crowded and disease killed people. Refugee
life was always the same: we lined up for food, tried to get
more, waited for supplies. It was like swimming against a strong
current and never moving. The only time I came alive was
when I was taken to see the main SPLA training camp, called
Bonga. There I saw soldiers shot once again in punishment for
crimes they had committed. My heart beat hard in the silent
moment before the guns fired. I felt afraid but excited at the
same time.

Things finally changed when I visited another refugee
camp. I was among about two hundred Lost Boys taken
to Itang for a soccer competition, and we realised that life
there was very different from at Pinyudu. Itang was a village
made of proper *tukul*s and compounds with neem trees
and gardens. Some of the shops were even made of bricks
and stones. The SPLA also had barracks about an hour outside the camp, the *jenajesh* wore uniforms, and many Nuer
people were there so I felt more at home. When I heard stories that the best boys were being picked to go to Cuba, a
khawaja land where they would be trained to be the highest
officers in the SPLA, I decided that I must run away to Itang.
Maybe there I would be used for what I had been trained –
battle.

I knew I needed money to travel to Itang because I had to buy a place on a truck going there, and that was how I became friends with Kai. I met him when I changed groups to join one full of boys from Leer – Baba's home. I did not miss Nyuol when I left my old group. I was a soldier now and Deng Deng and Malual had taught me that friends either left or betrayed you. So while I still played with Nyuol sometimes, I did not let him back into my heart.

Kai was a year older than me with big muscles and hard eyes, but what I liked most about him was that he knew many ways to earn money. For instance, we often used to go to the family section of the camp to find a woman and her children.

'We'll be your sons today,' we'd tell her, and together we'd line up for food.

When the *khawaja*s gave the woman extra, she'd either give us some to sell or pay us for our lies. We also stole clothes from the UN stores after making friends with a boy who worked there and told us when the guards would not be watching. It was hard to earn money though, and soon Kai and I had a new plan.

Pinyudu was fast becoming divided between rich and poor – those who lived in the dust and those who made it into gold. One of the wealthy was a woman who ran a restaurant in the marketplace that was always full. Kai and I spent some of our money eating there and for weeks afterward kept returning to watch the woman and her home. Day by day we became friendly with the children who lived nearby and met one of the woman's daughters. Like all young children, her tongue was loose and she told us where her mother kept her money – in a big box inside her *tukul*. Soon we had stolen into the hut and found the box. Smashing it open, we found a pile of notes and coins. Now we had enough to run away.

I felt excited as we paid to get on to a UN lorry going to Itang. I knew I was breaking a rule by leaving Pinyudu but didn't care. I was valuable to the SPLA – the *khawaja*s still came looking for me and I helped get food. Besides, I was going to Itang to be a better soldier.

Nobody asked questions when I arrived and told an officer I'd lost the piece of paper called a departure order telling me to move from Pinyudu. All he wanted to know was that I was trained, and after I showed him 'at ease' and 'attention' and told him about my training, he knew I was a real soldier. As I was given a gun, I told myself no one would ever find and punish me for what I'd done. I wasn't running away from war. I was running towards it.

Clouds raced across the moon and turned its silver light to black as it washed over me. I was standing on the road that ran around the SPLA base and guarding the camp. My eyes searched for enemies as the land stretched into darkness ahead. Trees rustled in the wind and I held my gun a little tighter.

I liked guarding the camp at night, just as I liked many other things about my new life at Itang. My unit was made up of *jesh a mer* as well as big soldiers, and we were always busy – jogging in the mountains, learning karate, and firing our guns. We were each given three bullets to practise shooting. Mine never hit the targets, fruit hanging from trees. I longed to be a sharpshooter because I knew they were treated like kings, but at least now I had a gun to hold every day.

One thing at Itang I didn't like. Soon after arriving I'd woken up one night to feel a hand holding me tightly and something pressing into the top of my legs. Reaching behind me, I grabbed it as hard as I could.

'What are you doing?' a big boy's voice hissed into my ear.

His hand clamped across my mouth as I tried to scream, but I struggled and kicked until he left my bed. All I saw was a shadow melting into the darkness. But after that I noticed things I had not before seen – bigger soldiers getting into bed with *jenajesh* at night, and pain in the boys' eyes the next morning. It was like a secret that everyone knew but no one spoke about, and officers told me I was dreaming when I tried to tell them about it. But I knew I wasn't, and after the night when the hand had tried to silence me, I learned to sleep with a paper bag inside my shorts and one eye open. The rustle of paper would wake me if anyone tried to touch me again. Long ago the *talemgi* had told me that I had to learn to never sleep, and now I knew he was right – enemies are sometimes closer than you think.

Guarding the camp, I focused my eyes on the darkness ahead of me. As a cold wind blew a little stronger, through the trees, the sound of the branches filled the silence. The darkness got thicker in front of me. I stared into it. I must make sure that nothing moved or changed. I must protect the camp.

A cold trickle of water ran down my spine.

I could see something in the black.

'Stop,' I shouted.

The shape started moving. I narrowed my eyes. It was huge, tall. *Jallabas*? Excitement rushed up inside me as I stared ahead.

'Stop,' I screamed once again.

But still it came – legs moving and head swaying as it approached. My heart beat into my ears.

It wasn't a *jallaba*. It was too big. It must be a *nyakuthunj*. I was going to be eaten just as boys had once been in the desert. I raised my gun and fired a shot, but still the *nyakuthunj* kept coming. I fired once more, but it didn't stop. The bullets cracked loudly in the air. Holding my breath, I pulled the trigger a third time.

The shape disappeared.

'Nyakuthunj,' I screamed as I turned to start running back to the camp.

My breath screamed inside me as I ran as fast as I could. I had to get away and warn the camp it was coming.

A light appeared in the darkness in front of me.

'What's going on?' a big soldier asked as he ran up to me with a torch. 'Why did you fire?'

'Nyakuthunj,' I said breathlessly. 'It's out there. It's coming for us. I fired and it disappeared. But it won't stop coming. It wants to eat us.'

Soon some more big soldiers had joined us to search the darkness for any sign of the *nyakuthunj*, but it had disappeared and they could find nothing in the night.

'This is your monster,' an officer shouted the next day as he threw a small rock at me. 'We went to check for animal footprints, but we didn't even find those. This was all there was.'

Looking down I saw a streak of white on the rock.

'Only one bullet hit,' he sneered. 'And you shouldn't be wasting ammunition on rocks that will never hurt you, little boy. You are just the same as the other *jenajesh* – quick to scare and shoot. But you all need to learn that you cannot waste bullets and create fear. What kind of soldiers are you?'

Shame filled me as he laughed. It burned hot inside. I was *jesh a mer* – the bravest soldiers who ran to the front of the battle. I had fought the Anyuak in Ethiopia and won. This man might be laughing at me today, but when tomorrow came, I would show him and others like him who I was.

Someone I knew lived somewhere in the SPLA base near Itang and always hoped that I would one day see her again. Fathna, the woman from the boat whose daughter I'd saved, lived in a big compound with her husband, Taban, who was the SPLA commander of the camp. At first I had stayed hidden and not seen them, but as the months passed, I'd become more sure I was safe. I had disappeared from Pinyudu and no one had missed me.

As time passed, I became as talkative as ever, and I'd once even spoken to Dr Riek Machar – a man so high up in the SPLA that he was friends with our leader John Garang. Riek came from Leer and when he came to Itang, I made sure I met him. His bodyguards had wanted to beat me, but I got past them to meet the commander. I made him laugh as we talked.

'How do you do it?' the boys asked when I went back to my unit.

'Because I have luck on my side,' I told them, but I did not really know.

I just knew that if I made officers laugh as I'd done with the *khawaja*s, then they would usually talk to me, and I was happy when I was told that Taban had asked me to visit him. I was sure he was going to thank me for rescuing his daughter from the river.

'Auntie,' I said as Fathna came to greet me.

In my culture anyone older than you is *uncle* or *auntie*; someone close to your age is *brother* or *sister*. Nuer are like a big family, and because Fathna had known Grandmother Nyapan Deng and Mama, I knew I must respect her.

'Jal,' Fathna shrieked as I arrived. 'It is so good to see you. Where have you been? What have you been doing? How is your family?'

'I don't know.'

A shadow flew across Fathna's face. 'What do you mean?'

'I have not seen them for a long time.'

'But your mother, your grandmother – how are they?'

'I don't know,' I said, suddenly feeling angry.

I looked at Fathna silently as she gave me a soda, but we soon started talking again until one of Uncle Taban's men called me to him.

'So you are the boy who saved my daughter,' he said as he sat on the veranda of his *tukul*. 'I am happy to meet you.'

'And I you. I want to go to Cuba where the *khawaja*s will train me to be a better soldier.'

'Really? Well, I am sure that one day I will help you, but first let us eat. Today we have a special guest and you must greet him with me.'

'Who is it?' I asked excitedly. Maybe Garang himself was coming to see us.

'It is Commander Jurkuch, and he is looking forward to seeing you.'

My stomach swooped. Commander Jurkuch was in charge of Pinyudu. The words inside me dried up. Would he know who I was? Would he be angry with me? But I felt safer when I saw the smile on the commander's face as he greeted me and we sat down to eat.

'So this is where you've been, Jal,' he said with a laugh. 'We've all been wondering what you've been doing.'

'He wants to become a better soldier,' Taban told him.

'I do,' I said excitedly. 'And I want to go to Cuba to learn.'

Commander Jurkuch looked at me. 'Well, I am sure that one day you will, but first you must do a job for us. The UN have been asking about you. Tomorrow they are coming to see us at Pinyudu with their video cameras and will want to see you.'

I did not speak for a moment. I did not want to leave Itang, where I was a soldier, and return to Pinyudu, where I had only waited to be one.

'Maybe you will see Mary again,' Commander Jurkuch said.

Mary? Happiness welled up inside me for a moment. I had never forgotten her and the day she took me to the market. Mary was the one *khawaja* whose memory had not been erased by time. But then I remembered how much I liked Itang.

'I cannot leave here,' I told Commander Jurkuch. 'I am a soldier now.'

'Don't worry. If you come with us, then I am sure Taban will let you come back to Itang. The *khawaja*s arrive tomorrow, so we must leave soon. We need you to make sure we get food supplies, Jal.'

I knew I could not refuse an officer's request, and soon I told my auntie that I must leave.

'Please don't go,' Fathna said with a worried look on her face. 'Stay with us.'

'But I have to. And I will come to see you as soon as I get back.'

*

Commander Jurkuch stared at me.

'You did well, Jal,' he said, and I smiled as I looked at him.

We had returned to Pinyudu the previous day and I had seen the UN. They'd taken a film of me as I'd told them we needed more food.

'I am pleased to help, sir.' I saluted and felt happy inside. I had helped my old friends at Pinyudu, and now I would return to Itang. 'When will I be able to leave?' I asked.

'Leave?'

'Yes. To go back to Itang as you said I would.'

'Not for some time, I'm afraid.'

I looked at the commander. 'But why?'

'Surely you know, Jal?' he said with a smile. 'Did you really think that no one would notice what you had done? Some boys might be able to get lost, but you are not one of them. You left us without permission, and even you must know that is a crime.'

I felt my stomach tighten. 'But I have helped you,' I said in a rush. 'And I am being a good soldier at Itang.'

'I don't care,' Commander Jurkuch shouted. 'Do you think that the rules of the SPLA don't apply to you? Do you think you're special just because you help with *khawaja* food that?'

I said nothing.

'Well, you're not,' Commander Jurkuch said.

I lifted my head to look at him.

'And now it is time for you to learn.'

I lay on the ground as I waited for the whip to bite into me once again. Days before I'd been told I was being charged with desertion, and a woman had also told my group leader that I had stolen some soap from her. He'd wanted me to admit all the charges, but I'd refused. I had run away but I hadn't stolen from this woman and so I wouldn't admit to it. Many people could accuse me of such a crime, but I knew I had never taken anything from her.

Now I was in Kover – the SPLA prison where soldiers were brought to die for their crimes. I felt afraid as I wondered if I too would be killed for what I had done wrong. Earlier that day I'd been brought before an officer who sat with two soldiers beside him. One was to give me twenty lashes with a hippo-skin whip, and I'd tried to protect myself by stuffing my overalls with plastic bags. But they'd been taken away, and now all I wore was a pair of shorts. My buttocks burned where the whip had slashed me. My skin felt hot and I could feel my heart pounding in my chest.

'Will you admit the charges?' the officer said as he stared down at me.

'No.'

I didn't care how much they beat me. I would not admit to something I had not done.

'Okay,' the officer said as he looked at the two soldiers standing beside him. 'Give him one-two.' The men stood on either side of me, and I heard their whips swishing through the air. I tensed as they rushed around. One-two, the whips cut into me. One-two, one-two, one-two. Pain filled me and I soon forgot I was a soldier as I started to cry. Just as I had on the day when I'd burned my foot during war many years before, I cried without tears.

The soldiers finally stopped whipping me after one hundred lashes, and my buttocks were swollen and numb as I was lifted up.

'Will you confess?' the officer asked once more.

'No,' I whispered.

'I think he needs some encouragement,' he told his men. 'Take him away.'

The ground moved in waves in front of my eyes as the men dragged me along. Pain ran down my legs and my eyes flickered shut. Were they going to kill me now? I wanted to be a good soldier. Why were they punishing me like this?

I opened my eyes to see a hole in the ground, and suddenly my feet were lifted into the air as arms pulled me up for a moment before the ground started swallowing me up. Down I went, down, down into the hole until the soldiers' hands let go of me and I fell on to the floor.

I looked around. The walls of the hole were made of wet mud. Dead cockroaches and scorpions lay scattered on the floor. A strong stench of rotting meat made me retch as I stared up at the clear sky above me. Darkness filled the hole as a blanket of thorns was pulled over the entrance, and I was left in suffo-cating blackness. I felt light inside as I tried to breathe. I was sure I would never leave this place.

CHAPTER 13

'Do they put *jenajesh* in front of the firing squad?' I asked the captain sitting beside me. Night had fallen, the other men were asleep, and it was dark in our prison, but I couldn't close my eyes.

'No, Jal. They wait until they grow.'

I shivered as I sat in the darkness.

I'd been in prison for many weeks now after being taken out of the small hole. My new home was a bigger pit where eighteen other men lived, and I had climbed down a ladder into it. The men were dirty and the air was full of the smell of them as they looked at me. Above, I could hear metal scraping along the ground as sheeting was pulled over the entrance.

At first I had felt afraid and kept quiet as I listened to the men talk. One had shot someone, another had slept with a commander's wife, and three had run away from the battlefield to a refugee camp. All had stories to tell. But while I slowly realised that the men would not hurt me, I knew I would not escape the dangers of my prison so easily. We were kept in the hole for a long time – gasping when we could feel the intense heat off the metal roof as it cooked in the sun, or sitting in mud when the rain fell and soaked us. The only times we were allowed out were to squat over a hole in the ground, for a lashing, or to do our duties. I had to sweep the camp for hour after hour but was always returned to the hole at the end of the day.

At first I'd tried not to think too much about how long I would be in prison. But as I listened to the other prisoners talk,

I understood that some knew they would end up in front of a
firing squad, and it scared me to think that I might too. I had
been whipped and beaten but still refused to admit to stealing, so
maybe Commander Jurkuch would want me dead. My head
ached heavily as I thought about it. I didn't know how long I
would be here or whether I'd ever be a soldier again.

'Why don't you tell me a story, Jal?' the captain asked as I sat
silently.

He was my friend now that we were in prison together. The
captain and I laughed when mud covered us or when another
prisoner farted, and then, when the guards tried to silence us, we
laughed even harder. Sometimes, just like tonight, we also told
each other stories to pass the time.

I turned my head in the blackness and began, 'There was once
a man who fell in love with a beautiful girl. But the man could
never meet the girl because she lived in a big compound guarded
by lions.

'And so the man would climb trees to sing beautiful songs to
the girl, and she would come out to listen to his voice. But no
matter how often she did, the man was always too scared to
climb down from his tree and speak to her because of the lions.

'Day after day he sang, and as the days turned into weeks and
months, the man told himself that he had to be brave because
the beautiful girl would never want to marry a coward who
stayed hidden up a tree. So one day he decided to climb down.

'But as his feet touched the ground, he saw a lion in the distance and he started running. Soon he was going so fast that his
legs flew in the air behind him and his ankles hit his head. As he
reached the compound where the girl lived, he was sure his own
feet were the lion's paws touching his back, and with a scream
he grabbed them, tripped himself up, and fell on to his belly in
the dust, where he fainted in fear.

'"Did I kill the lion?" he asked as he woke up.

'"What lion?" a voice asked.

'He looked up to see the beautiful girl.

'"The lion that chased me to you," he replied as she smiled at him.

'"The lion has gone for ever," she said.

'You see, the beautiful girl knew the man had never been chased by a lion, but she had already fallen in love with him because of his beautiful songs and wanted him to be her husband even though he was a coward.'

I heard a soft laugh in the dark. 'Well done, Jal,' the captain said. 'It is only in a story that a beautiful girl would fall in love with a coward.'

'Of course, Captain. But it is nice to think that songs can be so powerful.'

'They can, of course. Did you know there are soldiers whose job it is to make troops sing before a battle? Music puts courage into hearts and soothes them when they are defeated.'

'Yes, I have heard of such soldiers,' I replied.

'And one day you will hear them for yourself.'

I said nothing as he turned away to lie on the cold ground. There would be no more stories tonight. I thought of the songs once more. Once I had dreamed about singing them as I went into battle, but now I was sure I never would. Soon though, I would learn that when war finally found me, I would be silent as it roared in my ears.

May 1991 is the first certain date in my story because I fought in a battle documented in the history books when I was eleven years old. The SPLA's ally Mengistu Haile Mariam had been overthrown by rebels, and I was among many prisoners who were released and ordered to go and fight because, without his support, our army had to retreat out of Ethiopia. We were needed to join units to defend all that was the SPLA's – precious food, ammunition, and weapons had to be protected – and I was sent back to the camp where I had trained as a *jenajesh* two years before.

It was very different from the place I remembered ruled by the *talemgi*s. Now it was full of troops – some packing to leave, others handing out weapons – and chaos hung in the air.

'The Ethiopians have turned against us,' a Lost Boy called Diew told me. 'They have taken Bonga.'

It was the SPLA's main training base, where I had once watched prisoners being shot.

'But where will we get ammunition? How will we fight in Sudan without the Ethiopians' help?' I asked Diew.

'I don't know,' he replied as we fell silent.

On a battlefield just outside the camp, the SPLA were fighting the Ethiopian rebels, and all the *jesh a mer* were sent to the stores to get equipment. The younger ones had already been evacuated, and just the older boys remained. Even though I was one of the smaller soldiers, I had been left behind because I had been a prisoner and had to fight. I was wearing shorts and a T-shirt but was given boots, a mosquito net, and a gun. I felt excited as I touched the metal again. Did this finally mean that I was going to be a real soldier? I just wanted to shoot a bullet, know how it felt to hear it whistle out of the barrel of the gun towards my enemy.

But as the days passed and I watched bigger soldiers go off to fight, I felt something else inside. In the distance I could hear the sound of shells and guns being fired, and the noises reminded me of all I had seen long ago when I was with my family.

'They even have women fighting with them,' the big SPLA told us as they returned from the front line. 'They don't give up. We shoot and shoot and still they come for us.'

All around me, the wounded were being brought back into camp – some with bullet wounds, others with limbs blown off by grenades – and I remembered a man I'd once seen at Pinyudu. He'd lost an eye in battle and had a hole in his face where it had once been. His nose dribbled as he talked to us, and the sound of his rattling breath scared me. I thought of him now as I lay on the ground at night and tried to sleep as the battle screeched in the distance. There were whispers in camp that our commander,

Salva Kiir, had been ordered to leave but was refusing to. He did not want to show he was willing to run, and our job was to defend him. Soon it would be my turn to go to the front line just as other *jenajesh* around me were doing each day. I did not want to be shot in the eye or lose my leg. If I was wounded, I would rather die.

The morning air was still as I lay in the long, shallow hole. I rested my gun on a lip of earth in front of my face. Ahead was empty land that had once been cleared to keep mosquitoes out of the training camp. Now it was all that lay between our troops and the Ethiopians hiding in the trees beyond.

Diew was in a hole beside me, and I looked at him as we waited for the signal that the battle had started. We were not allowed to fire our guns until a soldier along our line launched an RPG and its deep boom signalled that we must fight. I felt sick and I wanted to pee as I waited. Beside me was a box of bullets that I must fire.

'Shoot straight into the bush,' an officer had told me. 'Don't get out of your hole, and don't raise your head too far.'

I crouched down a little more. I wished Diew were lying next to me. He seemed so far away even though I knew I could touch him if I just reached far enough. But I didn't want to move. The person who had been in my hole a few hours before must have died and that was why I was filling it. The Ethiopians were watching me now, hidden in the trees and waiting to fire at me.

I looked down the SPLA line – soldiers were lying in holes and pits all along it while others were crouched behind big guns on stands with belts of bullets slung around their shoulders. Ahead were the trees and long grass. The air was fresh as I breathed it in, but I knew death was close.

Boooooooom.

The deep explosion of an RPG.

War had started.

I squeezed the trigger and the gun kicked back against me. My feet flexed against the end of the hole as the firing started. A warm stream of urine trickled down my leg into the earth below me. The wind was bitter with the smell of bullets. I knew I had a choice: to run or shoot.

Again and again I squeezed the trigger.

T-t-t-t-t-t-t-t-t-t-t, the bullets erupted in front of me.

I closed my eyes as I fired, not knowing whom I was shooting at or where. I just wanted to feel the gun's beat as the air around me filled with the sounds of *jenajesh* screaming as they were hit.

'*Mamayo*,' they cried. 'Mummy.'

'Shut up,' I heard a big soldier shouting.

The world was falling apart. Screams, bullets spitting, and small explosions made my ears buzz. War was around me and inside me as my body shook.

I opened my eyes. The trees in the bush were moving, and suddenly Ethiopians ran out into the open ground ahead. They ran in a long line, diving on to the ground and firing at us as they moved as one. Earth flew into the air as a grenade hit the line, and I watched as men jerked before falling to the ground. For a moment, they looked as if they were dancing on strings, their bodies tightening in surprise before death took them. If they were hit directly, they were split apart. I closed my eyes again and pulled the trigger. All I could hear were the screams of the injured as I shot – *jenajesh* crying like cats, high and piercing, their sounds cutting through the deep cracks of my ammunition.

My eyes flew open and I saw more people coming out from the trees. Some were women, their mouths twisted in fury, breasts bared as they ran towards our lines. I closed my eyes to shoot again and felt a hollow click. My gun had run out of bullets. I reached into the box beside me to reload it. Around me soldiers were running forward into our lines to pull the injured out of their holes. I prayed that I would not be among them. *Please don't let them shoot my eyes, please don't make me blind.*

The Ethiopians were advancing. They were getting closer every second. I clicked the magazine back on to my gun and folded my hand around the trigger. Squeezing my fingers again and again, I fired into the gulf before me.

As the hours passed, I learned that battle is like music – it ebbs and flows, screeching and silent in turns. Some moments I thought my ears would burst as guns, grenades, and rockets exploded, then everything would fall silent as troops on both sides reloaded. I stayed in the hole all night, and by the time light was seeping into the sky above, the smell of blood filled the air as Diew and I were ordered to leave the front line.

'Get back to the camp,' an officer told us. 'It is time to evacuate.'

I did not feel angry as I heard those words. There were too many Ethiopians, and all night I had thought about the Arabs I'd seen in my dreams. Of course I was glad to have fired my gun, but it was *jallabas* I wanted to fight.

Diew and I were told that we were going to accompany a big soldier who was taking a commander's wife to safety. Her name was Nyakal and we were ordered to take her to Pochalla, a town just inside Sudan. The camp was under heavy fire by the time we got back, and people were running as they tried to escape. Bombs exploded close to us and fire was spreading quickly. We knew we had to leave as quickly as possible, but it was hard and we kept throwing ourselves to the floor as ammunition hit. My blood raced. We were playing a game with the enemy in the distance now – they couldn't see us any more and all we had to do was outrun them.

But Nyakal would not do as we told her. When we lay on the ground, she struggled to get up; when we told her to leave her bag, she held on to it. She ran like a chicken not knowing where it was going just as I had once seen people in my village do when war came. But now I knew how to run zigzag and felt angry that Nyakal didn't listen.

'Keep still,' the big SPLA soldier shouted at her as we dived to the ground during heavy firing.

But Nyakal tried to get up once again and I grabbed her ankle. 'Stay down,' I screamed.

All we could do was wait for the moments when everything went quiet and we could get up and run – past the injured who pleaded with us for help, the burning *tukuls*, and into the countryside. We all knew that if one of us was shot, then it was God's will.

The ground shook underneath us as we waited.

Bullets and grenades, rockets and shells – the sounds thudded in my chest. My stomach boiled inside me and my legs felt heavy when I finally got up – not light as when I was little and had to run from war. I had a responsibility now – our mission was to take Nyakal to Pochalla, and my legs were weighed down by it.

We finally escaped that night and left the war behind as the sounds of battle fell silent. I lost Diew and Nyakal as we walked in a big group of troops and civilians towards the border, and as the sky began to lighten, we reached a river that marked the entrance to Sudan. I thought of the day so long before when I'd looked forward to crossing a river to get into Ethiopia and reach school.

I knew I should try to find Diew and Nyakal, but my head throbbed and I felt dizzy. We'd left the road behind and were walking through long grass and trees where the hilly ground was rough and I kept slipping on stones. I had been awake for many hours without food.

Suddenly I heard a scream.

'They're here, they're here, the Ethiopians are here,' a voice shouted, and I looked behind to see a boy running from the direction of the main road. 'They're all over.'

An RPG went off near my right side, and civilians started running in circles. Diving to the ground, I unlocked my gun. Bodies were lying everywhere near where the grenade had hit – I could see a hand nestling in the grass, and the boy who had screamed the warning lay close to me. He'd been shot in the back.

As I lifted my gun, bullets started flying all around me as our soldiers returned fire. Ahead I could see an injured man. The small, round dot scars on his forehead told me he was Shilluk, and he groaned as he lay on the ground. He'd been hit by the RPG and his leg had been blown away. Blood seeped into the ground around him, bright red in the sun. My hands shook as I started to fire. I could not hear my bullets but knew I was firing because my gun was shaking.

I couldn't see where the Ethiopians were as I lay hidden behind a small hill, so I scrambled up the mound on my stomach to look through the grass. There they were. Pouring across the road in the distance. There were so many of them. We would never outfire them.

'Move, move,' the injured man shouted at me.

I stared at him.

'I'll stop them,' he screamed. 'Run.'

People started running, but I didn't know what to do. Those people were civilians. They were allowed to run when war came to find them. But I was a soldier. It was my duty to stay and fight. The Ethiopians were near us now – another few seconds and they'd be here. All around me other soldiers were firing as they tried to hold them back.

The man looked at me and lifted up a grenade in his hand. Sweat shone on his forehead and the ground around him dazzled crimson. He pulled the pin and held the grenade steady.

'Leave,' he shouted. 'Go!'

With a grunt, he threw the grenade ahead of him into a crowd of Ethiopians. Bodies flew up in the air as it exploded.

I did not move but started firing, pulling the trigger again and again. More Ethiopians were running up the hill as civilians ran for the river. My shoulder was numb now from the gun kicking against me. But suddenly it stopped moving. I squeezed the trigger but the gun didn't speak to me.

My bullets had run out.

I looked at the man. He was holding another grenade in his

hand. I knew I had to start running, but turning my head, I looked back at him. He was surrounded by Ethiopians who were kicking him as he lay on the ground. Suddenly a small dark cloud swallowed up the group as people were thrown back. An Ethiopian was cut into pieces as the grenade exploded. Carcasses flew into the air as the man and all those around him disappeared. Flesh shone bright white and red in front of me.

I stopped for a moment. The Ethiopians were everywhere – women running and diving on the ground as they shot, men holding up grenades as they screamed. I could hear helicopters and the deep growls of tanks or jeeps, see *jenajesh* and big soldiers starting to surrender, but I would not. Throwing down my gun, I forgot all the lessons I'd once been taught. My gun was useless, it had no bullets, it was too heavy, and if I was running with it, then I would be a target. If I was going to be captured, it was better to be captured without a weapon.

I ran to the river as people surged all around me.

'Don't go,' I heard an SPLA soldier shout. 'They're at the river too. They're shooting at anyone who tries to swim across.'

I didn't understand what he was saying. I was running away. I couldn't hear him, couldn't listen. I had to get to the river. I had to get back to Sudan. I carried on running.

My breath tore in my chest like claws as I saw the silver gleam of water. Running harder, I neared the riverbank and looked down. I didn't understand. Was it raining? Why couldn't I feel the drops of water on me? They were everywhere – falling into the water and leaving little pools on the surface that melted away.

I flicked my head around. I couldn't see the Ethiopians, but they were there. They were firing into the river. Again and again they did it until the surface was dappled with bullets falling like rain. I stared into the water. It was red with blood, the bodies in it so fresh that they had sunk as their life seeped into the river and stained it. People carried on jumping in as the bullets continued to shower down. I knew I would die too if I did the same. I had to find another way to cross.

Running into the trees, I followed the path of the river and joined a group of people running in silence as we tried to escape the guns. My heart beat heavy and fast and all I could hear was the sound of grass snapping beneath my feet. When the world was finally still again, I stopped in front of the river and, taking a deep breath, dived in.

CHAPTER 14

'Have you ever been to the battlefields?' the soldier asked as the truck drove along the muddy road.

'Yes,' I told him.

'Where?'

'Ethiopia.'

'Really?'

'Yes. And I killed many. There were many rebels trying to attack our base – thousands of them trying to get us. They were everywhere and had big teeth and red eyes.'

'You call Ethiopia a battlefield?'

'Yes.'

The soldier laughed. 'Well, soon you'll see the real thing *jena-jesh*. We're nearing Juba now.'

I had tried to run away from the war after pulling myself out of the river, and elsewhere 350,000 refugees poured out of Ethiopia to try to escape too. The rebels had attacked the refugee camps, including Pinyudu, and thousands of unarmed Lost Boys had died as they tried to escape – shot, drowned, or eaten by crocodiles as they crossed the huge river Gilo. I felt scared as I started walking with the swarm of people leaving the battle behind. I was a soldier who had thrown away his gun. I would be punished if the SPLA discovered what I had done. I didn't want to go back to prison – a cold, dark hole that I might never leave. The only way to keep myself safe was to hide among the Lost Boys and lie that I had never been trained as a soldier. Not every

Lost Boy had learned how to use a gun or been trained to fight as I had, even though we had all been under the control of the SPLA in the camps. If I could pretend I was just an ordinary boy, then I might escape.

I hid myself in a group of five Lost Boys who worked together to find food after we arrived in the town of Pochalla. People were starving all around us, and once again the *khawaja*s were there to hand out food to the weakest. They also started dropping it from the sky in planes, and my legs would shake when I heard the engines in the distance. People would beat each other as the huge packages crashed on to the ground, but there was still not enough to feed everyone. As well as aid planes, government ones also came often to bomb the town – sending fire from above as we ran to hide. I knew that when birds start flying, snakes start wriggling, and dogs start running, the bombers are coming, and when the throbbing engines go silent, it means they are finally above you. Many people were killed by the planes, as well as by mines planted in the forest near the town where they were hunting for food.

I did not want to wait to die with the refugees but was too scared to show myself to the SPLA as the months passed. So I decided to escape on one of the planes that flew out of the town and talked my way on to one by pretending to be an old woman's grandson. She told me that our journey would end in Kenya, but I had not heard of this place. I did not then know there were other countries with black people in them or how big the world was. I just wanted to fly in a *nyanking*. But, as the plane climbed into the sky and my stomach flew into my mouth, I could hear people scream. Something had got caught in the engine and my heart thudded as the big metal bird coughed and sputtered in the air.

I was happy when I finally stepped off the plane just across the border in Kenya. But I was soon rounded up by the SPLA and driven back to a southern Sudanese town called Kapoeta. I was taken to the compound of an important officer called

William Nyuon and no one asked about my gun as I had feared. The SPLA was finding all its soldiers because there was trouble in my army. Riek Machar – the commander I had talked to long before in Itang – had defected from the SPLA in August 1991. Like me, Riek was Nuer and had set up a rival group because he and his men were unhappy with our leader Dr John Garang. Garang was a Dinka and the split had caused much trouble between the tribes. Dr Garang dreamed of a unified Sudan but Riek Machar wanted a separate South because he believed the North could never be trusted. It meant that Dinka and Nuer soldiers, who had once fought together in the SPLA, were on opposing sides as some remained loyal to Dr Garang and others joined Riek Machar.

I was stationed in the commanders' compound, and as I cleaned shoes, ironed clothes, and polished guns, I listened to the big soldiers talk about the problems in the SPLA. Terrible whispers were in the air. The SPLA had attacked Leer as well as other areas loyal to him. Some of these were captured as villages were burned, people died, and the age-old rivalry between Dinka and Nuer, which had been overcome as they united against Khartoum, was sparked again. Convinced that Garang's Dinka supporters had targeted their tribe, armed Nuer civilians called the White Army, who supported Riek, and soldiers who had sided with him, rose up in revenge. They had attacked a Dinka area called Bor, and thousands had died – old people, women and babies, no one was safe. Those who had escaped were now wandering the country – thousands of refugees. Arab dictators in Khartoum were happy that our movement had been made weak by this fight.

Months passed as I moved from town to town with the SPLA. I wanted to go to the front line again now that I knew I would not be punished for losing my gun, but the commanders wanted to keep me with them because, just like the *khawaja*s at Pinyudu, they liked my stories and jokes. I had also learned how to play chess and dominoes, and they would laugh as I beat them. 'You have a bright future,' they'd tell me, but all I could dream of was fighting. I did not want to be kept away from battle. I had tasted it twice now and wanted to be part of our war against Khartoum. I'd heard that Lost Boys living in a huge Kenyan refugee camp called Kakuma would sometimes leave school there to go and fight. A seed had been planted in them that even education could not wither, and I understood how they felt. The need for revenge had been seared on to our hearts as we watched our villages burn and then beaten and starved into our bones at Pinyudu and training camp.

That was why I felt happy now as I sat on the lorry with the soldier who spoke to me of the battlefields. Finally I was going to war in a place called Juba – an important city that the SPLA was trying to capture. Many soldiers were going to fight, and I was at last going too. Capturing Juba would be a big loss for the *jallabas* – it was the capital of South Sudan, had an airport and the river Nile ran through it – and there were so many of us I was sure we would do it.

Night was falling as we drove. As the miles had passed, I'd noticed fewer and fewer civilians in the area and more and more soldiers.

'I will be happy to see the battlefields,' I said.

'Really?' he replied.

'Yes. I am Nuer – the tribe the British described as tall and fearless when they came to try and conquer us. I will not run away from Arabs on the battlefields. I will kill as many as possible.'

The soldier looked at me. 'Bravo little *jenajesh*,' he replied, then turned to stare at the road in front of us.

Arab army camps surrounded the main city of Juba while the SPLA bases were deeper into the bush. The biggest, called Kurki 1, was closest to the city, and Kurki 2 was smaller and farther out. I was taken to Kurki 2, where hundreds of other soldiers were also waiting. We arrived before dawn to find the camp completely dark. There were no cooking fires, cigarettes flashing red, or lights of any kind.

'We mustn't show ourselves to the *jallabas*,' a soldier explained. 'We must be hidden here in the bush.'

As the night turned from grey to light, I could see more of the base. It was next to a river, and small *tukul*s made of grass surrounded a parade ground. Jeeps and trucks were hidden among the trees in the forest, and ammunition boxes were every-where – some covered by tarpaulin, others dug into holes, more stored in tents. As the camp gradually came awake, injured soldiers started arriving in boats on the river. There had been a battle the night before, and a small town near Juba had been captured. Some men were carried off the boats with wounds bound with cloths, others walked with blood running down their faces, and some were still, their hands or arms missing as they were carried. I felt dark inside. I could smell death near.

'You guys are lucky,' an officer said as he walked up to us. 'We usually get shelling for breakfast. It's late today.'

I looked at him as I wondered what shelling tasted like. If he didn't like it, would I want to eat it?

'There are holes over there for you to use when it starts,' the officer continued. 'It shouldn't be too bad today. We did well last night so the *jallabas* will be feeling tired.'

I soon understood that shelling wasn't food. It was what I'd known as a child when little bombs had fallen on my villages. Now they were fired into our camp, and tyres burst on jeeps with a thud as they were hit by shrapnel, glass shattered, and *tukul*s burned as we hid in holes. After that day I became used to shelling for breakfast.

The next day I was transferred to Kurki 1 – even closer to the front line – and given a uniform. I had to cut it down to fit me and wished I had not lost my boots long ago. Instead I had to wear *mutu khali* – or die-and-leave-them – shoes made out of old tyres that never wore out. But I longed to have real boots again like the big soldiers. I was finally back in the heart of war, and all I could think of was fighting as I was given a gun. I had to keep it with me night and day except when I was doing duties such as cooking. I'd sleep with one eye open and my AK-47 beside me.

I was breathless as I listened to soldiers singing to prepare themselves for battle. But while troops were moved out of the base to go and fight, I was chosen with some other *jenajesh* to stay at Kurki 1 to be bodyguards for the camp commander, John Kong. Disappointment burned through me as I listened to my orders. I didn't want to stay here, far from the real war and with the commanders once again. I thought I had left behind all the months of waiting when I was rounded up for battle. But I did not argue as the other *jesh a mer* and I learned our duties. There were five of us in a unit of thirty-three who protected John Kong. If there was no war, we collected water and firewood, washed clothes, and sent messages. But when the shelling started, we would run into holes close to the one topped with cement where the commander hid. Each time I'd hope the *jallabas* would try to come into our camp so I could fire the gun that itched in my hand. The metal felt heavy as I raised my eyes over the edge of the hole and looked into the dark trees beyond with the sound of gunfire in my ears.

I did not want friends any more now that I was in Kurki 1. Sometimes I swam in the river or played soccer with the other *jesh a mer*, but I didn't talk as I had once done. We were in a war zone and there was no time for stories as news danced around us about the war and the injured were brought back into camp day after day – some with arms and legs missing, others with their ears shot off. I soon learned how to look but not see them. I only prayed that I would die when I finally went into battle.

Then a boy arrived whom I knew I wanted to talk to because I could see he was a real soldier. Lam was fifteen and had joined the SPLA after his father was killed as a suspected spy. He had been fighting for a long time until he got caught up in the tribal violence still dividing our army after the split between John Garang and Riek Machar. Lam and his captain, who were both Nuer, had been captured by Dinka SPLA. They were each told to dig a hole before their hands and feet were tied and machete blows cut into them. All Lam could do was pray as he watched his captain being buried alive in the hole he'd dug for himself. But God sent Lam a miracle when he realised the machetes had cut through the ropes holding him. He ran away covered in blood, and after some tribespeople had looked after him, came to Juba.

Lam had told his story to John Kong when he arrived, and I knew our commander was angry about it. Everyone under John Kong's command knew that Nuer and Dinka must not fight each other, and he told Lam he could be a bodyguard like me while he recovered from his injuries. I started talking to Lam, and as he told me his stories of war, I stared at the machete cuts on his arms, legs, and body. They were the true marks of a soldier.

'I've killed many *jallabas*,' Lam would say. 'You're scared the first time you do it, but after that you're not. It's easier than capturing them because then they shit in fear and cry like babies for mercy.'

Lam seemed tall as he stood beside me. He was so black he was almost navy blue, and his scars shone light pink in his skin.

'Have you ever been to war?' Lam would ask, and I'd feel ashamed.

'Yes, in Ethiopia,' I'd say in a rush. 'Where there are women soldiers whose breasts hang out as they shoot.'

Lam laughed. 'Ethiopia? Where our army lost? You couldn't beat women?'

'But you should have seen their breasts! We were all staring at them so hard as we tried to shoot that our bullets went soft.'

'I'd never let a woman beat me.' Lam clicked his throat as he always did after chewing *sawut* – a sticky tobacco resin that many of the soldiers liked. 'I don't want to kill women – it's their men I want. They took my father, and even if I kill ten thousand, it won't be enough.'

I felt bad when Lam said such things, a memory of Mama playing in the shadows of my mind, her smile like a blur somewhere in the distance. I could not even picture Mama's face properly any more. I just knew that death had been in my heart for so long I wanted to see it face-to-face one day soon.

John Kong sighed as a big crack filled the air. 'You are good at this job, soldier,' he told me.

We were sitting outside the commander's *tukul* and I was pulling on his fingers after he'd returned from war. Next I would move on to his toes and make them crack too. I did this job often, and sometimes John Kong would give me some tea if he had no visitors and the camp was peaceful.

The sun was setting and the commander's AK-47 lay close to me as I worked. Usually a stream of words rushed out of me when I saw John Kong, but tonight my mind was elsewhere. I'd seen Lam earlier and felt angry as he showed me his new boots. He was fighting now because his wounds had healed, and I stared at the rips on his uniform.

'Do you like my new boots?' Lam had said. 'I took them from a dead *jallaba*.'

I couldn't stop thinking about what he'd said as I sat in front of John Kong.

'I want to go to the front line, sir,' I said suddenly.

'The front line?' John Kong asked. 'But you're already on the front line, Jal. Juba city is so close you can smell it, and Arab encampments even nearer. You can hear the bullets, can't you? See the planes going overhead, feel the ground shake when the shelling begins? What other front line do you want to go to?'

'The one where I can see Arabs every day and shoot at them.'

'But you don't just fire your gun, Jal. There are tanks there and helicopters too.'

'I know about them,' I said angrily. 'I've been in war in Ethiopia.'

'I know, Jal, I know,' John Kong said softly. He looked at me as he sat up and a soldier handed him some tea. 'You are still a small boy, you are a junior, and you will have a bright future one day when we send you to school. We need you to go there and learn things to make our country great.'

But I didn't want to fly *nyanking* any more. I wanted to be on the ground with Lam, not high in the air looking down.

'Why can't I fight?' I insisted. 'I've heard the big soldiers talk. They are scared of *jenajesh* because we shoot so quickly. We are young and light too – they can use us to run across minefields and run at the front of battle.'

The soldier sitting by John Kong stared at me. 'So you think you can run as fast as me?'

'Of course.'

The soldier said nothing as he handed me a bullet belt. It felt heavy as I stood up and strapped it around my waist.

'Look,' I said.

The soldier stood up too and held out another bullet belt in front of me. I put it over my shoulder. He handed me a water bottle and a small box of biscuits. I put them into my pockets.

'Now run,' the soldier said.

I staggered a little as I tried to move. There must be rocks in this bullet belt. It was so heavy. I couldn't lift my legs.

'But I won't carry all these things into battle,' I shouted. 'I won't need them.'

'You will when your bullets run out,' John Kong replied.

Why wouldn't he listen to me? Why wouldn't he let me do what I'd been trained for? I'd spent months eating dirt, marching, and being beaten. I'd run away and gone to prison because I'd looked so hard for war, and for what?

'You must stay here,' John Kong told me. 'If we are attacked, then you can defend. But until then you are not going anywhere, little soldier.'

CHAPTER 15

We stood outside the *tukul* as the woman came to greet us. I was with Lam and four big soldiers in a village near camp, and we were looking for alcohol. I hadn't seen this woman before even though I'd been here many times to buy drink for the officers. Sometimes I had some myself in exchange for a few bullets. With a gun in your hand, you can get what you want.

I'd thought of Grandmother Nyapan Deng when I first drank the strange liquid. It burned my throat as I swallowed it, and soon my legs felt soft and my eyes fuzzy, but I liked the feeling. I would drink a whole bowl until my stomach felt like it would burst and I burped. Then I'd make music by blowing on grass between my thumbs or marching around as I made a trumpet noise with my hand, and the big soldiers laughed. The next day I'd have a headache, but I always wanted more alcohol. I liked coming to the village and seeing the fear in the people's eyes as they looked at a *jesh a mer* with his gun.

'Do you have any alcohol?' a big soldier asked the woman.

She looked at us. 'Do you have money?'

'Yes, yes,' the soldier said impatiently. 'Just bring us what we want and we'll pay.'

I knew we wouldn't. The officers bought alcohol with money, but we couldn't. We would have to take what we wanted.

I thought of Juba as we waited for the woman. Today was a Friday – the *jallabas*' prayer day. Soldiers had left camp this morning to go and fight, and I knew they would strike the moment our enemy's prayer chants rose into the sky. The Arabs were weak as they removed their boots, washed their feet, and knelt to speak to their God.

The woman walked out of the *tukul* holding two jerrycans – one brown, one white. She handed them to the soldier and we turned to leave.

'What about my money?'

'We don't have any,' the big soldier said quietly as he turned to look at her.

'What?'

'There's no money.'

The soldier stared at the woman as he lifted his gun towards her. Without a word, she turned to start running.

'Boom!' I screamed at her.

I looked at Lam and we laughed. The woman had run like a chicken, but this time she wasn't scared of war. She was scared of us. I smiled to myself.

Kurki 1 was usually shelled twice a day, and we got so used to it that we only ran to hide when the bombs were really heavy. Many soldiers were injured, but the civilians in the villages nearby were hit worst. I was cut once when a chunk of shrapnel flew into my leg, and another day I felt a hot wind blow over my cheeks as a piece of boiling metal flew past my face before burying itself in a mud wall.

I tried not to think about the shelling, but as time passed, I found it harder and harder to sleep as I waited for the camp to be attacked. Long, cold fingers wrapped themselves around my heart as I thought of all the stories I heard during the day. Rumors were that SPLA elsewhere were doing wrong to the villagers around them – taking food by force, killing people who attacked them, and catching women. The soldiers knew our laws but broke them. John Kong was too strict to allow such things to happen at Kurki 1, and we knew that if we hurt the villagers, their chiefs would come to see him. After we'd stolen alcohol from the woman, her chief had come to the camp, reported us to the commanders, and we'd all been punished.

But the stories I thought of most were those I heard about what the Arabs did to our soldiers if they captured them – pouring burning oil on to tongues, sticking broken bottles up arses, or killing us just for fun. As I lay in the dark, I would listen to the gunfire in the distance and think of the Arabs so near. I knew I would rather die on my feet than live on my knees and beg a *jallaba* for mercy.

As time passed, I didn't shake so much and my stomach stayed still – but my mind was still active. I thought about God often, and questions filled me. We were all created by God, but if God knew Satan would make so much trouble, then why hadn't He killed him? And who made God? My head felt heavy and I knew such questions could hurt *jenajesh* because I'd once seen a boy who'd asked too many.

'Is this our land? Does God love us?' he asked as he sat shivering on the ground. 'How did Arabs come here? Why are we fighting? How big is the world? Is it really round?'

Big soldiers had tied his hands and legs as he sat and laughed to himself.

'We are all going to die,' he said as he looked at me with ghosts in his eyes.

I was told such questions were useless but knew that in his wildness the boy was also wise. He was taken away, but sometimes I'd think of him as I tried to sleep. I knew I must control the thoughts that snapped like crocodiles in my head or I would become like him.

Planes came often to attack us, but the first time I saw a helicopter was early one morning. A warning had gone up and I'd started running to hide in a hole near the river. As I got to the bank, I heard a deep throbbing in the sky and a strange wind rushing around me. I turned my head to see a giant vulture in the sky. Bullets were pouring from it as soldiers ran to take cover and shoot. But I was too scared to. I couldn't remember where my gun was. The deep throb of the helicopter was moving closer and closer. It was coming to find me.

I got to the hole. Two bodies were lying close to it as I threw myself in. A soldier with bullet wounds in his chest lay on the floor; another was moaning next to him. My hand slipped on the earth and I lifted it to see blood running across my palm. No one was talking here, this place wasn't safe. I put my head out of the hole and looked at the helicopter. It had flown across the river and was turning around in the distance. It was returning for me. I had to find somewhere else to hide.

Jumping out of the hole, I ran towards the river. If I could stay underneath the water long enough, then maybe the helicopter would forget me. Throwing myself into the river, I dived down to look for a plant as thick as my thumb with a hole running through its stem that grew on the bed. I'd once used it to blow bubbles in Bantiu. Now it would save me from the helicopter.

I pulled at whatever I could feel beneath me. Green and brown shapes moved in front of my eyes. I felt something give and swam up to the surface holding on to it. Pushing the reed up but holding on to plants growing around me to keep myself underwater, my mouth closed around its end.

I breathed in and felt air flood into my lungs.

The surface of the water shone white above me, and dark shadows flew across it. The sound of my breath rattled in my ears, but I could hear deep booms as well. Everything was still as the minutes passed and I breathed through the reed, until I pushed my head above the water to see if the helicopter had gone. I could hear bullets and laughing, and I went back under the water. I had to stay here until everything was silent. But suddenly the river moved like a wave as plants bent all around me and I was pushed upward. I coughed as I broke the surface. Would the helicopter see me? Would it shoot me now?

I wiped my eyes. Ahead of me was the camp, but the sky above it was quiet. The helicopter had gone. I pulled myself out of the water and started walking back to my home.

'They will come on foot to attack us now that we have been weakened,' an officer told me as I arrived back, and he was right.

Soon the Arabs came and started attacking us from the forest. Around me faces were tight and eyes hard as we looked for them. Alongside other soldiers, I lay in a hole firing my gun again and again into the trees. The bullets seemed to go on for ever until finally the enemy was quiet. Later I would learn that Lam was among a flank attack that finished the soldiers our bullets hadn't reached. For now I watched as wounded *jallabas* were found in the forest and brought back into camp. Most were quiet and would soon be taken to fields nearby where they would work for us to grow food for the camp. But one would not obey as he stood with his hands tied behind his back.

'You will never win this war,' he shouted in Arabic.

A soldier walked up to him and kicked the Arab before raising his gun.

'*Allahu Akbar*,' the *jallaba* screamed in the instant before a shot ripped into his chest.

He fell to the ground and I looked at him. One day I wanted to be like the big soldier – looking into my enemy's eyes as I shot him.

Screams and gunfire echoed through the trees as I walked, and I was feeling scared. I knew now more than ever that I had to be brave. A soldier had recently been brought back to the base to be punished after trying to run from battle. He was called Mary and made to behave like a woman – cooking, sitting with his legs closed, and wearing a skirt – as his friends laughed that 'she' was a good wife. I knew war was like the *gaar* ceremony I'd watched in Luaal many years before; I had to keep silent however deeply fear cut into me.

Troops were walking through the forest to a village under attack from Arabs. Earlier we'd seen smoke rising in the air from the other side of the river and knew they were punishing villagers for helping us with supplies. About three hundred of us had crossed the river and started walking, soon coming to a place that had already been attacked and left. It was deserted except for the dead lying silently on the ground – blackened bodies, white bones and skulls, all huddled in the dust. Pictures of my village filled my mind as I looked at them.

At last I was going into battle, and this time there would be no trees or helicopters for the Arabs to hide in. They had tried to steal our guerrilla tactics by surprising the villages, and now we would be the ones to use them. We would surround the village and take it. At last I'd see my enemy face-to-face. Not Anyuak, not Ethiopians, but Arabs.

I moved silently, using my soldier skills to stay hidden and holding my gun tightly. I'd shortened the strap to make sure my AK-47 didn't hit the ground as I walked, and although I was carrying just thirty bullets, I hoped I would use them well.

With a sudden rustling noise a soldier dived to the ground. He was about to cough and someone next to him covered his head to smother the noise. We were getting closer to the battle. I felt brave inside. My stomach did not turn any more because all I could think of was the village I'd just seen like so many of my childhood. Today the hate inside me would finally be released against the *jallabas*.

The sharp crackle of burning got louder as the trees started to thin and the village came into sight ahead.

'Get down, line out,' an officer said, and we fanned out to attack.

Villagers were screaming as we moved forward still hidden by the forest. I could see women and children running and men tied up on the ground. But there were just a few Arabs there compared to us – about a hundred – and while some looked among the trees to check that no one was hiding, most were rounding up prisoners or slapping them as they sat on the ground. The Arabs thought this village was theirs now.

An RPG fired above me and I shivered.

'*U-lu-lu-lu-lu-lu-lu-lu-lu*,' I screamed as I stood up to run.

I tripped on the root of a tree and the ground flew up before my eyes. I looked up – soldiers were running on ahead of me as I scrambled up to follow them.

Troops ran forward as gunfire exploded through the trees. Big soldiers were firing as they ran, aiming at *jallabas* who fell as they were hit, but I could not run and shoot. My gun was too heavy and I might hit a fellow soldier if it rocked in my arms as I lifted it. Each time I fired a bullet, I had to stop – lifting my gun and aiming it into the camp before moving forward again.

I broke through the edge of the trees in a long line of troops following an officer. There was movement, noise, shooting everywhere, but I made myself listen as he screamed commands. The line was breaking up as the battle started. My heart rushed inside me, my legs felt weak. I was going to get shot or, worse, injured. I'd be taken back to camp like all those other injured men I'd seen.

I lifted my gun to start firing. Ahead I could see a group of *jallabas* standing between two huts, and I pointed my gun at them. I started firing as a big soldier next to me did the same. My gun kicked back and I closed my eyes as each shot rocked me back and forward, shells pouring from the AK-47 as it fired.

T-t-t-t-t-t-t-t-t, it screamed.

Suddenly I felt powerful, strong. My gun was speaking for me as it spat bullets. My gun was taking my revenge. The big soldier and I walked forward a few steps as we carried on shooting. The *jallabas* were trying to hide behind the huts, but our guns were too quick. I could see a man in the group had fallen and soon another had too. All over the village, soldiers were moving forward and firing. Snatches of sound and light pushed into my head. I fired harder. Two more *jallabas* fell, then another, and finally two more were injured. They were finally quiet.

'Well done, Jal,' the big soldier said as he walked up to the two injured men who lay in the dirt. 'Your bullets did this.' He moved his gun to point at the bodies on the ground. 'And it was your bullets that did this too. You are a brave boy.'

I looked down at the faces lying at my feet – eyes glassy and unseeing, blood seeping from wounds. One man had fallen on his back with his arms thrown out as if in welcome, another had been shot in the chest and his uniform was stained black with blood. The third was crouched against the wall of the burning hut, his eyes half-closed, and the final *jallaba* was lying face-down in the dirt. The bodies were blank, lifeless, just as I'd always dreamed they would be. The sound of the battle beat inside my chest as I stared down. The faces of the dead swam in front of me as I looked at them.

My eyes focused for a second. I felt breathless.

These were not Arab faces. They were black like mine. My stomach turned. Where were the *jallabas*?

'Who are they?' I asked as I pointed at the bodies.

'Black Muslims,' the big soldier said. 'Most of the army in Juba is black, only about a third is Arab.'

I stared once again before turning towards the big soldier. Confusion made my head swim. I didn't understand.

'They are *jallabas*, Jal, even if their skin is black like ours. And they are the worst kind. These are Sudanese who have joined our enemies against us, worshipping their God instead of ours. They are our own people and yet they hate us.'

A voice screamed in front of me. One of the injured men was pulling himself forward in the dirt, swearing and cursing as he tried to grab a gun. A crack filled the air and he fell back.

'See?' the big soldier beside me said. 'They are worse than

Arabs. And do you know why? Because they are betraying their own people, and for that they deserve to die like dogs.'

I heard a groan and turned to look at another injured man sitting at my feet. He had been shot in the leg and his hands were raised above his head in surrender. But I couldn't see his African eyes as I looked down – all I saw was his Arab heart.

CHAPTER 16

I longed to go to the front of the front line after that day – the area between Kurki 1 and Juba city where there were many small bases. It was here the SPLA and Arabs battled each other face-to-face to take camps and supplies, and where most of the heavy fighting took place. At last I got my chance to see it when I started carrying ammunition there with other *jenajesh*, and I was happy as we walked at night through the forest, carrying boxes of grenades and bullets. I could see things were different when I got there. The soldiers looked tired, the air was heavy, and as I unpacked the boxes I'd carried, I listened to *jenajesh* talking.

'Did you see his head explode?' one said, laughing.

'Yes. My gun ran out of bullets then because I'd killed so many.'

I stared at them. All the *jesh a mer* fighting at the front of the front line were older than me – boys of about fourteen upward – and they were bigger too. I was still so small, and however much I wished for it, my legs did not want to grow. That is why the officers wanted to keep me away from there. They thought I was too little to fight.

'You will soon go to school,' they told me. 'You are a clever boy and you must be educated so that you can help our country when the war is over.'

But I was twelve now. I had shot men. I was ready for more war even though life at the front of the front line was hard. In Kurki we slept in huts on beds made of wood; the soldiers slept in bushes. We cooked food for ourselves; here the soldiers were brought food, which was cold by the time they tasted it. At Kurki I had biscuits, a uniform, and the commanders spared me from doing the hard jobs such as collecting firewood or grinding maize with a huge pole called a *fundok*. In return I made sure I entertained them with my jokes or chess moves and brought back fish from the river whenever Lam and I went there to catch them.

'If you want favours, then this is what you've got to do,' Lam would say as we stood on the riverbank, worms hanging from hooks and dangling in the water.

Lam was now a bodyguard to one of John Kong's most important men and would go with our commander whenever he left camp for the front of the front line. Sometimes Lam would be gone days, sometimes a week, but whenever he returned, he would tell me his stories.

'You must always kill a *jallaba* with your bare hands,' Lam would say. 'Never let them trick you or believe their lies. You must capture them, kill them, and finish them.'

I'd nod as I looked at him, thinking of the other *jenajesh*, and sometimes I'd ask John Kong questions about the war as I did my duties for him.

'Why do we have to hide in the bush to fight?' I would ask. 'Why must we fight the cowardly way? In the villages, men face each other, so why can't we do this and fight the Arabs face-to-face?'

'Because the world has changed, Jal,' John Kong would say with a laugh. 'Our way of fighting is not the coward's way – it is the clever way because soon we will beat the Arabs.'

I hoped that by making the commanders like me enough, they would listen when I asked to go to into a proper battle. But they didn't want to, and on the days when I wasn't sent to carry ammunition, I would sneak down to the front of the front line in secret. I was usually caught but still kept trying. I wanted to feel myself being shaken inside as the tanks drew close and hear the click of guns as we started firing at *jallabas* who broke through our lines and tried to attack us. Then I lifted up my gun to fire with other *jesh a mer*, knowing we were admired by the bigger soldiers because we ran at the front of battle, were lucky running across minefields, and never took prisoners because *jenajesh* always killed the Arabs they found.

One of the most exciting days came when a commander gathered us all together to tell us we were going to make an important attack. Arab helicopters had fired at our camps every morning, and an officer told us he had a plan. Soon soldiers with RPGs and others with AK-47s like me were hiding in holes or trees as we listened for the deep throb. When they came, we fired again and again together until a helicopter exploded in a ball of fire above us. We cheered and cheered as it fell from the sky and knew that the helicopters would not come for us so often now.

My time at the front of the front line taught me just one new thing about war – the worst is when it is over. As the battle falls silent, only the screams of the injured can be heard, and when the guns stop firing and the smell of smoke fades away, the stench of flesh and blood fills the air. *Jenajesh* were always the ones who screamed most, and I heard them at night when I returned to Kurki 1 to try to rest. I never slept properly, keeping one eye open all night in case our enemy tried to attack and feeling the weight of my gun next to me. When the battle at the front of the front line had been very bad, I didn't want to eat meat for days as I remembered the smell. It reminded me of being a small boy and was so heavy I was sure it had sunk into my heart for ever, just as it had on the day I walked down Death Route with Mama and Nyakouth. I felt torn inside, knowing I was safer at Kurki 1 but still dreaming of seeing a *jallaba*'s face as I shot his heart.

I looked at Captain Yen Makuach. He was an officer at the front of the front line and I had got to know him on my visits

there. I liked him. Without tribal scars and able to speak both
Dinka and Nuer, Captain Makuach was popular with all the soldiers and, just like John Kong, kept the *jenajesh* close to him as
bodyguards.

'I want to come on an attack,' I said as I looked at him.

The eyes of Captain Makuach were hard to read as he looked
at me. 'Why, Jal?'

'I want to kill Arabs.'

He was silent as I stood in front of him.

I paused for a moment. I wanted to go forward into battle
for another reason too. For months now I had watched soldiers
returning with boots and clothes, radios and bedsheets, anything they could take from the bodies and camps of the
jallabas they had killed. Lam was the same – he often returned
to Kurki 1 with new things, and I longed for something to
show off.

'I want a bike,' I said as I looked at Captain Makuach.

I'd first ridden one during the months after Ethiopia when I'd
moved around with the commanders after leaving Ethiopia. I
was in Kafoeta when I saw it and asked the big soldier who
owned it to teach me to ride.

'You need to push the pedals with your feet, steer your direction with the handlebars,' he'd said as he took me to the top of
a hill where he'd let go.

'Hold on,' he shouted as the bike started to move, slowly at
first and then faster as the wind rushed past my ears.

The ground was bumpy and I didn't know how to drive the
bike so I just kept going down the hill – faster and faster until
the slope came to an end and I started pedalling up the other
side. I could hear people screaming. They must be cheering me
on, seeing how well I was doing. But as I turned my head to
smile at them, I saw a bomber in the air. Looking up, I felt the
bike tip and wiggle and I fell into the dust.

I'd never forgotten that day or the ones that came after it
when I practised more and more. I preferred the bike to a jeep

Here I am in the refugee camp in Ethiopia being interviewed by the press who came to report on the hunger strike in Sudan.

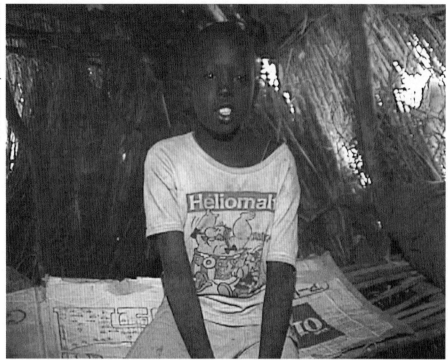

Top: This was my bed and I am sitting on my mattress, which was a piece of cardboard.

Bottom: Nual and I grinding maize for food.

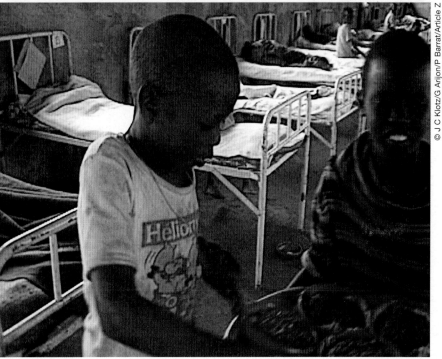

Top: Playing football with Nual. The ball was made out of bags and bits of cloth.

Bottom: This is the hospital in the refugee camp in Ethiopia and I am giving out food to the sick.

Top: Here I am in Nairobi and Emma is teaching me how to use the computer.

Bottom: This was taken in Nairobi at the home of a BBC reporter.

Top: Here I am visiting a school in Kariobangi, which is being supported by GUA Africa.

Bottom: On location in Juba, filming on an ex-battlefield for the documentary *War Child*.

Top: Me and Peter Gabriel backstage at the concert for
Nelson Mandela's ninetieth birthday.

Bottom: Here I am performing at a concert in Berlin, which was organised by
Oxfam in order to urge nations to keep their promises on aid, trade and debt.

Top: Ahead of the concert for his birthday I met Nelson Mandela to congratulate him on reaching his ninetieth year!

Bottom: Here is my performance being projected at the concert for Nelson Mandela's ninetieth birthday, which took place in Hyde Park.

From refugee to rap star. What a journey it has been!

I'd tried to drive once because I felt as if I were flying. But I'd lost the bike when I'd moved on from Kafoeta and had thought of it again and again as I watched soldiers bring back their prizes from Juba.

Captain Makuach looked at me. 'You are too small for battle, Jal – there are tanks, minefields, and big weapons. The *jenajesh* who fight are bigger than you. You are the smallest here, but one day soon you'll have grown enough.'

'But I want to kill Arabs. The *talemgi* once told me that this is what I'd do.'

'You've killed enough already,' the captain replied. 'You've defended the base, seen battle like any other soldier.'

'But I want to see it up close.'

'Why?'

I stared at Captain Makuach. I hadn't spoken of Mama and my village for so long, I'd tried to make myself forget what I'd seen there. But something made me speak and I told him my story.

'You have seen much,' he said as I finished. 'But revenge is not the reason we are fighting here. We are fighting for our freedom, our land and religion – not revenge.'

I didn't say anything. Captain Makuach spoke differently from so many of the officers who'd talked to me over the years – stoking the flames inside as they told me to remember my family and what had been done to them.

'I cannot send you into battle.'

I looked at him silently.

'But I will get you a bike.'

'Really?'

'Yes, Jal.'

The captain's word was good. A black bike was waiting for me when I came back. Happiness filled me as I looked at it. Now I could tell Lam that I too had taken something from battle. That afternoon I set off back to the base riding on the rough ground, and even though my legs quickly felt tired as I started riding up a hill, I knew I would be able to keep pedalling as long as my bike needed me to.

Boom! A shell landed next to me.

I jumped off the bike and started pushing it as another shell exploded nearby. Throwing down the bike, I ran behind a mound in the grass. I waited and waited until it finally went quiet again, then got up and took hold of the bike. Running hard, I started pushing it up the hill once again. My feet slipped and my legs hurt as I ran, but still I held on. Everyone in Kurki would want to ride my bike. I would have something to trade with them. I'd tell them I'd stolen it during an attack.

Boom! Another shell exploded. The *jallabas* had seen me. They were shooting at me. The bastards wanted my bike.

Ahead, I could see the top of the hill. I just had to get over it to be hidden. Digging my feet into the ground and pushing myself on, I kept running. I knew I would go quicker if I left the bike, but my hands wouldn't let it go.

Boom!

But still I ran.

Leaning on my bike and panting hard, I looked at the top of the hill as shells fell around me. Three steps, two steps . . . I was there. I stopped as I looked down at the slope running away below me. Now I would be hidden and safe. But for a moment I turned and looked back at Juba. One day soon the *jallabas* who'd fired at me would be the ones running. And then I would be like all the other *jenajesh* I saw at the front of the front line.

The officers were standing under a tree as they spoke. In front of them a map of Juba had been drawn on the earth with white chalk, and Dr Garang was talking to them. I had heard from other soldiers that the final assault on the city would soon start, and Garang was here to discuss it. I cannot be sure but think I'd been in Juba for about seven months by now, and it was the summer of 1992.

I stared at our leader as I stood near the group holding a clay pot of water. He had lost weight since the night so long ago when I had seen him at Pinyudu, and although I'd often seen John Garang with his wife, Rebecca, in the distance, I'd never been so close to our leader. I felt breathless as I looked at him.

'The enemy is weak now,' he said to John Kong. 'We must finish them soon.'

As the officers talked, I stood at the edge of the group, unsure of what to do.

'Where is the water?' I heard John Kong ask.

'Here,' I said, pushing my way through the bodyguards to stand behind him and Dr Garang.

Commander John Kong's back was to me as he stared at the map.

'We must take the airport,' he said quietly. 'That will stop their bringing in food, troops, and fuel. It will destroy them.'

'Yes,' Dr Garang said. 'But first we must unite our troops. The divisions between Dinka and Nuer are running too deep, and we cannot afford to keep up this rift. Not when we have come so far. Our troops must know that the SPLA is their first loyalty if we are to win this war.'

I listened as I filled some glasses. The battle for Juba had been long and hard and the soldiers were tired. Our singing was not as loud and fierce as it had once been when we sang our war songs in the mornings.

As Dr Garang, John Kong and the other officers talked, I worked my way around the group – handing out a drink to each of the men until I stood in front of John Garang.

My heart thudded as he looked up and took the glass of water I was holding. My hand flew like a dart to the side of my head as he did so, and my foot stamped on the ground. 'Sir,' I shouted as I saluted.

Dr Garang looked at the officers around him with a smile in

his eyes. 'Hello, soldier. What is your name and what are you doing here?'

It felt as if a thousand bees were flying around my brain. John Garang was talking to me. I wondered if I would ever be able to speak.

'My name is Jal Jok, sir, and I am *jesh a mer*, sir.'

'Well, soldier, it is good to see that you are learning here with Commander John Kong.'

'Yes, sir.'

Dr Garang patted me on the head before turning back to the map. I stood for a moment, wanting to talk too much but knowing I couldn't. The officers spoke in low voices as I walked away to start my duties.

Soon Dr Garang had to leave – spies were everywhere and the Arabs would try to take him when they heard he was at Kurki 1. Over the next few days it became clear that the big assault on Juba was close. Reinforcements had started to arrive, and bullets, ammunition, artillery, and jeeps with guns on the top were also being brought. Soon the camp was heavy with activity as Commander John Kong and many of the other officers left Kurki to move to the front of the front line with their units. A string of smaller attacks were being launched on the *jallaba* camps around Juba to see how strong they were, and soon news arrived that we were winning. Soldiers were sure that Juba would be ours this time – Arab messages had been intercepted that showed how scared they were.

Lam and I talked about it often as soldiers flooded out of Kurki. We knew he would soon leave with his unit, and I wanted to go with him.

'Will you talk to your captain and ask if I can come with you?' I said to Lam one day. I had to be there when the *jallabas* fell, but no one had given me a job to do yet. 'Commander Kong has left the camp now so he can't stop me from going. And the other officers won't say anything if your captain agrees that I can come with you. I don't want to be carrying ammunition and shooting as they come into our camp. I want to be on the front of the front line. Please, Lam.'

'This war will be like nothing we've seen before,' he said. 'It will be hard and fierce like no other.'

I knew it would be, and that was why I wanted to see it.

CHAPTER 17

Lam had done just as he had said he would. I was now in a unit of thirty-three going into battle alongside many others. The line of soldiers stretched into the dusk as troops walked through the forest. Lam was behind me but we didn't speak. I knew that he, like me, didn't want to open his mouth and let death slip slowly inside as we talked. All around us lay corpses, which the sun had warmed throughout the day. They were everywhere – bones, skeletons, and fresh bodies – and their rotten smell hung heavy in the air. This really was the front of the front line, and even the vultures did not fly away in surprise when they saw us. Death was everything here while the living went unnoticed. I wondered if any of the bodies still had life in them, if any of our soldiers lying on the ground were trying to whisper for help. I knew that not everyone hit by a bullet died. Maybe someone was lying close to me as the life ebbed out of them and I turned my back to walk farther into the forest.

About eighteen of my unit were *jenajesh* but I couldn't see them as we walked in the dark among hundreds of troops. We were nearing an Arab base around which we would hide before attacking when morning came. Our target was a camp near the river, which the SPLA needed to conquer in order to move troops into the centre of Juba. Our soldiers had been attacking the base for many days which is why the dead surrounded us. But we knew the *jallaba* camp was weak and all we had to do was finally take it as ours.

My foot slipped on the ground and I felt something wriggling inside my shoe. I gasped as I lifted my foot to shake it off. I looked down to see a rotting hand, crawling with maggots. The smell of flesh was so strong it made me feel dizzy. I shook my foot, fighting down the sickness that twisted my stomach, knowing I had to keep walking despite whatever I found in this dark place.

The skin on my neck shivered when voices and laughter drifted into the air. We were near to the camp now, and officers whispered to us to spread out silently to hide for the night. I knew I could not move again once I had lain down with Lam. We had been told the *jallabas* might fire into the forest to try to trick us. They wanted to find out if anyone was hiding, and if we shot back, they would know. The Arabs were in their base with spare bullets – we were carrying everything with us and could not waste ammunition. As well as bullets, I was carrying a water bottle, and these would be the only things I had with me when the morning came on which I would live or die.

My heart thudded, and the soft surge of blood rushed in my ears between each beat.

A tree rustled above me and I stared up. Faces were coming at me in the darkness. I shook my head.

I looked up at the stars hanging in the sky above. They seemed so bright and heavy tonight, as if they would fall out of the sky and spread silver across the land as it started to rain. I tensed as I heard rustling in the bushes. Something was running through the trees, and branches cracked as it came towards us.

'Lie down,' an officer hissed.

A muffled voice cried out and I heard the snort of a wild pig. Seconds later bullets fired from the base ahead.

'Do not retaliate,' the officer commanded.

Gunfire spit in a stream through the air. The boom of an RPG sounded near, and lights shone. I crouched lower and turned to Lam. Light from a small explosion washed across his face. I could hear a tank as it moved around the base, its deep growl throbbing in the earth underneath me and into my belly.

'We'll send someone in now to trick them,' Lam whispered. 'The *jallabas* know someone is out here, so a few will go in to make them think that's all there is. It's good for us. It will weaken them before we attack.'

He was right. Soon after the bullets fell silent, more guns started firing in the distance – ammunition streaking in blue, red, and green lines in the night sky. Using the bayonet on my gun, I dug myself deeper into the wet earth. The fight continued for a couple of hours as I shivered in my hole. I knew I should try to rest when it finally ended but couldn't. My teeth chattered as my mind tumbled over its thoughts. What if the tank came to find us? What if I fell on a minefield?

I had to close down my fear, push it into the place where I'd hide it. I knew what I had to do.

I thought of what was driving me: Mama screaming at me to run, Nyaruach crying as soldiers appeared in the distance, smoke rising from a village we were running from, the bodies of children lying on the floor, helicopters rushing overhead as I jumped into the water to escape them, Baba's face as he said goodbye.

'*Wakemale*,' he'd told me. 'Go in peace.'

I remembered Malual whipping me as I lay in the dust, *murahaleen* raising their guns to shoot at villagers, starving people lying in the sun as they waited in Pinyudu, the *talemgi*'s hand slapping my cheek, the bruises on Grandmother Nyapan Deng after the army had beaten her, the men on the bus whose hate poured slowly into me as I sat beside Mama.

This was what I had been waiting for. Now at last I would see the *jallabas* face-to-face. I was deaf to Garang's words. I would take revenge for all they had done to my family and my people. The cry of a chicken told me morning was close. Soldiers who had been sleeping heard it too and stretched as they woke. I put my hand into my pocket and pulled out some maize I had hidden there. I took a mouthful and forced it down with a sip of water.

Through the trees I could see the enemy moving as their camp came to life. I tried to remember what I was seeing – the holes, the positions – so that when I ran into battle, I would know what to expect. The sound of chanting drifted out from the camp. The Arabs were calling themselves to their God. Soon they would find no peace in their prayers. I had waited for ever for this moment. Fear had no place inside me now.

'*Ataaaaaaaaaaaack*,' an officer shouted as the RPGs started firing.

A shell dropped nearby and I saw a bloody ball fly through the air. A head. A soldier next to me turned and started running back into the forest, away from the enemy camp. I looked behind. A captain was standing in front of the soldier with a pistol in his hand.

'Where are you going?' he screamed. 'No retreat, no surrender.'

The butt of his gun flew into the man again and again as he beat the soldier back into line. Lam and I turned to move forward.

'*U-lu-lu-lu-lu-lu-lu-lu-lu*,' we screamed together as we started running.

I stopped to fire my gun before throwing myself on the ground. Up, firing, down, waiting, I could see soldiers falling around me. I fired one-two, one-two. I had to be careful with my ammunition. I shook as my AK-47 pulled me closer to the battle. I danced to its beat, rocking and moving as it pushed against me.

Ahead I could see SPLA surging into the camp as two tanks moved into the forest. They crashed through the trees as soldiers stood half-in, half-outside them, firing at us. Some big soldiers turned to run as the tanks rolled in, but I was *jenajesh* – we ran at the front of the battle, excited by the noise, not scared of it. But then I felt a quiver inside me and suddenly wanted to run as I watched the tank drive over small trees, snapping them like sticks as it came for us. An RPG flew overhead and fire exploded out of the top of the tank. I could see a body on fire as it flailed in the flames. The other tank tried to turn but it was too late – hit by an RPG, it was also blown up. We were going to win this fight now. Soldiers were scared of tanks but now we knew they had gone. I ran forward again.

Lam and I reached the edge of the forest. Ahead was a wide belt of grassy mud, a minefield. People screamed as they ran, the ground exploding beneath them. Bodies flew into the air before crashing to the ground. Smoke made my eyes water. I blinked quickly and looked at a soldier lying on the dark earth. His legs had been blown away. But I was small and light – these mines would not feel me as I ran above them, their teeth would not catch me.

SPLA soldiers poured into the camp on the other side of the minefield as I started running after Lam. I did not shoot. I wanted to save my bullets, and ahead I could see some of our soldiers shooting at *jallabas*. They would never run fast enough to escape.

As I reached the other side of the minefield, I could see *tukul*s burning and bodies lying everywhere. In the distance, a huge fire was blazing in the early-morning light. It must be the stores. The last Arabs left in the camp were blowing them up as they retreated. We'd won this fight before we'd begun, and I knew our soldiers would be following the *jallabas* as they tried to run. The enemy would not just leave this place. They would hide, set fire to whatever was precious, lie in wait to ambush our men. A retreat isn't quick. It is slow and dangerous. They were still close by – hiding in holes and waiting in trees for us.

'Go to the river and take up your positions,' an officer shouted as he pointed to the right of the camp.

Shots were being fired all around as Lam and I started moving with our unit – a group of around thirty soldiers. SPLA were aiming at *jallabas* hiding in holes while others ripped guns and clothes from bodies. Lam and I moved forward, covering ourselves with our guns and looking around in case the enemy surprised us. Noise roared, thick smoke clouded the air, the screams of battle lifted above me, and deep explosions rang out in the distance. I knew it took two days to capture a town properly. Just because we could not see the *jallabas* did not mean they were gone.

We started walking through long grass towards a small cluster of trees. Lam and I said nothing to each other, just looking all around us to see if the enemy was hiding somewhere near. I glanced at the trees. I could see something hanging in one. I looked at Lam and we held our guns even tighter. Were the Arabs waiting for us there? We walked slowly, moving quietly through the grass and watching the trees all the time. Gradually we moved closer, the black shape getting bigger, and I narrowed my eyes as I looked at it. What was it?

A soldier at the front of our group screamed as he stopped and looked up. I moved closer, raising my head to stare into the branches. A body was tied to the tree. A naked body. I stared at the face and knew something was wrong. This face was somehow uneven, strange. Then I realised. Instead of a nose there was just a bloody hole. Instead of eyes, just emptiness. My stomach turned as my gaze moved downward. Machete slashes covered the arms, whip marks burned the chest, and white threads hung from the groin, which was bare. It too had been cut and dismembered.

I looked around me. Burned bones lay in a shallow hole nearby, and three bodies were lying on the ground next to the pit. Each had been beaten, two had legs missing and one a hand. Bloody pools also lay where their eyes had once been, and each mouth was stuffed with a penis and testicles. Sickness burned my throat as I looked away. The stomachs were swollen with gas.

They had been lying there for a while. I looked at them again. I could see the marks of the Dinka on the forehead of one of the bodies. These were SPLA prisoners.

'*Aaaaaaaaaaaaaah*,' another soldier screamed, his voice rough and tearing out of him as he stood beside us.

Whatever fear I had felt as I ran into the camp was now gone. All I knew was a rage so strong that my body shook, and my heart hammered. Where were those bastard *jallabas*? Where were they hiding? I had to find them. I had to see them face-to-face. See the men who could do this, the men who could burn villages, rape women, steal children, and destroy their own people.

A bullet whistled close to me and a grenade exploded. Two of our soldiers were blown off their feet; another was shot in the leg. He moaned as we looked at a line of trees ahead.

'They're there,' a voice shouted.

'*Allahu Akbar*,' another voice screamed in the distance.

We spread out into a line, some helping the injured men, others taking up positions to search for the *jallabas*. Where were they? Lam and I kept firing until something moved on the edge of the trees.

'I've shot one,' Lam shouted as he got up to start running.

I followed him. I raised my gun, desperate to shoot as we ran into the trees. Two other *jenajesh* were with us as we ran.

Then we saw him.

The Arab was lying in the grass, his leg bleeding onto the green uniform he was wearing. He looked like an officer. His hand was injured as he lifted his pistol. It fell from his grip as he tried to fire.

I heard someone behind me and turned. The big soldier who had first stared up into the tree was standing looking at the *jallaba*; all around us others were pushing deeper into the forest to search for the enemy. For a moment, we were silent as Lam, the big soldier, the other *jenajesh*, and I stared at the man. I could see fear in his eyes as he looked at us.

With a grunt, the big soldier ran forward and kicked him in the head before stamping on his chest. The man screamed, words pouring out of him as he tried to reach for his gun again.

Pictures. Pictures. In my head.

'*Allahu Akbar*,' he screamed again.

Me. A child. Dust rising in the air as Arabs shot at us.

'What's the best way to make this fuck feel pain?' I shouted at Lam.

'We have to cut him,' he said.

We looked at each other for a moment and our rage stared back at us from the other's eyes. I turned my head. Lying nearby was an old brown machete. I put down my gun and walked a few steps to lift it up. I turned back to the *jallaba*. His eyes pleaded with me, staring out from his pale skin. Lam's eyes – black with hate. I looked at my hand – my black skin holding the machete. Both Lam and I marked by our blackness, which had made us this *jallaba*'s enemy. I did not think of my God in that moment who had also pitted us against each other. He was lost to me now.

I walked towards the man, lifting the machete in my hand as I moved closer with the other *jenajesh* beside me. They too had machetes in their hands, and our enemy's eyes were begging us now for mercy as he moaned and cried.

I lifted my machete as the other boys raised theirs and smashed them into the *jallaba*. Blood spurted on to my face.

Pictures. Pictures. In my head.

I hit the man twice more. He gurgled and slumped back. Blood ran down his face as he writhed on the ground. He wouldn't die. The other boys had also cut him, but why wouldn't this *jallaba* die?

'Leave him alone,' the big soldier suddenly shouted. 'We are supposed to take these *jallabas* prisoner. If you are found, then you will be punished.'

'But he refused to surrender,' Lam said. 'He was trying to shoot. What are we supposed to do?'

Lam turned away as he steadied the Arab with his leg before plunging his bayonet into his stomach. The man screamed and Lam lifted his gun. A bullet sang and I looked down. Blood roared through me.

'He's dead – leave him,' the big soldier said to us.

Lam, the other boys, and I stared at the body. He was still moving, twitching as he lay on the ground. Was he really dead? Or would he come after us?

'Move,' the big soldier ordered, and Lam and I turned to run.

We went deeper into the forest. Shots were being fired close to the river ahead, and our eyes searched the thick undergrowth for enemy faces. I slowed to a walk. I couldn't speak.

Pictures. Pictures. In my head.

A crackle of branches. A *jallaba* standing in front of us. Hands held in front of him. Surrendering. This time skin darker. A mixed-race Arab. African and Arab in one.

Lam and I lifted our guns. We fired together at the man's legs and he fell to the ground.

We walked up to him.

Pictures. Pictures. In my head.

First we shot his hands. We had to make sure we finished him. He was stronger than us, quicker. He cried as he lay on the ground. Lam raised his machete and looked at me. I lifted mine. We held our hands up together. The blades plunged down as one.

Blood covered my legs and shorts. I felt my chest heave and my throat contract. I was going to be sick. Everything was blurred. I heard a laugh as I breathed deeply, gulping air down into my lungs to stop my stomach from revolting. I stared at Lam, silent for a moment, before I too started to laugh and found I couldn't stop.

The battle had finally ended and soldiers were singing and dancing in celebration. I sat with Lam as we rested. I felt drunk as I looked around at troops wearing clothes they had taken from the *jallabas* or carrying bags of food they had claimed as their prize for this victory.

'I'm going to get some things,' Lam said as he stood up above me. 'There won't be much left but I'll look. Do you want anything?'

'Yes,' I said, too tired to go with him.

'What?'

'A bike.'

The one I had been given at the front of the front line was broken, and now I wanted another to show I had been to battle.

Lam walked away. I stared around me once more as I lifted some maize into my mouth. For a moment I thought of nothing as I chewed, but then the taste of gunpowder spread bitterly over my tongue. I spat out the food before lying down to rest. My mind was blank as sleep finally took me over.

CHAPTER 18

'*Nyigat*,' the Dinka soldier said softly to the Nuer trooper. 'Thief.'

The Nuer man said nothing, but his eyes were full of anger as he walked away.

'Didn't you hear me, *nyigat*?' the Dinka insisted.

The air stilled as the Nuer soldier stopped and turned around. Everyone was watching to see what he would do. It was like this now at Kurki 1 because a few days after Lam and I had returned from the raid, the SPLA had been forced to withdraw from Juba. Ammunition and supplies had run out after many days of heavy fighting, and we would have to attack again to win the city. I was sure John Garang would be able to motivate exhausted soldiers to fight once more, but some were angry that so many men had died for nothing. Now they were turning on each other as the trouble between Dinka and Nuer SPLA worsened. Troops were arriving at Kurki after being attacked with machetes, while stories were told that some were being shot by their own comrades during battles.

I watched as the two soldiers in front of me fell on to each other – fighting and punching, reaching for their guns as they defended their tribes. Soon they were pulled apart, but Lam and I said nothing as they were marched away and we turned back to our game of dominoes. I felt calm inside as I waited for my next battle, and Lam and I talked about the day of the raid. We knew we were supposed to have kept the *jallabas* alive and could face trouble if we were discovered, but sometimes we could not stop our tongues.

'We killed them easy,' Lam would tell me. 'We should have hurt them more.'

'Wake up,' a voice whispered close to my ear.

I snapped my one eye open, ready to fight. Were the Arabs attacking?

I looked up to see Lam above me.

'Come on. We're moving out.'

As I did every night, I was sleeping in my khaki shirt and shorts, so I just got up, picked up my gun, and followed Lam out of the *tukul*. Troops moved silently in the darkness like ants. Tying bags of maize, wrapping bullet belts around their waists, or loading bags on to their backs, each had a job to do.

'What's happening?' I asked Lam as we walked to a store. 'Where are we going?'

'Shhh,' he said.

I looked at the bag slung over his shoulder. He must be moving out too. I did not want Lam to go into battle without me.

'Take these,' a soldier said as we arrived at the store, and I was handed maize and ammunition.

Weapons were never given out from this store. Maybe this was something to do with the important commander Wang Chouk, who'd arrived at Kurki earlier that night. But I was learning how to keep quiet now when I needed to, so I said nothing as I strung my AK-47 around my shoulder.

I couldn't carry the big bag of maize I'd been given and ran to get my bike to rest it on. As soldiers started marching in lines towards the river, I joined Lam. Ahead I could see Yen Makuach, the officer in charge at the front of the front line who'd got me my first bike. I wondered why he was here with us now instead of in battle.

Reaching the riverbank, we waited in the darkness as troops

moved on to the big wooden boat used to transport soldiers and supplies. There were so many of us, and the boat could not take everyone so we had to go across in groups. The night was black as I stood on the bank, but as Lam and I edged forward, I could see a soldier lying on the ground. He was in charge of guarding the boat, but his hands had been tied together, his mouth gagged, and a gun was being held above him. I looked at Lam but he stared ahead without seeing me.

We boarded the boat and once more everything was silent as it moved across the water. Still Lam did not speak, but finally, when we'd left the boat and were waiting for the rest of the soldiers to cross, I couldn't hold my tongue any longer.

'What is happening?' I whispered.

Lam only lifted his finger to his lips as three SPLA river guards were dragged before an officer. They too had been tied and gagged.

'Where are your radios?' the officer said roughly. 'We need them. Give them to us.'

The guards stared at the officer until one shook his head. A gun smashed into his temple and the man staggered a little as the order to move out was shouted above our heads. As we left the guards behind, I heard gunshots ring out in the distance. One. Two. Three.

I didn't understand. What was happening? Why were shots being fired at our fellow SPLA? Were they spies?

'Where are we going?' I asked Lam again.

He looked at me. 'Defecting,' he said in a low voice.

I stared at him. What did he mean? Leave Kurki? Leave John Kong and the battles we knew were waiting for us there?

'We are going to join Dr Riek Machar. I could not tell you before, Jal, because I knew you would never keep silent.'

I remembered the man I'd met so long before at Itang. Then he had been one of John Garang's most important friends, but now he was his enemy, just as Dinka and Nuer SPLA were turning into enemies before my eyes.

'We are not safe here,' Lam continued. 'You've seen what is happening to Nuer troops like us. We are part of the SPLA, but we are getting killed by our comrades. Those guards would have warned others if we hadn't captured them first. I have dug my own grave once before, and I will not wait here to do it again.'

'But where is Riek?'

'His camp is in Waat. He has a new army there called SPLA Nasir, and we are going to march to join them.

'John Garang will accept nothing but victory over the whole of Sudan and he will fight this war for ever. But Riek wants autonomy for southern Sudan away from the *jallabas*, and this is something we could win. It is better for us that way.'

I stared at Lam. Waat was far away to the north, between Leer, the area where Riek and Baba had both been born, and the Ethiopian border.

'You won't be able to bring your bike,' Lam told me.

My stomach twisted. Leave my bike? Leave Kurki? Leave all the things I had collected as my own during the long months there – a mosquito net, a blanket, and two pairs of shorts?

'Don't worry,' Lam said, reading my thoughts as I stared angrily ahead. 'I've got most of your stuff. I packed it for you.'

My body relaxed for a moment. Lam was my friend. He was right. I did not understand what was happening, but I would follow him.

At first we marched through hills and forests, often travelling at night to avoid attacks by Arabs or other SPLA, as a soldier with a compass showed us the direction to walk. When the marching ended, we would eat some maize before lying down on our sleeping mats. There was plenty to look at as we walked – birds, flowers, fruits, and trees – and also a lot of food. We killed animals and ate guavas, mangoes, and bananas we found growing on trees. The land was not always kind to us, though, and minefields caught some of our soldiers as we walked. A boy's leg was blown off meters away from me, and he had to be left behind to be looked after by villagers. But mostly our march was peaceful as Lam and I walked side by side. Still I did not question where I was going. If Lam and Yen Makuach believed it was right, then I would follow them. We would join Riek and find war again. Kill the *jallabas* as before.

Soon we had made a new friend called Lual, whom I'd seen at Kurki but never spoken to. Lual told us he was fifteen and from Bahr al-Ghazal, one of the areas worst hit by the war because that was where the oilfields lay. Now he was a bodyguard to Wang Chouk, the commander who was leading our defection, and he, Lam, and I talked as we walked. Lual and Lam both dreamed of returning to their villages one day, and soon I did too. I hadn't thought about home for so long, but away from the battlefields in the quietness of the countryside, memories flitted into my mind like flies dipping into water.

'We will search for your father,' Captain Yen Makuach would tell me when I ran ahead in the lines to find him. 'And if he is alive, you can return to your village.'

I felt mixed inside when I thought of Baba, but as the days turned into weeks and we walked for hours on end, I remembered Nyagai, Nyakouth, Nyaruach, Miri, and Marna. Where were they now? Were they still safe in Luaal? Nyakouth would be a woman now. Was Nyaruach still talking as much as ever? Miri and Marna must be boys instead of the babies I remembered.

I asked the officers many questions as we walked, and they spoke to me of why they had chosen to leave the SPLA. It was hard for me to understand as I thought back to the *talemgi*'s lessons about loyalty.

'We are not choosing to do this, we have been driven to it,' they said. 'John Garang doesn't want anyone to question him, and the Dinka call the SPLA theirs. We used to fight with one spirit, but now the Nuer are labelled thieves. That is why we must join Riek and fight for an independent southern Sudan.'

I learned to agree with them as I thought about what they

said. I did not want to fight my fellow soldiers, to waste energy
on arguments between tribes, when all I wanted to do was kill
jallabas.

When the forest started to thin and dry savanna stretched in
front of us, things changed. After about a month of marching,
our maize started to run out and we were ordered to eat the little
we had left uncooked so it filled us up more.

Wang Chouk urged us forward every day. 'We are no more
than a week from Waat,' he would say, but I knew soldiers
believed our commander had brought bad luck with him
because his wife was the only woman among us. We all knew
she refused to carry a stone to ward off bad spirits because Lual
slipped one into the pocket of her dress or trousers day after day,
but she always threw it away.

As food became scarcer, the officers told us to use our soldier
skills, and we searched for plants we could cook or leaves on
trees to eat. They didn't taste good, but I had learned long ago
on the march to Ethiopia and at Pinyudu to take food wherever
I could find it. People got poisoned by eating the wrong things,
others got weaker as we walked, and bellies grew round as
bones started to lie like sticks under thin skin.

Lam though refused to eat what we found, saying, 'I am not
an animal. I eat maize and meat, not leaves on the trees. Soon we
will be in Waat and I will eat everything I want there.'

The boy lay under the tree as the line of troops moved away,
leaving him behind as they marched into the dusty savanna. He
knew that he would soon be alone on the plain, lying beneath an
empty sky that never seemed to end.

Lam, Lual, and I turned to look at him. The boy was a little
older than me and had got a fever after injuring his leg. Big soldiers had carried him, but now they only had strength to lift
their own limbs on this hard journey. They had left the boy sitting under the tree with a mosquito net, a sleeping mat, and a
G3.

'They say they'll go back for him when we reach Waat,' Lam said quietly.

The boy's voice was weak like a whisper as he pleaded with passing soldiers to carry him.

Lam, Lual, and I said nothing as we stopped walking.

'What should we do?' Lual asked.

'Wait with him,' I said.

The boys nodded as they looked at me. We all knew that if any of us were left sitting under such a tree, we would want someone by our side, waiting for help to return for us.

'What are you doing?' a big soldier said as we stood talking. 'Get walking and keep moving.'

Lam, Lual, and I stared at each other, unsure of what to do. We wanted to help the boy but had to obey orders.

'Do what I say and don't look back or you'll be punished,' the soldier said.

His eyes told us that we could not argue. We turned away from the boy. We had to get walking. Keep moving.

I felt scared as I started to walk. If this boy was left because he was too weak, then what would happen to me if I became so? Would Lam and Lual carry on while I stayed still?

A shot blasted into the air and I turned to look back. In the distance I could see the body of the boy slumped against the tree. Half of his head had been blown away, and the gun lay on the ground beside him.

Get walking, keep moving, the soldier had said, so I did, but I knew I would never forget what we were leaving behind.

A body may scream for food and water, but a mind will always shriek louder. As the dusty weeks in the savanna passed and our march continued, I watched as boys and men were driven mad by hunger and thirst. Soldiers fought over scraps of bone if we ever found an animal to kill, and I stayed silent as a *jenajesh* drew his gun on a younger boy and threatened to shoot if he did not piss into a cup. Many men shot themselves when they realised they couldn't go on, while others simply lay down and never got up again. There were also arguments among the survivors as the soldier with the compass disappeared and no one knew which direction to travel in. Wang Chouk used the sun and the stars, but some refused to listen to him and broke away from our group.

At night and in the early morning, we would wake and lick dew from desert plants – the drops of liquid bursting on to our tongues as we gasped for more. But when the sun rose higher in the sky to beat down on us, my bones would again feel as dry as the earth beneath my feet. Sometimes we ate the hyenas and vultures that followed our lines and were shot as they fought to snap up the bodies lying in the footsteps behind us. But soon even they disappeared, knowing death would take them just as surely as it was taking us if they came too close. I became used to hearing the shake and rattle of a man's last breath as it whispered into silence and he died on the ground beside me as Lam, Lual, and I grew thinner and weaker. When I looked at them, I saw myself: bones sticking out and lice running through our hair and across our skin.

Life was slowly draining from inside me. My stomach burned and I would pull my belt tight around my shorts to ease the pain. The sun beat white-hot on my head, and thirst made my tongue feel heavy. My feet turned purple and one of my little toes became infected. Soon it started to rot and I laughed one night when the tip fell into Lam's hand as he massaged it. But I felt scared inside because I knew that if I did not keep walking, I would die. The only thing that strengthened us was the words of Wang Chouk as he urged us forward. We knew we would soon reach Waat.

'Only a few more days,' Lam would tell me. 'Then we'll be there.'

'And we'll have all the milk we want to drink and goat to eat,' Lual would add.

*

Lying underneath a tree, I could hear the magician chanting for rain. He was a soldier we called Bullet Proof, and everyone knew that he used magic to protect himself from guns. I turned my head to look at him as he threw shells on the ground. His voice sounded muffled and blurred, as if my ears were full of water after swimming in a river, and I could see two of him standing before me. Lam and Lual lay silently nearby. Too weak to talk or move, we were resting, and I knew many among our group would never get up again. It had been many weeks now without proper food, days without water.

I stared up at the white sun. Black and red spots burned into my eyes and faded pictures of home flashed in front of me: watching Nyakouth hit a small ball made of palm-tree leaves with her hand before running around a pitch of eight holes as we played *kurai;* hearing Nyaruach's cries as I chased her one day after discovering she'd told tales on me again; looking at my mother's swollen belly and asking her where I had come from as a baby. She'd told me she found me in the bush, and I'd wondered if Baba would give me a brother or sister too as I thought of his fat tummy.

The magician continued to softly chant. I knew soldiers all around me would be praying to their gods to bring rain. I thought of Mama's God, whom I'd long ago forgotten. I was tired of the war, the fighting between men, the comrades turning on each other with guns in the dust. I wanted to go home to die with my family.

Something stirred inside me. I thought of Mama's God again. 'Please bring us rain,' I prayed.

I licked my lips and felt a thick crust covering them. My throat was dry. I couldn't swallow. My head felt dizzy and light.

A shadow fell across me as something landed on my skin like the touch of a cool fingertip, then another touch, another and another. I lowered my eyes to see dark stains smearing the white dust on my arm. I lifted my hand and licked. Water.

'It's raining,' I heard someone shout.

There was a roar of thunder, a crack of lightning, and men screamed with joy as rain started falling – some stood with their mouths open, others lay laughing in the mud that quickly formed. Sitting up, I clawed into the earth with my hands. I knew I must dig a hole and line it with my sleeping mat to collect this rain, which had come like a miracle to save us. The savanna in the distance was as dry as ever – rain was only falling above the tree where we lay. All around me soldiers were claiming it was their God who had brought the rain, while others praised the magician. I wondered if it was Mama's God who had done this.

'He will always look after those who believe,' I remembered her saying to me as I stared at the water collecting in the hole I had dug.

After that day the parched savanna gave way to a wetland where we walked between swamp, marsh, and papyrus islands, our skin turning white and shrivelled as we pulled ourselves in and out of the water. Snails, rats, and frogs filled this watery place, and at night we feasted on them after building fires of grass and gunpowder. But still Lam refused to eat. The only thing he carried now was his gun. His bag was too heavy for him to lift as he staggered on his skinny legs.

'Do you want some?' I asked him as I pulled a piece of rat from the fire.

'No,' Lam insisted. 'We are so close to Waat, and what would I tell the people in my village if I ate such things?'

I thought of the men who were dying with the pride of a lion as they refused to eat whatever food we could snatch from the grasp of this starving place. I wasn't like them. Snails lined my pockets because I knew that we'd soon return to the graveyard of the savanna. Death came for us once more when we did, but still I kept walking. Keep moving. Don't look back. Something inside keeping me standing as I watched big soldiers and *jenajesh* stagger and fall to the ground in the midday sun.

There must have been about forty of us left when stories

about the magician started to be whispered from ear to ear. It was said he was surviving by sinning. The worst sin a person could commit. A sin that entered you, became part of you, and would never leave you. Flesh becoming flesh – the magician just like the vultures that had once stalked us was feasting on the dead.

One night I woke and lifted my head to look at him in the distance. I could see the magician crouched on an anthill before a fire burning orange in the blackness. Something lay on the ground in front of him, and he lifted it to the flames. I turned my head away.

Lam's face was drawn and his bones stuck out from his body. Lual and I tried to feed him porridge made from the seeds of the *buaw* tree. Smearing the food on the inside of his mouth, I closed his lips before stroking his throat. But Lam's mouth fell open and the porridge fell in a soft lump on to my hand. He had to eat.

I dug my hand into the porridge once again and took another piece. Pushing it into his mouth, I stretched my fingers to the back of his throat – anything to get the food inside him and keep it there. But the porridge fell from Lam's mouth again. Despair burned inside me. I felt weak and tired.

A hand touched my shoulder and I looked up to see Wang Chouk standing above me.

'Leave him,' he said.

I looked back at Lam. His breath was ragged and shallow and his eyes flickered as I took another lump of porridge and guided it into his mouth.

'He cannot eat now,' Lual said. 'He is too weak.'

My hand was still and my heart slowed until I heard the sound I had come to know so well – a soft hiss and then silence. I lowered my ear to Lam's mouth. Nothing. No breath, no life.

Later that night Lual and I asked Yen Makuach to help us. We knew what we had to do. Soldiers were finding food by killing and eating hyenas that came for the bodies. Lam would help us now. The moon lit up the dry ground as the three of us carried his body out into the savanna. We could hear hyenas in the bush, laughing together like women as they started to hunt. Silently, Yen Makuach showed us how to tie Ugandan grenades to Lam's body. Taking out the pins and holding the safety lever tightly in place, we tied rope around his belly, neck, and legs before securing the grenades to it. The hyenas would pull the rope when they came for Lam and trigger the explosives. Then they would be ours to eat.

I did not look back at my friend as we left him lying in the dark savanna. I felt nothing as I returned to lie on my sleeping mat and waited for the hours to slip slowly by until the sound of the grenades came. I felt as if I would eventually disappear as my body wasted away.

When the explosion finally came, I moved to get up. My head felt heavy, weighing me down, as I tried to lift it. My skin was grey and my hip bones jutted out on either side of me. Sluggishly, I lifted one foot to start moving. I staggered a little and my shorts slipped to reveal lice eggs lining the waistband.

I walked slowly. I just had to claim the dead hyena, feed myself, give myself enough energy to keep going.

Keep walking. Get moving. Don't look back.

But when I reached the place where we had left Lam, I felt anger tug in my belly. There was nothing where he had lain. The hyenas had outwitted us – after eating their fill, they'd left us hungry.

Soon after that day, Lual also died. We had been lying together under a tree for many days, too weak to walk any farther as we waited for Yen Makuach's nephew to save us. He had left us two weeks before to search for tribespeople with whom we could barter guns and bullets for food. For now there was no strength left to keep walking and we rested for many hours at a time.

It was dark as I looked at Lual and knew that he too would soon leave me. Death was coming quickly for him, rushing out of the night as the day disappeared. I was not surprised. I knew it could come in an instant when it chose you.

I lowered my head and pushed my nose into the crook of Lual's arm. His skin was warm, soft. It smelled like dry meat. Saliva rushed into my mouth.

Could I do as the magician had done?

I pulled my head away, turned my face from Lual.

Mama, where are you? Mama, are you near?

A soft rattle hissed before Lual's silence filled the air around me.

He was dead. Gone.

Could Lual save me where Lam had not?

I closed my eyes and a shadow danced across the back of my mind. I heard sounds –

Mama singing hymns, the voices in church raised together in praise.

Mama had prayed during the war and the bombs had never hit us.

I had prayed under the tree and rain had come.

I knew that if God didn't save me, I would feed myself by morning. Lual was so close. His body still warm and the smell of him in my nostrils. I needed him. I would die too if he didn't help me.

But could I do this terrible thing?

My eyes flickered shut as I rolled on to my side away from Lual.

I could feel him so close, feel his smell reaching inside me and clawing at my stomach. It was so good. So sweet.

Help me, Mama.

God, if you are there, then show me the way.

The hours of the night slid slowly by as I lay next to Lual. Minute by minute, hour by hour, I lay awake as my body and mind fought a war inside me, and I told myself that if God had not saved me by morning, then I would eat. I would wait just a little longer to see if He would hear my prayer.

Our Father. Help me.

Our Father. Who art in heaven. Hallowed be thy name.

Our Father. Forgive us our trespasses.

When the sun shone warm on my skin and light filled the sky, I turned my head to look at Lual lying beside me. God had not listened.

I knew what I must do now.

I stared up at the sky as a black shadow streaked into the corner of my eye. A crow. I reached for my gun. If I could kill the bird, then I would feed on that. I would survive on its flesh. I would not commit a sin that would stain my soul for ever. But my arm was too weak to lift the heavy AK-47 as my fingers closed softly around it.

Our Father. Who art in heaven. Where are you now?

Suddenly a shot cracked into the sky and I saw a boy ahead collapsing to the ground with his gun. I knew he had hit the bird as a burst of black feathers fell to the ground. The boy didn't move and neither did the bird. Slowly I pulled myself on to my knees and started crawling towards the crow. Food. God had done as I asked. He had delivered me from evil. And soon He would save me again.

CHAPTER 19

I was marching in a line of troops with my gun tall beside me. I had been in Waat now for several weeks – just one of about a dozen who'd survived the desert journey from Juba. The bird I had eaten on the day God saved me had kept me alive long enough to be found by Yen Makuach's nephew, who had returned with the tribespeople he had left us to search for. Bartering Lam's gun with them in return for a goat's leg, I was stopped from filling my belly too full by a tribesman who tied me up before feeding me pieces small enough for my shrunken stomach to digest. Other boys were not so lucky and died that night after eating too quickly and too much.

Wang Chouk, his wife, and Yen Makuach were also among those who reached Riek Machar's camp, and we arrived to find starvation stealing the villagers there just as it had taken our comrades. On the outskirts of the camp, I saw a bony toddler crouched on all fours with its head resting on the ground as a vulture pecked at the diarrhoea seeping from its body. The child's mother lay nearby, too weak to do anything but softly push a stick against the ground to try to scare the bird away. As I ran to chase it, I knew both mother and child would soon be taken.

Many refused to eat vultures, which feasted on the dead, but I ate their meat to survive in Waat. Starvation had left its mark on me, and pain tore into me when I filled my stomach, even though I wanted to eat continuously. I'd see food and shake as I picked it up, but things got better when *khawaja*s brought refugee food.

Just as at Pinyudu, the aid workers did not know that the Sudanese who assisted them giving out the supplies were often soldiers, this time from Riek's compound. We were welcomed there after our long journey, and I soon found a way to make myself popular by using the writing I'd learned in the refugee camp to make a list of names as the soldiers gave out food.

Gradually I'd grown stronger, but my heavy gun still dragged on the ground beside me as I marched today. We were going back to the compound after giving out food, and I could see two *khawaja* women standing in the sun ahead of me. I knew who one of them was. She was called Christine, and I'd met her at the food-distribution point soon after arriving in Waat, but I didn't recognise the other woman. Christine was short with hair the colour of dried savanna grass, while the woman with her was tall and dark.

'*Khawaja*s,' I shouted as I marched past. 'How are you?'

They smiled as they walked up to me, speaking in those strange voices I'd heard at Pinyudu.

'You want to go to school?' the dark *khawaja* asked as she bent down to look at me.

'Yes, school, school,' I replied with a smile as I stopped.

She pointed at me, then at my gun. 'You school. This gun stay here.'

'Yes, yes, school, school.'

Christine and the other woman laughed as they started talking again.

'You America?' I asked as I remembered Mary.

'No, no, England,' the dark *khawaja* replied.

As the women talked, although I did not understand the words, I could see they were arguing as they looked at me.

'Whoever wins? I go school,' I said with a laugh.

The dark *khawaja* leaned down once again to look at me. Her eyes were kind as she took my dusty hand in hers. She was not scared to touch me. Just like Mary.

'You want to go to school?' she asked.

I looked back at her. It had been so long since I'd thought about school. I'd forgotten all my dreams of learning to fly *nyanking*. But as I opened my mouth to speak, a voice started shouting and I turned to see a big SPLA running towards me.

'You,' he screamed. 'What are you doing with those *khawajas*? Get away from them and get back to the compound.'

As I turned to start running, an officer walked towards the soldier and said, 'What are you doing? Leave these women alone.'

'But they are trying to talk to Jal,' the soldier replied.

'Well, they can do what they like.'

'Why? These *khawaja*s should not be speaking to our soldiers. They are here to give out their food and that's all.'

'Not this woman,' the officer said, pointing at the dark *khawaja*.

'What do you mean?' the soldier demanded.

'She is different.'

'Why?'

The officer looked at the woman standing tall and proud and said, 'Because this is Riek Machar's wife.'

I looked at the *khawaja* for a moment before I turned to start walking away. There was something determined about her. I could see fire in her eyes.

I saw the *khawaja* wife often after that day. She was called Emma, and everywhere she went, her red-and-white dog called Come On followed. It had been given the name because that's what Emma always said to it as she walked and the dog trotted after her.

She soon started teaching me English. I knew little about her other than that she was a *khawaja* with many smiles and pockets stuffed with biscuits. But I would later learn more about Emma McCune. The Englishwoman had fallen in love with Sudan on a visit in 1986 and returned three years later to help aid agencies set up schools. Nothing, not even war, would stop her. Emma travelled through deserts and battle zones to talk to villagers and deliver supplies, and thousands of children were educated thanks to Emma's efforts. Fearless, independent, and sometimes reckless, she was different from any other aid worker and soon earned herself a reputation among them for not following the rules. But Emma didn't care – all she wanted was to bring education to a people desperate for it. War, though, was the constant enemy in her fight, and after becoming frustrated about not being allowed into certain parts of the country by the SPLA commanders, she requested a meeting with Riek Machar in January 1990.

'Do you have any idea how frustrating it is when the children I am trying to teach keep being marched off into the bush to become child soldiers?' she told him.

The next time Emma saw Riek was a year later when she had travelled more than fifteen hundred miles – and hacked her way through eighteen kilometres of acacia forest – to reach where he was. The army commander fell in love with the adventurous *khawaja,* and the couple married in June 1991. Of course, the union was controversial. John Garang's supporters viewed Emma as a spy, and she was sacked from her job because people believed she could no longer be impartial about delivering aid. But Emma was loved by Riek's people and immersed herself in all aspects of traditional village life – even accepting the existence of Riek's first wife, Angelina, who was living in England because he had taken her there when he studied at university. Emma knew it was a Nuer man's right to have more than one wife, and it wasn't just her open mind and tall, slim figure that made her like a white Sudanese. She was one in her heart and lived uncomplainingly with my people among the malaria, food shortages, and violence of war zones.

Maybe Emma picked me, or maybe I picked Emma – I cannot be sure now – but I knew that something about me made her care fiercely. Maybe it was because she had tried to turn the tide of war's hopelessness for so long that she wanted to know for sure that she had saved just one person, or maybe it was because in me her life's passions – children, education, Sudan, and Riek – were united. Like every other southern Sudanese child, I had once been desperate to be educated, and Emma awakened the dream again inside me. I was also part of Riek's family, which bound us together. I'd discovered soon after arriving in Waat that I was related to Riek through Baba because both men came from the Leer area. In Africa's extended families, it meant Emma and I were tied to each other by kinship.

Part of me liked the *khawaja* woman who brought me biscuits and gave me medicine when I was ill. I was sure to make her laugh at my jokes just as the *khawaja*s at Pinyudu and the commanders at Kurki had laughed, but I didn't understand why Emma had picked me out. She never told me, just as she never asked about my life in the SPLA. Instead we talked about Sudan, its people and customs. Emma called me Emmanuel – one of the names I'd been christened with at Pinyudu – which I liked because someone had told me it meant 'God is with us', and also because she was Emma and now I was Emma-nuel.

But another part of me did not trust the strange *khawaja* who got upset about things I was used to, such as taking food from the places where I knew it was hidden.

'You mustn't steal,' Emma would tell me after I'd found the *tahnia* in a plastic box in her compound. 'You only have to ask and I will give it.'

She also didn't like it when I arrived late for my lessons.

'If you are going to learn better English, then you must come to see me,' she'd say. 'You have to keep time.'

But I didn't listen to her, and the next time I would cook another story to explain why I'd arrived late again.

Day after day Emma talked to me of school. I listened as she spoke, thought of the *nyanking* I had once dreamed of flying, and knew that Riek also wanted *jesh a mer* to be educated. He had arrived in Waat about a month after we finished our desert trek and promoted Wang Chouk before sending the commander

and Yen Makuach back into battle. But Riek was not going to
do the same with the *jenajesh*, and fear had filled me as talk of
the Kakuma refugee camp reached me. I knew there were
schools there, but I didn't want to go back to fighting over
khawaja food and waiting. I'd rather go back to war.

'I'll take you with me,' Emma would tell me, and I would
smile as I thought about the white people's land.

Maybe if I went there, I would finally learn the things I needed
to take my revenge on the *jallabas*. Riek might not want me to
go back into battle, but that didn't mean I'd stopped wanting to
kill Arabs. I wanted to take my revenge just as much as I ever
had, and hatred still scratched the back of my throat at night
when I lay thinking of all I'd seen. Ever since the raid on Juba
with Lam, I'd realised that I must find a new way to fight
because I'd seen how well equipped the *jallabas* were, and as
Emma talked to me, I asked myself if going to school in a white
land would help me.

'You are too small to live in war, too young to see the things
you have,' Emma would tell me. 'I am going to make sure you
go to school.'

But how could I ever leave Sudan with this *khawaja* woman?
Was this what God wanted for me?

'Trust me, Emmanuel,' Emma would say in a low voice. 'I'm
going to take you away from here.'

She kept her promise after Riek agreed that Emma could take
me. In early 1993, a small plane landed in Waat on the way to
Kenya, and hidden among bags carried by four big SPLA bodyguards, I scrambled up a ladder into the plane and buried myself
among the luggage as Emma kept the pilot busy by laughing and
joking with him. Soon I felt my stomach swoop away with the
land falling beneath us and crawled forward to where she was
sitting. Climbing into a seat next to her, I smiled as she looked at
me. I didn't know where I was going or what was happening – I
just knew that war had taught me to take whatever path you
find.

'I told you we would do it,' Emma said as she squeezed my hand. 'I told you.'

I stared around the white room until my eyes came to rest on Emma. She was holding something in her hand.

'This is soap.'

I took it from her hand and lifted it to my nose. It smelled like fruit and I opened my mouth.

'No, no, Emmanuel,' Emma said as she tried to grab my hands.

But the fruit was already in my mouth, and suddenly a taste so strange it made my throat tighten spread over my tongue and I coughed.

I spat out the fruit. 'This is no good.'

'I know. You cannot eat this, Emmanuel. This is soap. You use it to wash yourself.'

I thought of the river plant I'd sometimes used in my village. This place called Kenya was very different even though it was full of black people.

After arriving in Nairobi earlier that day, we had come to stay with a friend of Emma's called Sally. I'd stared at the city as we drove from the airport – there were tall buildings and more lights than I'd ever seen, coloured in blue, green, red, and yellow. Sally's house was big, with flowers in the garden, and I'd watched in silence as she told her dogs to sit down. Emma was not the only *khawaja* who spoke to dogs as if they were people. But Emma and Sally did not notice me staring as they hissed and laughed together.

'Emmanuel?' Emma said, and I looked at her.

She was pointing to a big white chair in the room with a special name – the bathroom. The chair looked like a gourd sitting on a drum and had a lid on top. With gestures and actions, Emma showed me how to lift the seat, sit down, and do what I had to do there before reaching for some white paper on a hook beside her.

'This is toilet roll,' she said.

I stared at Emma. How could a room so clean be used for something so dirty that I had always done in the bush? How could anyone use paper to wipe themselves instead of sticks or leaves? But before I could ask, she pushed a metal lever on the side of the white chair and I watched as water roared through it. How did the river reach this room?

'Now it's your turn,' Emma said gently as she walked out.

I pulled down my shorts as I stared at the white chair before sitting down on it. It felt cold on my skin and I wondered what would happen if a snake came to bite me from the river.

I stood up. This chair was dangerous.

Silently, I climbed up on to the chair and put my feet on either side of the seat before crouching down over the hole. Staring between my legs, I was happy now that I could watch for snakes.

Emma and I were with each other all the time in those first few weeks in Kenya. She took me to see friends, bought me clothes, slept beside me, and gave me paper and pencils to draw with. She showed me how to use a knife and fork, gave me my first toothbrush, and silently wiped up the black marks covering the white bathroom when I used charcoal to clean my teeth just as I had always done.

But questions filled my mind as I looked at Emma. Why was she so nice to me? Was she going to sell me just like I'd heard about some white people who took children did? I knew I made many mistakes in this strange place. When I was given a cup, I broke it; when I ate food at a table, I threw chicken bones over my shoulder on to the floor; and when I played with white children, I would make them cry.

Emma and I had terrible fights sometimes. I wouldn't listen to her or I'd do bad things to test her. But Emma never laughed or shouted back at me.

'You are my little brother now,' she would say. 'And that is why I am looking after you just as every Sudanese looks after their family. I want you to go to school, to have a future.'

'But don't you have your own children?' I'd reply.

'No.'

'Women in Sudan have their own babies when they have a husband.'

'I know, and when the time is right, I will have children with Riek, but for now I am looking after you.'

And so I took without thinking what Emma, and other people around her, gave because I had forgotten what love was. Smiling and happy, Sally looked after me too and was like another mother. Soon after we'd arrived in Kenya, Emma's mother, Maggie, also came to stay, and I called her Granny just as I'd been told to. I liked the woman with twinkling eyes who gave me something I'd never before eaten called chocolate, which made my mouth thick and full as I ate, and a real soccer ball. But nothing was enough in this place full of new things. When I saw a Game Boy for the first time at a friend's house, I liked it so much that I sneaked back to take it, and when Emma put me into bed at night, I would get out of bed to return to the adults because I had done as I pleased for so long.

'You're a young boy,' Emma would say as she put me back. 'You must sleep and grow.'

It made me angry when she said such things. I wasn't a boy. I was a soldier, and at night my dreams haunted me more than they ever had. I would see pictures in my head – machetes cutting, mouths screaming, helicopters firing – and wake up covered in sweat as I shook in the darkness. Sometimes Emma would try to cuddle me, but I didn't like it. She was a woman, who should not see my fear.

'There is no war here,' she'd whisper in the dark. 'You're safe now.'

But I knew I wasn't and still slept with one eye open to make sure I could see my enemy. I missed my AK-47 and wanted a pistol to keep me safe. I didn't understand why all the *khawajas* didn't carry them, and as I lay awake at night, I would think of returning to Sudan. I had seen for myself now what had been taken from my people. All around me was the life the Arabs didn't want us to have – food, cars, schools, and peace – and I promised myself that I would learn everything I could at school before destroying the *jallabas*. Some of Emma's friends who came to see us were Muslim, and although she had explained they were not the Arabs from my country, I'd look at them as we ate dinner, stare down at my knife, and want to cut them.

I wondered if they knew what I was thinking because, just as I'd once learned to smell battle as it approached in Sudan, I could sense some here did not understand me just as I did not understand them. One night we went to a barbecue when we were staying with another of Emma's friends, and as people ate and listened to music, I saw a *mawuna*. Did the *khawaja*s here use it to throw shells as we had done in Sudan?

I walked up to the *mawuna* and, stretching myself upward, put my eye to it. The moon shone white and huge; I could hear wind rushing past my ears. The shell must be about to drop. Covering my ears and turning away, I closed my eyes.

'Bang,' I shouted.

I opened my eyes again to see the *khawaja*s staring at me, their food stopped on its journey towards their mouths.

'It's a telescope,' I heard a voice say.

'No, *mawuna*,' I replied.

But I could see the white people did not understand, and I'd sometimes hear them talking in low voices to Emma.

'What are you doing?' they'd say. 'You live in a war zone, can only just keep yourself alive, and why have you brought this boy here so far from what he knows? You're wasting your time. Just put him in a refugee camp and visit him when you can. He's too wild.'

'No, he's bright, he's special,' Emma would reply. 'And I am going to make sure he goes to school.'

*

I ran across the grass, holding my gun in my hand as I shot.

'T-t-t-t-t-t-t,' I screamed as the bullets flew past my head.

Arabs were nearby, hiding in the bushes and waiting to shoot at me. I dived to the ground and stayed still, lifting my head a little to stare down the garden.

I knew I was safe to be a soldier while Emma and Sally were out. They didn't like it if I hid in the dark and shouted to surprise them when they turned on a light or when I pointed at anything that moved and pretended to shoot. I found it boring when we went to game parks to look at animals – I'd seen them all before and all I could think of was shooting them. Emma also didn't like the pictures I drew of jeeps, tanks, and houses on fire instead of hippos, birds, and crocodiles.

'You must draw beautiful things,' she would say.

I stared across the grass again and started pulling myself forward, holding my gun in front of me. I could see it even though it wasn't there – the barrel black, the brown handle, a small box of spare bullets in a bag tied to my waist. I crawled silently forward until I reached the bushes. Looking deep into them, I saw the Arabs had gone. For today.

I walked back to the silent house and sat down on a chair in the sitting room. It was boring waiting for Emma to come home, and soon the cat started to wind its way around my feet. But I didn't chase it away as I had done when I first came here. Then I had not liked cats that were fat while my people were starving, but Emma had explained it to me.

'People have pets to love,' she told me one day. 'You must care for them and look after them.'

After that day I'd learned to be a friend to the pets – throwing a ball for the dog or rubbing the cat – and now I looked down as the cat pushed against me. It was so hairy and its whiskers were long and I wondered if I could help it as I looked at it. A few days before I'd looked in the mirror and hadn't liked what I'd seen. My eyebrows were like spiders crawling on my face, and I'd taken a razor to cut them off. Now I stared at the cat. It was ugly too.

Stroking the cat and lifting it into my arms, I went to find some scissors. I would cut its hair to show it I loved it. I stroked the cat, which purred as I looked after it. It would not know that it looked nice when I'd finished, but Sally and Emma would. Small tufts of fur dropped on the floor around me as I snipped and cut off the cat's whiskers.

'What are you doing?' I heard a voice say, and turned to see Sally.

'The cat is ugly. And I am making it beautiful.'

But Sally had a strange look in her eyes as she stared at me. I had done something wrong again. I got up and walked out into the garden to look for the *jallabas*. I didn't understand this world and I never would.

CHAPTER 20

'We are nearly at the sea,' Emma told me as we drove along the road. We had left Sally's house and were going to stay with more of Emma's friends near a place called Mombasa. 'What is the sea?' I asked.

'It is a big place with a lot of water which you can sail across to find other countries.'

'Is the sea bigger than a river?'

'Yes.'

'Does it have crocodiles and hippos?'

'No. But it is full of fish to eat.'

I heard the rolling of the sea before I saw it, a low crashing that started like the whisper of rain before growing to the roar of a storm. Gazing ahead, I saw white dust stretching into the distance and on the other side more water than I had ever seen – water that danced and moved in white rolls, water that sparkled blue in the sun.

I could see people in boats or swimming in the sea, others lying on the beach with their families. But the sound drew me in most – the roar like a slow beat as the water whooshed and sucked on the sand. I stared and wondered how many fish there were, how many days it would take to cross this sea.

'How far is it to the other side?' I said to Emma.

'It is very far.'

'Does the sea go to the end of the world?'

'If you cross this sea, you will get to India.'

'What is India?'

'It is another country, like Sudan and Kenya are countries.'

I turned back to stare at the sea. I felt its rhythm inside me, bewitching me and making my mind slow down, making the thoughts that tumbled and jostled inside find space from each other. The roar of the sea was making me quiet inside.

I did another bad thing soon after we arrived in Mombasa. The house where we were staying had a security button, and Emma told me it could only be used when there was a problem. But as soon as I was alone, I pushed the button, and the security people arrived. My disobedience cost three thousand Kenyan shillings – or about £30 – to put right, and I knew Emma was angry as she spoke to me about it.

'Do you know how much this cost, Emmanuel? You were asked not to touch the button, and we have had to pay a lot of money because you used it wrongly.'

I stared at her. The only money I'd ever seen was in Ethiopia.

'We have had to pay many, many shillings,' Emma said quietly.

I did not understand.

'It was three *bathdor*,' Emma added.

I sucked in my breath. In my tribe, numbers only went up to one thousand, and the word for that was *bathdor*. It meant lost in the wilderness, a number so big you could never find the end of it.

I didn't feel bad inside at first when Emma told me that. I felt nothing even though I knew I had done wrong at Sally's and I was now doing it again. But something about Emma that day confused me. Why didn't she beat me? Why didn't she scream at me? Why didn't she kick me out of her house?

'You must realise that when I ask you not to do things, it is not just for fun,' Emma said softly. 'You are in a different place now and you must let me show you the way here.'

I said nothing as she spoke to me, but I could not stop thinking about that day when Emma dropped me off at her friend's house while she went shopping. Within hours, I had slipped out of the garden and started walking back to the house where we were staying. Even though many little paths led off the beach to all the different houses, I had learned as a soldier to remember what I saw and followed the sea until I found the right one. The walk took me about two hours in the heat of the midday sun, but I didn't mind. Emma, though, was surprised when she found out what I'd done.

'Emmanuel, how did you get back?'

'I came by feet,' I told her.

'But you might have got lost. You cannot just leave somewhere and not tell anyone where you are going.'

I looked up at Emma as she spoke to me. Her eyes were soft and her voice kind. I knew I had wanted to find her.

Within weeks of arriving in Kenya, I was sent to a school called Sawa Sawa Academy in a place called Meru in the centre of the country. Emma took me there with a big metal box fitted with a padlock to put my new clothes in. The uniform I had to wear was black shorts, a white shirt, a black jumper, and shoes. The clothes felt tight, the shoes pinched, and I thought of the die-and-leave-them shoes and shorts that I'd worn for so long. I tried not to think about the war now that I was going to school. I knew that I would tell no one about where I had come from because I did not want to see the looks in their eyes that I'd seen in Nairobi. I was still a soldier in my heart but would keep my secret close.

It was dark as Emma and I stood outside the school office to say goodbye. Buildings were scattered down a hill below us. I was finally here. I was really going to school. I had forgotten how much I'd once wanted to go, but now the dreams that had kept me marching to Ethiopia suddenly came alive again. I could see how good this school was. Emma wasn't sending me to an ordinary place, but a good school where rich children were educated.

'Work hard,' she said as she smiled at me. 'I'll phone and see you in the holidays when I'm back from Sudan. But I want you to study when I'm not here and do well.'

'I will.'

I remembered sitting by Mama's side reciting ABC, and the *tukul* in Pinyudu where I'd learned my first lessons. This place was so different, so far, and now Emma was leaving too.

She bent down to give me a hug and I stood still.

'Take care of yourself,' she said as she took my hand.

I drew it away. My heart was shaking inside me but I didn't want Emma to see. I had to be strong. A soldier.

That night I slept in a dormitory filled with beds and the next day was tested in maths and English. I knew I would fail as I stared down at the marks on the papers that I did not understand, but when a teacher later told me that I was going to be put into class one with the five-year-olds, I begged not to be. I was thirteen – if I were still in Sudan, I'd soon be receiving *gaar* – too big to be with the baby children.

'Put me in a higher class,' I pleaded. 'And if I fail the first term, then I will be sure to pass the next.'

In the end I was put into class four with eight-and nine-year-olds, but the other children my age still made fun of me.

'Are you stupid?' they would ask as they gathered around me.

I knew I was different to them. My body was long and skinny, my hair lightened by all the years without proper food, and my face the colour of roasted coffee beans – not like the Kenyan children with their chestnut skin.

'Look at you,' they would say, laughing. 'Your hair is lighter than your face, and your skin is so black you need a licence to drink white milk.'

I disliked one boy in particular, Abdul. He was from Tanzania, and his Muslim name and light skin made me hate him even more.

'You're so black that if you stood at traffic lights in the dark,

then all we'd see would be your red eyes,' he would say with a
laugh, and my hands would itch as I longed to punch him.

I told myself that I was at school to study, but then came a
night when the big boys organised a fight in the dormitory. The
winner would receive a loaf of bread, and as they looked at it on
a table, everyone was excited. Soon Abdul challenged me to
fight him, but I didn't want to.

'Are you scared, Sudanese boy?' Abdul laughed.

Boys circled us and started chanting softly. 'Go, go, go,' they
sang.

I looked at Abdul. He wouldn't laugh if he knew what I could
do. He wouldn't smile if he'd seen the *jallabas* I'd killed. I stood
still as he walked up to me and slapped my face. His hand was
hard on my skin, the bitter crack just like the *talemgi*'s
all those years before. He made a fist and I held up my arm
to block him. He tried again. I blocked him once more before
throwing a punch at him. But Abdul was too big to be moved by
my fist and hit me again. This time I could not stop him and fell
to the floor.

Anger rushed through me in hot waves, making my heart
beat fast and my breath shallow. I stood up and Abdul punched
me again. I knew these children would never respect me unless I
showed them who I really was and proved to this Muslim boy
that I could beat him.

Abdul laughed as I jumped up and turned my back on him.

'Had enough, black boy?' he jeered as I ran towards a wall.

Forcing my feet into a run, I jumped at the middle of the wall
and, using one foot to push myself into the air, spun around and
kicked out at Abdul with the other. I pushed all my strength
into my leg as I flew at him, and my shoe smashed into his nose.
Blood ran down his face.

'Yeah, yeah,' boys screamed in excitement as Abdul fell to the
ground.

For a moment, fear rushed into me when he didn't move and
I wondered if I had killed him. But happiness burst warm inside

me when he coughed and groaned, because I knew that no one would want to fight me any more. After that day, I became more popular and started to make some friends, but I still felt like an outsider – so different from these rich children whose parents came to collect them during the holidays. When I returned to Nairobi, I went to stay with a Sudanese family, and once again my path crossed with that of Fathna, whom I'd last seen at Itang camp and who was now living in Kenya as a refugee like me. No one else wanted to look after me over the holidays, but Fathna had agreed to.

'Jal,' she shrieked when she saw me. 'I always knew you were a strong boy and here you are.' Fathna was as kind as ever, but I soon learned when I returned to Nairobi that it wasn't just Emma's white friends who didn't trust me.

'Lost Boy, *jenajesh*, outsider,' the eyes of the Sudanese community in Nairobi silently spoke to me.

On one trip, Fathna took me to a big school meeting where one of her neighbour's sons was being given an award. The ceremony was being held in a playground, with a microphone to make sure everyone could hear. As I stood looking at the wires and boxes leading to it, a boy walked up to me.

'Do you want to be a hero?' he said. 'Do you want the town to talk about you? To be seen on TV? Well then, all you have to do is flick this switch and you'll get super-energy like in the cartoons.'

I'd seen those on television and thought of the brightly coloured animals and people who jumped walls and fell off buildings as I pulled the switch. But the crowd went into an uproar as the microphone system shut down, and someone soon found me standing beside it. The police were called to make sure I was punished, but I could hear the voices talking to them as they arrived.

'He was a child soldier, he's crazy,' they said, and the police stared at me before leaving.

Emma was the one person who did not judge me. Travelling

between Sudan and Kenya, she came to see me whenever she could, sometimes taking me for a few days to see friends, or called me at school.

'You must submit to the rules,' she'd tell me after I got into trouble again. 'I know it's hard, but you must be humble towards the people who are teaching you. If you want to help your people in the future, then you must be a good student and a child like all the others at school. If you do well, then one day I will take you to England to study just as Riek did. He went to university there and look at him now – he's an important leader.'

A voice still told me not to be soft as I listened to Emma talk, but sometimes I felt anxious now as I thought of her in the war I had left behind. Emma was with Riek as much as possible, even at the front of the front line, and I knew death threats had been made against her. In April 1993 I'd visited her in the hospital after she'd run from an attack without her shoes and her feet and legs had been badly injured by thorns that had slashed them. Her bodyguard Forty-Six had saved her.

'It was a heavy attack but I'm glad to be alive,' Emma told me with a smile. 'Luckily for me, Forty-Six was there to carry me with one hand.'

When I returned to school, I tried once again to concentrate on learning, and soon both my Swahili and English improved. I liked learning new things, just as I'd known I would when Emma talked to me of school, and I enjoyed science and geography, arts and crafts. The only subject I did not like was music, when the teacher tried to show me how to write notes down on paper. Why did music have to be written? It was something you learned in your village, which filled you as you marched in army lines, not a science. Again and again, I thought back to the freedom songs I'd sung in the army and knew I would never imprison them on paper.

Just one thing threatened my learning – a girl called Janet. She was a year older than me and I'd noticed her one day as she sang in the school choir at church. I'd forgotten God once more now.

I knew He had saved me in the desert, but for many years before the night beside Lual's body God hadn't heard my prayers.

But I found myself thinking of Janet more and more. At night I would dream of dancing with her, and in the day my heart would beat faster as I passed her in the corridor. She made my head feel strange, as if I were standing on the edge of a river and watching the water rush past. I thought about it often, wondering how just one person could make me feel so different, until I realised what had happened. Janet had bewitched me. I had to stop her. She couldn't fool me. I didn't like this feeling.

'You!' I shouted at her one day as I waited for her after class. 'I came to this school to study, not think about girls.'

Janet looked shocked. 'What are you talking about, Emmanuel?'

'You,' I shouted again. 'You're a witch-doctor.'

For a moment her face was still before she started laughing. 'Don't be so stupid,' she giggled as she looked at me.

I reached out to slap her but suddenly a foot tripped me up and I lost my balance as hands started hitting me. I pushed them off to see Janet holding a stick with one of her friends standing beside her.

'Leave me alone, refugee boy,' she said in a low voice as she stared at me.

Later I told a teacher about what had happened.

'A lot of money has been paid to help me study, but this girl has bewitched me. When I go to sleep, I dream of marrying her; when I go to eat, I cannot.'

The teacher smiled at me. 'But, Emmanuel, this girl is not a witch,' she said with a smile. 'And she has certainly not bewitched you. It is simple. The feeling you have is called love.'

I stared at the woman. Love? I must push down the feeling, crush it inside me just as I had when I was a young boy and war had taken everyone from me. I knew how love had once made me feel.

*

Emma's smile was bright as I opened the car door and got in beside her. It was November 1993 and I had come to Nairobi on the school bus.

'I have good news,' she said. 'You won't have to go anywhere else when you come back from school in the future because you are going to live with me. I have a house, Emmanuel, a beautiful house.'

It was true. Emma had found a home, which she'd named Peace House, and I was excited as I looked around it. There was a big garden with tall trees, servant's quarters, and a veranda for lying on to hide from the sun. Emma had even picked out a room for me and bought a chessboard so that I could play with the bodyguards.

'I have other news, Emmanuel,' she told me that night. 'I am going to have a baby.'

I looked at Emma. I'd never seen a half-black, half-white person. 'What colour will your baby be?'

'It will be gold. And you, little brother, will be here with me to watch it grow.'

I could see how happy Emma was, and for the next few days we were with each other all the time just as we had been after I arrived in Kenya. But about a week later Emma left Peace House one afternoon to go and see her friend Roo, and I didn't go with her because I wanted to finish the game of chess I was playing.

'Okay,' she told me as she looked down at me. 'I'll see you later.'

A strange feeling, like a cold touch on my spine, came over me as she walked out of the room. It was like a shadow inside because I usually went wherever Emma did. But I pushed it down and turned back to my game. When I'd finished it, I took a shower and went to sit on the veranda to watch TV with the bodyguards. I liked being with them and wanted to hear their soldier stories as I waited for Emma to come home. But the afternoon turned into evening and still she did not arrive.

Then Riek's nephew Kuany came to see me. 'There's been an accident.'

As I looked at his face, I could see tears streaking his cheeks, and something twisted deep inside me. Kuany was crying. A man should not show his tears.

'What do you mean?' I stared at Kuany.

'It's Emma.'

'What about Emma?'

'Her car has been hit by a bus. They say she's not going to survive.'

My head rushed as I looked at Kuany. What did he mean? This could not be true. Emma was happy and laughing, Emma was having a baby, Emma was living here at Peace House with me. Emma was my home now.

Silently, I went to my room and waited for more news. I'd wanted to go to the hospital, but someone had told me I couldn't and I thought of Emma alone in that white place. I wanted to be with her just as I had been when she'd hurt her feet. But as the night got darker and the stars were hidden by the blackness, Kuany came to my room.

'She was a gift to us,' he cried as he looked at me. 'She helped our people, our children, and she is the mother of our community.'

'What's happening?' I asked anxiously. 'Where is she? When is she coming home?'

'She's not,' Kuany sobbed. 'Emma is dead.'

My legs went weak as I heard those words. Emma could not have gone. She could not have been taken from me. We were not at war here. We were safe. Kuany was lying.

But I knew he was not the next morning when Sudanese women started arriving at Peace House and crying as they threw themselves on to the ground. They believed Emma had been murdered by Riek's enemies, who hated the strength she'd given his people. She was an angel who had helped them just as she'd helped me, and now she was gone. As I looked at the women, I remembered all those years ago when others had done the same for Mama. The cries, the tears, the twisting bodies as grief poured out of them – it was just as it had been so long before. Mama had been taken from me, and now Emma had too. I was alone once more.

CHAPTER 21

Six years later, I closed the door to a room in Peace House and turned off the light. Sitting down on the floor, I pulled my knees up to my chest, put my arms around my legs, and curled myself into a ball. A pain was in my stomach, something was crushing my lungs, squeezing the air out of me until I could hardly breathe, pushing me down into myself as the blackness surrounded me. My skin felt cool, a layer of sweat on it making me shiver even though the night was warm. A moan twisted out of my mouth and I gulped to stop another from escaping me. My head rushed as someone outside turned on a light and a crack of yellow shone under the door. In its path, I could see a pistol I had taken from the gun store. Should I shoot him? Should I use it to destroy the future I knew I didn't have, six long years after Emma's death? I stared at the gun as memories filled my mind and I closed my eyes .

I am fifteen and it is two years since Emma's death. I am clinging to the boy's back as he twists and turns to try to throw me off. I hold on to him as he rocks and sink my teeth into his shoulder. Biting as hard as I can, I hear him scream. He throws his hand back to hit me and I bite his thumb. He turns his head and my teeth chew into his cheek.

'*Aaaah*,' the boy screams as I dig my fingers into his eyes, just as I was taught at training camp.

I know I will never beat this bully with a punch. I am still too skinny and he is big and fat like a rich kid. Again and again, I bite him to teach him a lesson he will never forget.

'Black boy, gorilla boy, refugee boy,' he and others like him taunt as they laugh at my clothes and skin.

I feel hands pulling me and I cling to the boy's back even tighter. Once more my teeth sink into him.

'What are you doing?' a teacher shouts as he finally pulls me away.

The bully is crying like a baby now as he bleeds.

'Take this boy to hospital,' the teacher says. 'And you had better come with me, Emmanuel. What will the headmaster do with you this time?'

I am eighteen and my friend Daniel is standing in front of me.

'Fuck you, fuck you,' he screams at the men who've chased us.

He puts his fingers inside his trouser belt, and I know he is closing them around his metal in this moment. His metal, his gun, the one thing these men don't know we have as they chase the Lost Boys through the streets. They want to drive us away, banish us from their church. They are scared of the boys from Sudan who've fought in wars and killed. They want nothing to do with the Lost Boys who now roam the streets of Nairobi with me.

The priest takes a step forward. Traffic buzzes around us in the street, *matatus* beeping, trucks growling. I see Daniel's hand move deeper into his pocket before he starts to pull it out. The gun.

'No,' I shout. 'Not the priest.'

I grab Daniel's hand and we wrestle for a moment before the pistol goes off, a bullet ripping across the edge of my shoe as people start running. I look up at them. Helter-skelter – just as they'd looked when I was a child in villages being attacked.

'Run,' I scream, and turn to move.

Daniel and the other boys follow me. We have to get away.
The police will soon come and we cannot let them find us.
We are Lost Boys, worth nothing, but if there is one place
where we will be forgotten even more completely, it is jail.

It is a few months later and I stare as my past rises up to
greet me in a room in Riek's house in Khartoum. Since
Emma's death I have moved from place to place, and now
I am here until I move again to somewhere new.

Baba is in front of me. He isn't as big as I remembered.
He looks smaller, shorter, as he stands in civilian clothes –
a grey top and trousers with sandals. He has lost weight.
He looks old. White hairs are on his head.

He is not here to see me. He has come to visit Riek, who,
along with leaders of other rebel groups, has signed a peace
deal with Khartoum. People are calling Riek a traitor
because they say the promise of the Khartoum Peace
Agreement is worth nothing. It will supposedly allow
southern Sudan to govern itself just as Riek has been
fighting for, but opponents say all it has done is hand the
Arabs permission to start drilling for oil. John Garang didn't
sign the agreement because he wants to win the whole of
Sudan, and his supporters hate Riek for what he's done.

I have been in Khartoum for several months and hate
every moment here. I can feel the Arabs around me, see
them on the streets, watching people with skin like me
living in cardboard huts. I see little boys begging, women
washing clothes on the streets to earn enough to eat,
southern Sudanese being whipped in the sunlight as Arabs
drive past in nice cars, and shanty towns full of thousands
of forsaken refugees with skin the same black as mine.
Being here has changed something inside me, and I know
just two things: that one day I will help my people by
fighting again, and I want to kill the *jallabas* still.

Now I stand in front of Baba all those years after he sent me away. He is an army commander now.

'My son, my son,' he says as he pulls me to him.

It is eleven years since I've seen him, and my eyes are on a level with Baba's as he looks at me. Regular food has made me grow since leaving Sudan.

'You have grown big and strong,' he says. 'How healthy you look! I've heard about you from Riek and you've made me proud.'

I don't speak as Baba talks. My mind is telling me to but my body will not listen. I just stare at him silently.

He looks at me. 'Jal, don't you understand me? I am proud of you.'

For a moment rage fills me as I look at Baba. I am back in the shed after the boat accident, waiting for him to come for me, hoping he will want to take me home to my brothers and sisters. But instead he left me all alone just as I have been ever since. The rage dies though almost as soon as it comes, and then I feel nothing. My father stands before me and my heart is cold.

I moved from place to place in the years after Emma's death as I fought to survive. At first I'd returned to Sawa Sawa Academy after Riek sold Emma's car to pay for my expensive school fees.

'There is no money, but we have your mum's car and we are going to sell it,' he told me.

But I returned to Peace House when the money ran out about six months later. Riek was not there, and I was soon driven out by the whispers and stares of soldiers who called me 'bush boy' and beat me. By then I had started going to church, knowing I'd meet good people who would share what little they had with me, and I was right. When I left Peace House, I went to stay with the mother of my church friend John Paul. She was called Petrolina and lived in one room with her family of eight children in a slum called Kangemi.

'You've survived the worst and God is with you,' Petrolina would tell me, but I didn't believe her.

Kangemi was full of every shade of life – birth, death, and everything in between teemed in the tiny streets filled with noise, dust, and dirt. Most people survived on $1 a day, but even though Petrolina and her family also lived in poverty, I could feel the love in her house like a breeze blowing around me. For the next few years I stayed with her on and off or returned to Fathna's for a few days. I also sometimes went back to Peace House, which Riek had kept after Emma's death because all the top SPLA commanders had homes in Nairobi. SPLA Nasir soldiers and other Lost Boys lived there, and I still did guard duty when needed. From there, I sometimes stole a gun, which I showed off to the rich children in the area. Their eyes would open wide as they looked at it, and I would laugh at these soft kids with my Lost Boy friends. There were hundreds, if not thousands, of us living in Nairobi, and in a way we were like a family to each other. But we also knew boys would come and go and never got too close.

Compared to many, I was lucky because Emma's friends tried to look after me and used money from a fund set up in her name to send me to school again. But they were used to Africa, used to children like me who roamed wild, and can't have been surprised when I got expelled from my next school for fighting. It was always the same during the years when I grew from a boy to a young man – I went to a good school, was expelled, or simply left to roam again. I tried as hard as I could to study, sometimes passing exams, but finding it difficult to concentrate and never catching up with the other children my age.

I knew I was different because I was a soldier, and although other children never knew my secret, I think they could sense it. I had dreams at night that made me shake and sweat in fear as the war buried inside me came alive again. I would see heads being cut off, babies crushed, and helicopters flying overhead with bullets pouring from them. My dreams haunted me, and news of the war in Sudan fed my hate because I knew how my people were suffering. Surviving took all my energy – finding food to eat, a place to sleep, and breath to fill my body when despair filled me. I had ulcers in my stomach, backaches, and sore eyes. Hatred was all I felt inside – if the *jallabas* had not destroyed my country, then I would not be a refugee taunted by children who told me I was black, ugly, and useless. If Mama's God were strong, he would have heard the prayers of the southern Sudanese, but instead Allah was allowing his people to oppress mine, to force us to be the slaves they believed we were destined to be. Why should I worship Mama's God with my heart when I went to church? I would never allow Him in. Instead I knew I must fight the madness that was trying to steal my mind because, just as I'd once felt life draining from me in the desert, I could feel hope finally dying inside me.

I am eighteen and lying on a mattress on the veranda at Peace House. It is night and I have been asleep – dreaming, dreaming of bullets and helicopters, guns and fire. I open my eyes as a bright light shines on me and lower my head to shield myself from its glare as fear fills me. Suddenly a picture comes into my mind – people on a journey, following the light. I feel afraid and curl up, wanting the light to fade. It is taking all my strength as a feeling of shame sweeps over me. I will not be able to follow the light. I will go to hell.

'Forgive me,' I say inside my head.

Suddenly I stand up and, not knowing why, take a step forward. I see a man in front of me, wearing long robes whose bright colours burn into my eyes. Two men, on either side, are with him. Peace fills me as I see him and kneel. He puts his hand on my head.

'I bless you,' a voice says in my mind.

'In the name of the Father, the Son, and the Holy Spirit,' I silently reply.

We repeat these words three times until the voice tells me: 'Keep quiet.'

I am silent.

'I bless you in my name,' it says.

Shoots of happiness spring up inside me, reaching into my heart.

'How am I going to live if you are not with me?' I ask.

'Everything you need was given to you in the beginning,' Jesus tells me.

I look up. I am alone again.

I opened my eyes to stare at the gun once again as the memories flickered away. It was October 1999 and I could hear soldiers' boots outside as they walked in and out of Peace House. My head ached and my chest was tight as I sat in the dark and remembered, trying to push down the feelings inside me, the despair that made me curse the day I was born.

Should I kill him? I thought as the words the teacher had screamed at me earlier that day echoed in my head.

I'd started at the school after returning from Khartoum and tried hard after the night I saw Jesus in the darkness. Slowly I'd become more popular and found I liked science so much that I'd even won chemistry and physics awards for my work. Then, after beating the two most feared school bullies in a fight, I'd been chosen by the pupils to be head boy. But trouble had found me once again after the students went on strike over conditions at the school and some went too far by vandalising the headmaster's house. He blamed boys I knew weren't responsible and so I'd tried to tell him he was making a mistake. But I could see my past glaring back in the headmaster's eyes as he shouted at me. However well I'd done, he knew I was *jenajesh* and would never forget it.

'You were the cause of this rebellion,' he said. 'It is your doing that these boys misbehaved.'

'But I had nothing to do with it and neither did they. They are innocent, sir. You must listen to me.'

'Keep quiet,' the headmaster shouted. 'This is nothing to do with you. I am in charge here, not you.'

I was mad now. Who was this man to disrespect me? I was a soldier. I was a man. I was nineteen years old now.

'You are wrong,' I shouted back as I pushed my face close to his. I could feel my hands tingling, my body longing to hurl itself into him and beat him. 'You are punishing innocent boys,' I carried on. 'Why don't you know I am telling the truth?'

'Because it is not your place to question me. I am the headmaster here and I have had enough of your attitude. Don't you see? You'll never be anything or go anywhere. You are just wasting your time here. You're nothing but trouble. You are rude, disobedient, and now you even stir up the other pupils against me.'

I stared at the headmaster.

'I've had enough,' he spat. 'And this time I'm going to expel you for good.'

I moaned softly as the memory became more vivid. I hugged my knees even tighter, feeling a cold trickle of blood running from my nose to my mouth. It happened now without warning when I fought to keep my feelings under control, as if my body was trying to expel all the pressure inside me. How could the headmaster do this to me when I'd finally been doing well at school? How hard did I have to try before luck came to me? I was tired of fighting, tired of living a life with no one to look after me, tired of being alone. Petrolina had moved and I had lost her. I felt I had no one to look out for me now.

The people I met at school were from a different world. The Emma Fund had paid for me to go to good places, but no one there could understand what I'd seen. I was a soldier.

My hands shook as I thought of the headmaster again. I would never get into another school now I'd been kicked out. I'd never get the education I needed to help my people. I had nothing now because the headmaster had taken it from me.

I stared at the gun. I wanted to kill this man, take the pistol and travel in the darkness to find him. I knew I could do it without anyone knowing because I had been trained to. I would find him and see the fear in his eyes as I raised the gun at him. He should know who I was, see that I was a soldier, understand I had a power over him that he couldn't even begin to understand. Then he'd be just like all the others, crying and begging the moment the gun was lifted to his heart and he realised his life was going to end.

I kicked my foot against the floor and a pain – sharp and long, like a bayonet – ran up my leg. I knew what was causing it. An old injury. My foot had been weakened on the day of the raid in Juba, and it had never become strong again. Now I rubbed my ankle to try to ease the pain that came back to haunt me from time to time. A pain that told me I'd never outrun my past.

I am twelve years old and Lam and I are running towards the river. We have left the second Arab where he fell and are going to rejoin our unit. We know they are heading for the river, and I see *tukuls* near the water as we come out from the trees. Soldiers from our unit are standing near them, and several other men are there too. They are thin, sickly looking, and as we get closer, I see that some have been beaten while others have fingers missing. SPLA soldiers who have been tortured. I remember the body on the tree and rage rises up in me again.

'We need to search and sweep the area to make sure we've captured it,' a big soldier tells us, and troops spread out as Lam and I start walking.

I am trembling. My head spins, my breath quickens, and my mind is blank. I stare down and see blood on my legs and arms as I hold my gun tightly. For a moment the faces of the two *jallabas* we have just finished come into my mind, but I push them away. We must move forward slowly. We cannot run. A retreat is slow, like a game of chess, we must wait to see what move the *jallabas* make.

A gun fires and a soldier nearby falls to the ground. Two others follow him as Lam and I throw ourselves to the ground and start firing. I lift my shoulders and see heads peeping out from a hole near the river. The *jallabas* are in there, they are near now. Suddenly three figures fall in the hole and we know we have a chance. As a grenade explodes, Lam and I get to our feet and start firing.

We run to the hole, screaming our war cry.

'U-*lu-lu-lu-lu-lu-lu-lu-lu-lu*,' I shout, the sound making me brave again and giving me energy. I am light, I am quick, I am my bullet, and my bullet is me. My bullet is my people and my people are me.

The Arabs try to run as we get near, and soldiers split to chase them. To my right, I can see a *jallaba* limping, trying to get to the trees near the river, and Lam and I run at him. He tries to fire but no bullets fly. He is ours now.

We catch up with him on the edge of the river. Lam shoots one of his legs; I shoot the other before we both put a bullet into one of his hands. The man is crying now as he lies on the ground. He sees me, knows me, and I feel a current pumping through my body as I look at him. Turning my gun around, I hit him on the back of his head with the butt.

Pictures, pictures in my head. My village, my family, my country . . .

Lam pulls the gun from his hand.

'No, let me do it,' I scream.

I look down at the *jallaba* as I raise my left leg to kick him in the head. Every ounce of strength I have left flows into my foot as it smashes into his temple. But suddenly a pain like a shock of electricity runs up my leg, and something cracks in my ankle. Blood runs out of his nose and mouth as I stagger back. The pain comes in a wave again as I step on to my left foot, and it gives way beneath me. Exhaustion suddenly rushes over me as I look at Lam.

'He's mine now,' he shouts, and raises his gun.

The bullet hits the Arab in the head and I stare down at him. I feel nothing now. One, two, three . . . Three *jallabas* whose lives I've taken for all those I've lost. No pain, no disappointment, no regret, no guilt. All I know is that I want to kill again and again.

My heart thudded inside me as I opened my eyes and stared at the gun. Should I use it now just as I did all those years ago? Should I allow it to release the hatred I feel inside me for this man who'd taken everything from me once again? I breathed in deeply. My mind was racing, my head was hurting.

I looked into the blackness and saw faces before me – Mama and Emma, like ghosts in the dark. Minutes turned into hours as I stared into the night, thoughts rushing through my head until at last they became quiet and my heart stilled.

I stood up and looked down. Should I be a soldier once more? I was silent inside.

I was not in war any more. This man was not a soldier shooting at me in battle. He was a civilian, an ordinary man, not my enemy in battle.

I kicked the gun away and walked towards the door.

CHAPTER 22

It was late afternoon as my friend Andrew and I walked home together. I had met him at school after I started studying again when Emma's mother, Maggie, had given me a final chance.

'I will help you do your exams,' Maggie told me on a visit to Nairobi. 'But after that you must get yourself a job and learn to support yourself, Emmanuel. The time is coming that the Emma Fund will not be able to pay for you any more.'

I was grateful to Maggie and liked my new school, called Arboretum College, even though I was still behind other people my age because I was twenty and only preparing to take my GCSEs. I had become friends with Andrew, who was a year younger than I and about to sit his A-levels, and we talked as we walked the same way to and from school.

'Would you like to come home with me?' he asked one afternoon in early 2000, and I agreed. Dust danced in the deep golden sunshine as we stood outside a grey stone house. I knew Andrew's father was a professor of medical research at the University of Nairobi and his mother was a teacher, which was why their home was beautiful. Outside was an avocado tree, a small garden, and a tap, and inside I could see a living room with sofas and a table with chairs around it.

'Hello, Mum,' Andrew called as we walked in, and I saw a woman sitting on the sofa reading a Bible.

She was round, small, and her face broke into a big smile as she saw us.

'This is Emmanuel,' Andrew told her. 'And this is my mother, Mrs Mumo.'

'Welcome, welcome,' Mrs Mumo said as she stood up. 'It is nice to meet you, Emmanuel. Come and sit with me. I'm always pleased to meet Andrew's friends. Would you like some tea or maybe something to eat?'

Andrew left the room to get us a drink.

'So, Emmanuel, tell me a little about yourself. How did you come to Nairobi? What subjects are you studying at school?'

I stared at Mrs Mumo. I wasn't used to people asking questions and wanting to know who I was because I was no one. But this woman's eyes were shining with smiles as she sat beside me.

'I am from Sudan and I am a refugee here.'

'Aah,' Mrs Mumo said softly. 'That is a difficult life for any young person.'

I looked at her again. Life is hard in Africa, and my story was only a drop in an ocean made up of millions of tears. But, as questions poured out of Mrs Mumo, I told her I had been brought to Kenya by a British aid worker and was hoping to finish school soon and pass my exams. I also spoke about the other Lost Boys in Nairobi and the organisation I'd started to try to help us, after realising on the night I stared at the gun that I would never outrun my past if I sat still and let it flood over me. Like all the Lost Boys, I needed an education if I ever wanted to fly *nyanking* or become an SPLA commander or a doctor who helped my people. And so, in the months before I knew the Emma Fund would send me back to school, I'd formed a group called the Consolidation Association for Southern Sudanese Youth, or CASSY for short, to try to find money for fees. I might feel as if I were collapsing on the inside, but the other Lost Boys saw me as lucky because I was related to Riek and the *khawaja*s had helped me, so they looked to me for guidance and that was how CASSY came to life.

The first people we went to see were the Americans at their embassy, but they turned us away. Then we went to other embassies and big aid organisations that we'd known at Pinyudu, but no one would help us. Frustration rose inside me again. The other boys were looking to me for help and I couldn't do it. All we could find were scraps of money by doing odd jobs that would never be enough.

But as I told the story to Mrs Mumo, I found myself relaxing. She was full of life and a kindness inside her shone out.

'Your future is bright,' she said as she looked at me when we'd finally stopped talking. 'You are an intelligent boy and are going to do well in life, I am sure. You are already showing that you are a leader, and I would be happy to help you with your work.'

I stared at Mrs Mumo. I hadn't heard anyone say such good things about me since Emma and the commanders in the SPLA.

'I hope you will visit us again, Emmanuel,' Mrs Mumo said as I stood up to leave. 'You are a good boy, and from now on you must be like another son for me – come here if you want to eat, and come here when you want to relax. You are welcome to stay with us if you would like to.'

I couldn't believe what was she saying? She didn't know anything about me or who I was, otherwise she would never ask me into her home.

'What do you mean?'

'That I want you to treat our house as your own and feel at home here.'

I wanted to laugh as I looked at her. She must be mad. She didn't even know me and she was inviting me into her home? Of course it is common in Africa to share whatever you have, but, even so, Mrs Mumo was being more generous than most.

'But why?'

'Because I can see that your life is troubled and you do not know what is ahead of you,' Mrs Mumo said with a smile. 'But I know just one thing: God has big plans for you.'

I stared once again. Mrs Mumo really was nuts.

'Do you know what you are saying?' I said slowly.

'Yes.'

'Do you know that I do not come alone? There are many refugee boys here with no mothers, so if you take me, then you take us all.'

'Yes.'

The next Saturday I went back to see Mrs Mumo with about ten Lost Boys, and she fed us all. Then I returned with even more of my friends, and once again she welcomed us. This was Mrs Mumo's way. The house she lived in with her husband, Jasper, and her sons, Andrew and Michael, was always full – the bedrooms and sitting room packed with teenagers and orphans who came for help. Drug addicts would also come in the middle of the night, and Mrs Mumo would feed and pray for them. By day she raised money for the children's home owned by her church and even went into the slums to talk about God to the gang leaders.

'He is here to help us all if we are willing to listen to Him,' Mrs Mumo would tell me.

From the moment we met her, Mrs Mumo started helping the Lost Boys and CASSY. She was like an engine bursting into life, and soon she became known as Mama CASSY. With her help, we started raising money for school fees by cleaning people's houses or repairing their fences for a fee. She also helped me write nice letters asking people to help us. Within weeks we had enough to pay for uniforms for the Lost Boys who had got scholarships to go to school and convinced Arboretum College to take two boys. Mrs Mumo even persuaded a friend of hers who worked at a college in Nairobi to allow four Sudanese boys to study there.

'We just have to work hard and God's path will open before us,' Mrs Mumo would tell me, and sure enough it did.

After sitting my GCSEs in June 2000 – getting two low passes and failing three others – I went to live mostly with Mrs Mumo. I still moved around and went back to Peace House sometimes, but I liked being at Mrs Mumo's because she treated me like one of her sons. By now she knew a little about my life as a *jenajesh*, and sometimes I wondered if she could see the shadows inside me. But it seemed as if nothing I said could shock Mrs Mumo. To repay her kindness, I had started going to her church, the Kileleshwa Community Church, because I knew it would make her happy. I could not let God into my heart, but as I listened in church, I thought of the desert and the way He had helped me. In so many ways I wanted to believe in Him because the happiness on Mrs Mumo's face as she prayed reminded me of Mama's. Although my life had changed since the night I'd stared at the gun, my anger had not disappeared. I prayed with my head but not my heart, and Mrs Mumo's faith drove me on, not mine in God. Buried deep inside me, the spear of hatred still burned, and sometimes I thought it would burst out of me. The war in Sudan was still raging, my people were dying, and news of it always made my heart pound. Why did God make my people so desperate? Why did the Lost Boys have to knock on doors and beg to find help even after they'd escaped war? It depressed me still, and I wondered if I would ever leave the bitterness behind.

I stared at the black-and-white picture on the television. A man was speaking, his voice full of passion as people listened to him. His name was Martin Luther King.

'And when this happens,' he said, 'when we let freedom ring, when we let it ring from every village and every hamlet, from every state and every city, we will be able to speed up that day when all of God's children – black men and white men, Jews and Gentiles, Protestants and Catholics – will be able to join hands and sing in the words of the old Negro spiritual, "Free at last! Free at last! Thank God Almighty, we are free at last!"'

The crowd cheered and clapped – thousands of people stretching into the distance as Martin Luther King finished speaking, faces full of joy, eyes shining with belief. Their cries echoed in my head as Mrs Mumo stepped towards the video and turned it off.

'You see, there are many whose lives are full of struggle like yours and other people who have suffered just as the Sudanese have,' she said as she turned to me. 'This man was the child of slaves in America, people who were taken from lands across Africa and transported across the ocean in terrible conditions. Some died on the journey, and the rest were sold when they reached America. Only the strongest survived the brutality.'

I thought of Martin Luther King and the crowd listening to his words, black and white faces turned upwards like flowers in the sun. I hadn't known before that other people in the world had troubles like mine – even in places like America. The only stories I knew were about southern Sudanese boys taken by the Arabs.

'Martin Luther King will be remembered forever for his message, that peace, and not war, is the way to win battles,' Mrs Mumo said, looking at me as I sat silently on the sofa. 'He knew he lived in a land where different tribes were unequal, but he did not let bitterness poison his heart. He was a holy man who understood that the peaceful fight was the one which would win, and he was right. Black and white now live as equals in America.'

I looked at Mrs Mumo. Did she know about the struggle inside me? Did she believe, just as all the others before her, that I was stained deep down in my soul?

'Martin Luther King chose the most powerful weapon in the world – love – to break the chains of hatred,' Mrs Mumo said softly. 'He knew bitterness for past sins would destroy him and his people from the inside. He had a dream – do you have one?

'Look at the other leaders we have talked about – Mahatma Gandhi and Nelson Mandela – none of these men preached hatred, and all believed in forgiveness.

'Remember what the Bible says, Emmanuel: "For if you for- give men when they sin against you, your heavenly Father will

also forgive you. But, if you do not forgive men their sins, your
Father will not forgive your sins."

'And the Lord's Prayer says the same: "Forgive us our trespasses as we forgive those who trespass against us."

'You are a young man now, and it is time for you to realise
that this is the most important lesson you will ever learn.'

I said nothing to Mrs Mumo that day as I wondered if I
would be able to do as she said. I had lived with hatred for so
long that it was part of me, bleached into my bones and scarred
on to my heart. But as I sat and thought about what she was
trying to teach me, I could hear a voice whispering to me.

'Let us not seek to satisfy our thirst for freedom by drinking
from the cup of bitterness and hatred,' Martin Luther King had
said. 'Again and again, we must rise to the majestic heights of
meeting physical force with soul force.'

Music was all around me in Kenya as people sang in church or
at prayer meetings in Mrs Mumo's house. On the streets and in
school I started hearing other songs that also spoke to me. The
soft lilt of Bob Marley brought back memories of the commanders in Juba who'd listened to him; the heavy beats of Tupac
and Ice Cube made my chest throb; the modern African rhythms
of Kofi Olumide and Kanda Bongo Man reminded me of my
childhood; and the R&B of artists such as Mary J. Blige, LL
Cool J, and Chaka Khan made me want to dance. The first time
I heard 'I'm Every Woman' at a school dance, I closed my eyes
and jumped to the beat as my friends stared at the bush boy
hearing disco for the first time.

Although I loved music of nearly every kind, I never thought
about making my own until the day I heard a song by Puff
Daddy. I was on a bus travelling to a slum for a CASSY meeting
and my mind felt heavy. We were still raising money for boys to
go to school, but there were no fees for me yet. I'd been through
British schools in Kenya that were expensive, and although I
wanted to do A-levels and go to university, there wasn't enough

money to pay for me. My chances with the Emma Fund had come to an end, and I knew as I sat on the bus that I was going to have to encourage the CASSY guys to be positive even though I didn't feel it.

A song started playing on the radio as I stared out of the window at the streets passing by. It was by Puff Daddy.

I was surprised as I listened to the words. I'd listened to American rappers and gospel songs in church, but I'd never thought the two could mix. Puff Daddy was saying Jesus had helped him. This was something different from anything I'd heard before, and I thought of Mama as the song went on.

'God loves everyone, Jal,' she'd told me as we ran during war. 'And He forgives their sins.'

I thought of all the testimonies I'd heard in church, the smiles on people's faces as they spoke of how God had helped them, and now Puff Daddy was saying the same. As the streets of Nairobi rushed past the windows, I remembered sitting under the tree in the desert and the bird that had fallen from the sky as I lay beside Lual. Could I ever truly believe in God again? Could I let Him into my heart?

I had thought about forgiveness more and more since Mrs Mumo had started teaching me about great men such as Martin Luther King. I knew it wasn't a light that could be switched on in an instant – it grew day by day, week by week, month by month – but something was changing inside me now during the hours when I sat alone and tried to calm my feelings. A seed had been sown, and I sensed that, just as I'd once faced a choice about whether to use violence on the night when I stared at the gun, I now had another choice: to remain trapped in the bitterness of the past or to find peace in the present. I had always thought I would help my people by again fighting for my country one day, but now I began to see a different way – a path to peace just as Martin Luther King had believed in.

I thought of the stories of men such as Gandhi, Mandela, and

King that I'd read in the books Mrs Mumo had bought me. Day after day she spoke to me about God's love and his message of forgiveness, and as I looked around Nairobi, I saw Muslims and Christians living together, marrying each other, and working side by side. There were Muslim children at school who wanted to be my friend even though I rejected them. If people here could live in peace, then maybe I should learn from them.

'All you need is Jesus,' Mrs Mumo always told me, and I thought of her now as the song finished.

I stared out the window again. *All we need is Jesus Christ*, I thought to myself as notes started playing in my head. I could hear phrases and sounds as words started forming in my head.

All we need is Jesus Christ
'Cause he died for you and me
Come rejoice 'cause he is alive
Ain't a thing too hard for Jesus.

By the time the bus journey ended, a plan had come to me about how we would help CASSY. I would write my song and we would use it to form a group to raise money. Andrew agreed with me, and we soon found other boys to join us. We called ourselves JAEEEM – the first letters of the names of the group members, who were Andrew, Emmanuel, Edward, Eedo, and Mark – and of the person we would be singing about, Jesus. All the boys loved music as much as I did, and from the day we started, lyrics flooded into my head as I remembered my aunt Nyagai and the words I'd written with her long ago for the rapping competitions in my villages.

God loves us 'cause He has shown us
How to live right, how to imitate Christ
You wanna be like Jesus in every way?
Try to live right and pray every day?

All the JAEEEM boys knew CASSY needed as much money as it could get and were happy to help. To make ourselves sound as good as possible, we found a friend called Junior who mixed our beats on a keyboard and taped them so we could rap over the top. I wasn't the best singer – the other boys were taller, more handsome, and found rapping easier – but I was better at English, and as the weeks passed, I felt more and more words coming into my head. I'd lie in bed and think of them or walk along the street and hear them inside me.

From the moment I started writing songs, the feeling they gave me was like nothing I'd ever had before. I'd always tried at school but never concentrated properly. With songs, though, it was different and I enjoyed what we were doing. We practised until we felt able to perform in front of people, then started doing shows in our church or at youth clubs. Suddenly I was busy again. I hadn't had much to do after finishing my exams, but now my mind was completely occupied, and the busier I got, the calmer I felt – my nightly dreams diminished and the feelings of frustration inside me started to weaken. Now, after getting to know England and the USA, I have learned that this is called music therapy, but all I knew in Kenya was that music made me happy in a way I hadn't felt before. It was the one thread running through my life – from being a child watching Mama in the church choir, to listening as village people celebrated life, to singing soldier songs to put courage into my heart – music, along with Mrs Mumo's teachings, fed something inside me that gave me peace.

In the winter of 2000 we performed at one of Kenya's best schools, Brookhouse International School. Mrs Mumo was teaching there and had spoken to the headmaster, who agreed we could perform for the Christian Union. We went on a Sunday and I felt happy and sad when I got to Brookhouse; happy because we were raising money for CASSY, but sad as I looked at the children in their uniforms and wondered if I would ever go to school again. Brookhouse was beautiful, with a soccer field, children relaxing on the grass in the shade of jacaranda trees, clean buildings, and a kind staff. I longed to go to such a place.

'I am going to ask the headmaster to give you a scholarship to this school,' Mrs Mumo said soon after we'd visited.

I smiled as I looked at her. Mrs Mumo liked to think big, but this was too much even for her. I'd lived in Kenya for seven years running on the streets and surviving from day to day. I'd dropped out of school after school, hardly passed any exams, and had no money even to buy a uniform. I didn't know what I was going to do with my life now, but however much I wanted to, I doubted I'd ever go back to school.

'Yes, Mrs Mumo,' I said as she looked at me seriously.

'All we must do is trust in God and He will listen.'

The white man's eyes were serious as I sat opposite him. Mr Mantz was the head teacher of Brookhouse. Earlier that day I'd sat some tests for him and knew I hadn't done well. I might be able to rap a little, but my English wasn't strong enough for the British-system tests, and I didn't understand a lot of what was asked. Now I was sitting in Mr Mantz's office, a room filled with books and trophies like no other I'd seen before.

'So what do you want to be when you finish school?' he asked.

'I'm not sure. A doctor maybe, or a pilot. All I know is that I want to help my people.'

'And why do you want to come to Brookhouse?'

'Because I want to get the best education possible and I know that is what you give here.'

Mr Mantz continued to ask me questions, and I tried to answer them as well as I could. But I knew I had failed the tests and would never fit in at this place where the children came from Kenya's best families.

'Your grades are too low, I'm afraid, for you to attend this school, and your test result was poor as well, Emmanuel,' Mr

Mantz said at last. 'I think it may be a waste of time for you to come here. Maybe you're more suited to doing carpentry at a college or another course that would prepare you for a job.'

I nodded as he spoke. Even Mrs Mumo's faith wouldn't be enough this time. But my heart felt heavy when I left the office and told Mrs Mumo what Mr Mantz had said.

'This place is not for me. We will have to find another school I can go to.'

'Emmanuel!' she insisted. 'This is just the devil trying to block the door.'

Mrs Mumo refused to take no for an answer and went back to ask Mr Mantz once more to give me a scholarship. But he told her he could not take a chance on a boy like me, with a past like mine, a pupil unlikely to obey authority.

'Emmanuel is a good boy now,' Mrs Mumo said firmly.

'I am sorry but we cannot help you,' Mr Mantz replied.

Still Mrs Mumo did not want to listen. She returned the next day to see Mr Mantz and this time he told her: 'I thought I had made my decision. But while my mind says no, my heart says yes.'

Mrs Mumo looked at him seriously.

'Do not do anything in a rush,' she replied. 'Let your mind and heart agree and maybe you will give Emmanuel a chance. If not, we will find him another school.'

Mrs Mumo was happy when she told me Mr Mantz was thinking hard about his decision.

'You are going to that school,' she told me. 'You must have faith that God will provide.'

I did not want to listen as I tried to put Brookhouse out of my mind. JAEEEM had just done a big concert that had raised a lot of money for CASSY, and we were also going to perform at a huge Christian event on New Year's Eve. But I couldn't stop thinking about it as I wondered if Mrs Mumo was right. Should I trust God to help me? She seemed so sure. It was then that Mr Mantz asked to see me again and I returned to Brookhouse before leaving the headmaster and Mrs Mumo to talk. I was back at home when I heard footsteps coming up the path.

'Well, Mr Mantz and I have spoken,' Mrs Mumo said as she walked in.

I wished she would stop talking about school and let me concentrate on my music. Mr Mantz was right. It was time to give up on her dream.

'You are going to Brookhouse.'

I looked at Mrs Mumo and breathed in as she smiled at me. I could feel the bottom of my heart begin to dance.

I was going to school? I was going to the best school in Nairobi? Mr Mantz had decided to take a chance on a boy like me?

Mrs Mumo was right. After all the months of questioning and praying, God had saved me once more: He had opened a door to the future for me. I knew now that my heart believed in Him again.

CHAPTER 23

All I could see were faces – thousands of people in a crowd that stretched like a sea ahead. Hands were waving in the air and cheers were flying above me as JAEEEM stepped on to the stage. We were performing at a big Christian event on New Year's Eve 2000 – one of many acts supporting a popular gospel group called Milele – and the crowd was the biggest we'd ever seen. It was a world away from the church audiences we usually played to, and my heart thudded as our backing track started. My throat tightened as I looked at Andrew and the other boys beside me. I just had to think of the lyrics, the rhythm of the music, and let them open me up inside as I knew they could. A wave of sound from the crowd washed over me as we started to rap, and the bass boomed inside my chest like the beat of shells dropping into the earth. But war was not surrounding me now. Hate was not filling the air I breathed. It was love. Love from a crowd who cheered as we sang and stilled my pain in a way I'd never before known.

Brookhouse was everything I'd thought it would be. There were music classes, a swimming pool, basketball, and table tennis. It was just like a British school, and I joined the soccer team, started swimming, and ran the 10,000 metres. I was twenty-one by now and still had to work hard at my lessons. Many teachers there were kind to me – Mr Mehta, the school's owner, not only gave me a scholarship but even money for bus fares because he knew I couldn't afford it – and Mr Nyoro, who taught accountancy, befriended many children, including me. Both men knew about my past and always encouraged me. When I failed in class, Mr Nyoro would push me on, and when I was full of regrets about how much school I'd missed, Mr Mehta would tell me I'd soon catch up. Surrounded by children from wealthy families, many of whom planned to go abroad to university, I felt frustrated that I was so far behind as my desire for education grew stronger. I wanted to be like the other pupils – go to university and learn enough to help my people.

I tried as hard as I could in class, but music often disrupted my thoughts. Boys were still coming to ask CASSY for help, and so JAEEEM needed to do fund-raising concerts to help them. Lost Boys were being taken from Kakuma refugee camp to a new life in America, and some came to Nairobi on their way. They'd arrive at Peace House or Mrs Mumo's with eyes shining about the new world they were going to, and many would ask for help. We started collecting clothes at concerts for the boys, or I'd give whatever money I had. One Lost Boy on his way to America even took my coat, which had my passport in it.

But as time passed, it became clear that I wanted something different from JAEEEM than the other boys. We argued more and more as they turned up late or with girls by their side and I felt that they weren't as serious as I was. I also wanted to get time in a studio, but the other boys didn't seem as disappointed as me when we were turned away.

'I can't waste my time on you guys,' a producer told us. 'You're just no good.'

I may have been a Christian now, but I still felt like hitting him.

In the end JAEEEM split. Music meant something to me that the other boys could never understand because the responsibility I felt for helping others ran so deep. But it was hard to perform alone because, with no one beside me, no one shared the sadness if the song stopped and the audience were silent – which happened often. All I knew was that I had to rap, just as a fish needs water and a bird needs air, and so I started performing alone.

In late 2001 Mr Mehta gave me permission to do a concert for the Brookhouse pupils. Just one stood up to clap for me as I started singing, but by the end the pupils were cheering and I raised about £200 which I gave to Mrs Mumo for the orphans.

'Emmanuel, you are so ugly but I love you,' a little girl told me as she handed me a flower when I finished singing at Brookhouse. 'You sound like Puff Daddy. You know Jay-Z?'

'Yes,' I told her.

'Well, he is ugly too, but his music makes him look beautiful.'

Mr Mehta also smiled as he stood before me. 'You have talent, and there are those who have big careers in music.'

'But I am doing this for fun,' I told him. 'I don't want to be a musician. I want to go to university someday.'

'Well, you should give your music a chance.'

But I didn't think about music as a job. I just knew it was helping me. Small things could still trigger my bitterness, and sometimes I'd wonder if there was any good in the world as I thought of all the evil I'd seen in my past. But then I'd start to sing and remember Emma, the angel who'd saved me, Mama, Mrs Mumo, and Mr Mehta, and I knew there was good. I had to carry on learning to forgive until the feeling stretched right into my heart and settled there forever.

Riek Machar also inspired me. I still saw him sometimes when he was visiting Kenya from Sudan, and in January 2002 he and John Garang united to start peace talks with Khartoum. It seemed as if the war in Sudan might finally be coming to an end, and I looked at Riek – the friend he had made of a man who had once been his enemy and the Arabs who visited him at Peace House – and knew he had no bitterness in his heart, which helped me keep trying to conquer my own through music and prayer.

Soon after, the husband of a Brookhouse teacher who owned a studio offered to help me, and I used pocket money given to me by Mrs Mumo and Mr Mehta to cut my first CD. I was excited to stand in front of a proper microphone for the first time to record 'All We Need' – the song I'd written on the bus – and pressed around fifty CDs to sell at concerts to raise money for CASSY. The track even got some airplay on Christian record stations and the BBC World Service thanks to a friend of Emma's who'd helped me over the years, Peter Moszynski. He was a journalist I'd spoken to about my story, and he had been a good friend to me in the years after Emma's death – sending me pocket money and visiting when he was in Nairobi. But the excitement over the track faded quickly, and what I earned from the CDs soon disappeared because I gave most of it away. I'd grown up in a place without money and had yet to learn that while it may seem like a road to freedom, you are quickly trapped again if you spend it too fast. There was also resistance to me in some churches because rap was seen as the devil's music.

Months passed, and as 2002 turned into 2003, I began to learn how hard it was to do music. I would go to shows and no one would turn up, or I'd collect money for CASSY and not have enough to pay for a bus ticket home. A band called the Reborn Warriors had started performing with me, but even they could not soften the humiliation I felt if no one applauded. It was one thing to get the crowd in your own church on to their feet and praising you, but another to ask total strangers to do so. Audiences didn't respond to my lyrics about God in the way my church friends did. They just stared at me, almost confused at what I was saying. I wanted to tell them about the hope Jesus had given me, but they didn't want to listen. I knew what they thought. I sounded bad, like a boy impersonating Puff Daddy, because however hard I tried, I just couldn't find my own voice.

Music was also beginning to interfere with my studies. Surrounded by wealthy children, Brookhouse continued to feed the ambition inside me, as did my friend Peter Moszynski, who continued to help me and told me about a place called Oxford

University. In December 2002 Peter had paid for me to visit him in Britain, and we went to see record producers to talk about my music. Although no one was interested in me, Peter had promised to help find sponsors if I wanted to study in the UK. He knew his friend Emma had wanted me to get the best education possible, and a university degree from Britain would go far in Africa. I was a strange creature, a boy who'd lived in the slums and relied on strangers to support me, but surrounded by wealth and privilege that made me want to achieve. So I didn't question going to England because, just as I'd learned to do as a child, I only looked forward as I took every opportunity that came.

'Nothing is impossible,' Mrs Mumo would tell me, but I knew that devoting myself both to music and my studies was so.

As the time for my exams approached in the summer of 2003, I decided to give up music. I was working hard for the AS-levels in chemistry, physics, and maths I was about to take, and as I pored over my books, I remembered the words that Mama and Emma had so often told me. Education was all that mattered.

'Hello?' I said as I picked up the phone.

The line crackled as a man started speaking. 'Jal Jok?'

It was a long time since anyone had called me that. I was Emmanuel Jal now, just as I'd become after meeting Emma.

It was the winter of 2003 and I was in London. I had passed my exams just as I'd promised myself I would and was studying at the University of Westminster. I'd enrolled in a year's foundation course in electronic engineering, and Peter, his girlfriend Jill, and his friends Andrew and Jennifer Shand were funding my studies. I hoped I was repaying them well by working hard, even though I found England a strange place. The food tasted bad, the trains that ran underground didn't blow out smoke, and people never looked each other in the eyes. Sometimes I'd play games trying to catch someone's gaze, but it was impossible. Maybe everyone was sad because it was so cold all the time. I looked as big as a bear most days dressed in jumpers, T-shirts,

and jackets – more clothes than I'd even owned for most of my
life piled on to keep me warm because I knew the sun in England
lied. One day it was shining outside and I'd left the house in a T-
shirt and sandals to find it was still cold. I missed the African sun
that warmed me as it shone.

'Who is this?' I asked the voice on the phone.

'I am here with your sister,' the man said.

'What do you mean?'

'Your sister. Nyaruach.'

Memories rushed into my head as I stood holding the phone.
My little sister, Nyaruach? The girl I hadn't seen for sixteen years?
The sister whose face I couldn't even remember? My heart raced
as I listened to a woman's voice. It was small and worried.

'Hello? Jal?'

'Yes. It's me.'

'It's Nyaruach.'

How had my sister found me? Surely she was dead? I held my
breath. I couldn't understand. I'd lost my family years before.

'I am so glad to hear your voice,' Nyaruach continued when
I fell silent.

'But how did you find me?'

'I heard you speaking on the BBC radio when your song "All
We Need" was played. I couldn't believe it was really you.'

I stilled my mind as I thought. 'I am a student now, not a
musician. And where are you?'

'In the Dimma refugee camp in Ethiopia. I have been search-
ing for you ever since hearing the song and it's taken so long. But
now I have found you, thank God.

'I traced you through the Sudanese community in Kenya and
had to save to pay for the phone calls. I need your help, Jal.'

I swallowed as I listened, unsure who this woman was. I
didn't understand. How could a ghost come to life? How could
a child be a woman now and know me?

The woman's voice grew faint as she talked, slowly and haltingly,
telling me she had been in Dimma for many years. Questions

rushed through my mind. How did she get there? Did she know
where the others were? Nyakouth, Nyagai, Miri, and Marna? But
suddenly Nyaruach's voice quickened as she talked.

'I must go now, Jal,' she said in a rush. 'But remember, I want
to come to you. I have to leave this place.'

I was silent for a moment as my chest heaved inside me.
Could the words come out? Could I claim a sister who was all
but dead to me?

'Please, Jal,' she said urgently. 'I need you to help me.'

I thought of Mama when she was near me, when my blood
beat the same as hers. I didn't know what to do. How could I
help a sister when I had nothing to give?

I closed my eyes as I remembered a girl I had known in my
grandmother's village during the war. It was hunger season and
she had nothing to give her brothers and sisters as they cried for
food. So the girl put an axe in a pot over a fire and told the little
children to wait many hours for it to cook. As the children
stared at the metal axe, which was never going to soften, the
pains in their stomachs disappeared because they were filled
with hope, and their sister was able to find food while they
waited. Now I must do the same.

'I will bring you to me,' I said slowly. 'I promise you,
Nyaruach, that I will bring you to me.'

The voice said nothing as the line went silent. A world away,
my sister was trapped in the prison of a refugee camp and I had
promised her freedom.

'We cannot issue you with a visa,' the white woman said.

I felt my temper quickening. I was sitting in the British embassy
in Nairobi after returning to Kenya for the holidays. My visa
for Britain had run out, and I needed another one to continue my
studies at the University of Westminster. But I had been refused
again and again, and no one would tell me why.

'But please,' I insisted. 'I have friends in England, sponsors
who will look after me, and a place to study. I am getting good

grades there. I got a hundred per cent in my maths exam, I am a top student.'

'I'm sorry, Mr Jal, but I am not able to issue you with a visa.'

My anger got the better of me.

Fuck her. Fuck white people. Fuck Britain.

She was like the headmaster who'd thrown me on the dust heap all those years before. I had to get back to the university, study hard, and provide for my family. I'd heard nothing from Nyaruach in the weeks since the phone call from Dimma, but I knew more than ever now that I must do well. I had a sister to look after.

The woman's face was blank as she sat at her desk. 'If that's all?' she said as she gestured for me to leave.

I stood up, blood beating in my temples and in my ears. Stumbling out of the door, I walked into the busy street, silently praying that a car or bus would hit me. I couldn't take my own life, but someone else might. How could this be happening again? Just as the future opened before me, it had been snatched away yet again. Looking around at the beggars on the street, the rubbish piled high, the trucks roaring and voices shouting, I wondered how I would ever escape.

CHAPTER 24

That was one of the worst days of my life, as the hope I'd worked so hard to create inside was destroyed and I wondered how I would ever find the faith to keep going. When my friend Mr Mehta discovered what had happened, he offered to let me return to Brookhouse to study for A-levels. I didn't know what I would do now, but if I couldn't get a degree, then I should try to get as many qualifications as possible. But Mr Mehta could see I was like a boat drifting in the sea now that my dream of university had gone. I would never be able to afford it, never get another chance as I had in England thanks to Emma's friends.

'You should make music again,' Mr Mehta told me. 'Maybe it will help you as it did before, and remember what I once told you – some people make it big with music in places like America.'

My best friend at Brookhouse, Philip Gitoni, and the Lost Boys told me Mr Mehta was right. 'Come on, Emmanuel,' they said. 'You're good, you've got talent, and you're gonna make it big. You shouldn't have given up so easy before.'

I wondered if they'd been seeing a lot of Mrs Mumo in the months I was in England but knew they were right. Bitterness had threatened to overwhelm me again since the day I'd felt hatred biting into my soul once more as I stared at the *khawaja* in the embassy. Music had once given me peace in a way I had never before known, and although I'd given it up, maybe I could use it again to crush the despair inside me. Remembering the

words of Martin Luther King and the happiness that forgiving
had given me, I wrote a song to give myself hope.

When I am lonely
I just have to praise the Lord
When I am broke
I just have to praise the Lord
When no one loves me
I just have to praise the Lord
When things go bad
I just have to praise the Lord
As I walk through the valley of the shadow of death
As things go bad I won't turn back
Because I know Jesus Christ is there for me
He died for me, he paid my price

As soon as I started writing again, I felt peaceful and decided to
give my music one hundred per cent to see where it might take
me. Making it a success lay in my hands alone because the music
industry is different in Africa than in Britain and America. A few
artists are signed to labels, but most are their own producer,
manager, distributor, and promoter, and I was going to have to
do the same. Once more I saved up my pocket money and
Brookhouse also sponsored me when I asked for money to make
a recording of 'Praise the Lord'. When it was done, Philip and I
visited radio stations across Nairobi with the CD. If I wanted to
be serious about music, then I needed fans and so people had to
hear my music. New friends I had made also helped me –
another Lost Boy called Lam, and Manaseh, the son of a
Sudanese pastor, visited stations with the CD – but we all got
knocked back.

'Who are you? What kind of artist? What kind of music?'
people would say as they threw my CD into a box full of them.
I was a no one with no fans, and people didn't take any notice of
me.

'Keep going,' a voice inside told me. 'Don't give up.'

I knew I wouldn't. Music and God had saved me once before and I hoped they would do so again. I wanted to share my songs, tell others what I'd learned.

Soon there was just one chance left – a DJ whose support could turn any tide. There are many different music charts in Kenya, but the biggest for gospel music was on *Kubamba*, a show presented by DJ Moz. He was the best-known gospel DJ in Nairobi, and you were guaranteed fans if you got to number one on his show. Month after month in early 2004, I studied by day and went to see DJ Moz whenever he played at night. Saving my pocket money and walking to and from shows to save bus fares, I tried to meet him.

'Can you play my record?' I'd ask at the end of the night as I handed him a CD. 'Can you listen to this?'

'I'll try, I'll try,' he would tell me, but week after week 'Praise the Lord' never made it on to his show.

But Lost Boys are good at finding ways around rocks in the road – we learned well as we fought for food and life in the camps – and we came up with a new plan. We had to convince DJ Moz that Emmanuel Jal had fans who wanted to hear his music, and so while none of us had mobile phones, we borrowed other people's or used a pay phone to make a call or text.

'Could you play "Praise the Lord" by Emmanuel Jal please?' we'd ask in one voice before phoning and using another.

I don't know how many calls we made, but eventually it worked because DJ Moz played 'Praise the Lord'. I could only wait as my song started climbing his chart and other stations picked it up. Young gospel fans liked it, and as the song started getting attention, I knew it was time to use the rest of the money I had been given by Brookhouse to shoot a video for the song at school featuring the kids there. When it was done, I sent it in to *Stomp*, a gospel music programme on the Kenyan channel Nation TV. Like DJ Moz, it was the biggest of its kind, and when people at school saw me on TV, they started voting. For a week I waited as the video climbed the *Stomp* charts and for the next week wondered what would happen as it edged into the top ten.

Then Philip rang me: 'Man, you've made it. You're at number one.'

I stood in front of the hotel door and lifted my hand to knock. I'd got a phone call earlier that day telling me Nyaruach was in Nairobi. I didn't know how she'd escaped the refugee camp, and since the phone call all those months before, I'd wondered if I would ever find her again to keep my promise. I'd also asked myself if the woman I'd spoken to could really be my sister. How had she survived the war? And was this stranger on the phone really her or someone who thought I had money after the success of 'Praise the Lord' and claimed to be my kin as others falsely had? If she was a fake, then she would be disappointed. People may have voted me on to DJ Moz's and *Stomp*'s charts but I hadn't made any money.

My life had changed in other ways though. I was doing more and more performing now that people knew my name, and I even had fans – young people who called out my name on the streets and asked for my autograph. I didn't like the attention, I was used to being no one, but I was becoming a little star in Nairobi. My friend Peter Moszynski was still trying to find me a record deal in Britain, but I wasn't too hopeful after what we had been told when I visited England. I just wanted to keep making music because now during gigs fans would shout the lyrics of 'Praise the Lord' back at me as I sang and I felt their happiness just as I felt my own.

I stared at the door again before opening it and walking into a room with a couch and a TV with two women sitting before it. One stood up as I entered.

'Jal,' she said. 'Is it really you?'

I stared at her, not sure what to say as she stepped towards me. I tried to smile.

'I have come so far,' she said.

The woman was small and slight, her clothes dirty and torn.

'How did you get here?' I asked.

'Somebody who knows you through your music helped smuggle me out of the camp. Ever since I spoke to you on the telephone, I've been listening to the BBC World Service hoping for news of you.'

I couldn't remember Mama's face. Did this woman look like her? Was it really Nyaruach?

'It was a terrible journey,' she whispered. 'We were attacked as we walked through the bush and I met a lion as I ran. I was sure it would eat me but I spoke to it as it came for me. I told it that I had to meet my brother, and the lion looked at me before it turned away and ran after the people chasing me instead.'

I stared at her as she started crying, eyes so like my own. She too had been saved just as I had been when I sat under the tree in the desert and prayed for rain. Something inside me stirred. This must be my sister. The woman standing before me was part of the family I had cried for at Pinyudu until no more tears would come.

'I am happy you are here,' I said slowly, and smiled again.

But Nyaruach looked at me with sad eyes as she held on to me and wept.

'I know you are a Lost Boy,' she whispered. 'And I have heard what has happened to men like you. Lost Boys don't feel anything for their families, they have learned to deaden their hearts, but I hope you will help me.'

Her words cut into me and her tears burned me as memories of all the sadness I had seen as a boy moved inside. She was right. I felt a rush of responsibility for my sister, but my heart was not moved in the way it should have been. Nyaruach was part of the family I'd mourned so long ago, but just as on the day I'd seen Baba in Khartoum, those feelings were lost to me now.

Today I understand why. To open my heart fully to my sister

would have taken me back to my childhood – a place to which I could never return. I had never told anyone, not even Mrs Mumo, the whole story about what had happened to me or what I had done, and as I looked at my sister, it felt as if that story was about another boy in another life. I had locked so much of my history away, and seeing Nyaruach took me dangerously close to being flooded with the hate I had worked so hard to rid myself of.

But somehow my sister understood the distance between us. Her story, like mine and so many others' in Sudan, was full of pain, and neither she, nor the Lost Boys I knew in Nairobi, ever asked about another's. I was careful not to ask Nyaruach exactly what had happened to her, just as she never asked me. We both knew it would be too hard to hear. All I learned then was that Nyaruach had been separated from our brothers and sisters as they ran from war. From the little she knew, she believed Nyakouth, Miri, and Marna were alive and living in Bantiu, where Grandmother Nyapan Deng was also. She had seen four children die in the war and only one survive.

In the weeks that followed I found Nyaruach a place to stay and promised to find money to put her back into school. Sometimes I'd stop to think about the miracle that had brought us back together and wonder what others might lie ahead for us. But then I'd feel sad when I listened to Nyaruach weeping at my coldness.

'You don't even want me here after all I did to reach Kenya,' she would tell me.

As time passed, Nyaruach and I learned to accept each other, and I knew that now, more than ever, I had to find success because her life was in my hands. I was still working hard at my music and writing song after song as I dreamed of recording an album, but Nyaruach didn't like it at all.

'Why are you doing this?' she would sometimes cry. 'Making music is for drunks to earn money for alcohol, for singing in the villages, not to earn yourself respect. You should be getting educated, Jal, and looking for a job in an office or learning to be a doctor. That is how you will get a name, not by singing.'

'But this is what I do now, Nyaruach,' I told her. 'Music makes me and other people happy.'

She couldn't understand it and I had no words to describe why music was so important in my life. But meeting Nyaruach was to change both of us for ever.

The beats calmed me as they filled the studio. It was the music to a new song I'd written called 'Gua'. The word meant 'power' in Arabic and 'peace' in my mother tongue, Nuer, and the lyrics were a mixture of Arabic, Nuer, Dinka, and English – all the languages I'd used growing up. 'Gua' was unlike any other song I'd ever written.

For so long I'd thought only of writing songs about God, wanting to thank Him for His help and too afraid of the past to risk talking about it and making people pity me. But I'd thought again and again of what I saw in Nyaruach's eyes every time I sat down to write after she'd arrived in Nairobi. War had scarred her, just as it had me, and we were just two among a people who all knew death by his first name. The despair was like the never-ending desert I'd once marched across. Should I speak of such things in my songs?

At first I had felt afraid. My Christian music made Mrs Mumo happy and I didn't want to cause her any trouble. Her husband, Jasper, had recently died and it was hard for everyone, but most of all for her. There was not enough food in the house, not enough money for rent, because Mrs Mumo gave it all to her work in the community, and life was a struggle. I also knew the Christians who'd supported me liked my songs. Religious music is popular in Kenya, and I doubted if my fans would want to listen to something different from a singer who'd made his name with it. I had a responsibility to CASSY and had to keep raising money.

But the thoughts of my family and country would not go

away. The peace talks between north and south Sudan that had started in 2002 were coming to an end even though hunger, destruction, and bloodshed still stalked black Africans. In 2003 Khartoum had started attacking an area in western Sudan called Darfur after rebels, angry at the government's neglect of a region that had supported it, had risen up. To crush them, government planes had started bombing as an armed Arab militia called the *janjaweed* slaughtered men, women, and children in violence echoing all I had seen as a child. But where Muslim and Christian had once fought each other, the government was now killing its own – black Muslims who'd fought and died for it in the war against the South. Thousands had died, even more forced to flee, and as I looked into my sister's eyes, I felt more and more that this was something I wanted to write about. I understood now that the war in Sudan wasn't simply about Islam against Christianity, one tribe against another. Muslims, angry at what Khartoum had done, had joined the SPLA, and Khartoum was attacking Africans who'd supported it. I had learned to stop hating *jallabas* in the years since I started learning to forgive, but how could such despair ever be defeated? Martin Luther King had believed in soul force, and maybe I should use it now to talk about peace.

Andrew Mumo and Philip had encouraged me to write 'Gua', but it was Mrs Mumo who'd finally convinced me.

'Happy are the peacemakers, for they will be called the children of God,' she'd told me. 'Remember Martin Luther King – he chose love and brotherhood to fight his war, and in this way many white people joined his fight.'

Now my sister Nyaruach, and my friends Lam and Manaseh, were all preparing to sing with me. I'd asked her to make this record with me because I wanted her to be part of it, just as I wanted Lam and Manaseh, who'd seen war as I had, to sing too. We were all witnesses and, like so many children of Sudan, wanted our people to return to their lands, for the killing to end.

As the chorus started, they sang:

I will be so happy when there's peace in Sudan
When people come back to Sudan, my heart will be filled
*   with joy.*

Manaseh started to rap:

Just hold on a minute, wait for a minute
How will it be if there is peace in Sudan?
Our hands will be raised, our God will be praised
When my people will plant seed in their land
When my people will be free in their land.

I took over the lyric:

I can't, I can't wait for the day
When I will see no more tears, no more fear, no cry
No tribalism, nepotism, and racism in my motherland
I can't wait for that day when the wonderful people go
*   back home*
And plant their nation in this generation.

I shivered as the song ended, and I looked at Lam, Manaseh, and Nyaruach. This song was powerful, but would people want to listen to us?

I had sat my A-levels at Brookhouse in June 2004 and passed with low grades. But music was the most important thing in my life now, and I'd learned Mr Mehta had been right – some people made big money from it. I'd been paid $300 to perform for just one night after the organisers of a women's rights event asked the man who'd sung 'Praise the Lord' to perform for them. My eyes nearly fell out of my head when they handed me the money. I'd never earned so much before, and although it soon disappeared after paying the band, taking Lam out to eat and to watch a movie, buying clothes for Nyaruach, and giving some to Mrs Mumo for her work with street children and CASSY, it proved to me that music might be something I could do as a career.

Writing 'Gua' had also inspired me and I'd recorded enough songs for an album with money given to me by Brookhouse and Peter Moszynski's friends Andrew and Jennifer Shand. It included another peace song called 'Why?' as well as 'Praise the Lord' and 'All We Need'. But of course there were hurdles to overcome. The studio where I'd recorded was robbed and the whole album disappeared. Luckily I still had rough cuts that I could use, but money was an even bigger problem. Just as I'd needed it to release and promote 'Praise the Lord', I had to find more if I was to do the same for 'Gua'.

I wondered if the charities that had helped me in Pinyudu when I was a child might help me again now. Peace between north and south Sudan was soon to be signed, and aid organisations were keen to help ordinary people be part of that. But they wouldn't support individuals, so Lam, another former *jenajesh* called JKP, and I set up the South Sudanese Artists Association and went to an American development organisation called Pact, which gave out USAID money. We asked for funds both to help the release of 'Gua' and to pay for Lam and another Lost Boy to record their own peace albums. The people at USAID could see we were serious and CASSY had done good work, but in inter- view after interview we were asked about our music, what we wanted to do, and how we would spend the money. I under- stood that some might try to cheat on such grants, but it was frustrating all the same. Finally, though, in late 2004 we heard the news we'd been waiting for – we'd been awarded $10,000. Now I just needed to know if people would like my new songs.

The ninth of January 2005 was a historic day for my people as the Comprehensive Peace Agreement between north and south Sudan was signed in Nairobi. Although the fighting continued in

Darfur, it was said it would never end without peace between north and south. Years of negotiation had finally finished between the SPLA, other rebel groups, and Khartoum, and the agreement granted autonomy to the South for six years, at the end of which a referendum would take place on full independence. Both sides kept their armies but agreed to a ceasefire and how oil revenues would be split in the future. I didn't feel any hope, though, because I believed Khartoum was only making peace to prepare for another war against my people. Peace for us wouldn't be real until roads, schools, homes, and hospitals had been built, families reunited, and children educated to be leaders. Peace may be negotiated by politicians, but it is something written in hearts and minds, not on pieces of paper.

To celebrate the signing of the agreement, I was invited to be one of the acts performing at a big concert in Nairobi. The fame that 'Praise the Lord' had brought me had not disappeared, and I was quite well known now. But I felt anxious about performing in front of all the top leaders from Khartoum and the SPLA. I'd performed at another signing ceremony in Naivasha a few weeks before and been warned to watch my mouth before I went onstage – just as I had been years before after speaking to Peter Moszynski and other journalists about the use of *jena-jesh* in Sudan. I'd felt intimidated as I'd sung and was worried again when I arrived with the Reborn Warriors at the stadium. I was right to be because I was arrested and only released when Nyaruach, my friends, and fans stood outside the cells and asked to be arrested themselves. No one told me why I'd been held, but I wondered if my new songs were going to cause me even more trouble.

Later that day I left for Kakuma refugee camp, where I was going to shoot a video for 'Gua'. DJ Moz and a big group called the Gospel Fathers were also on the trip because we were all going to perform for the children at the camp. Being there – the dust, heat, and smells – reminded me of the boy I'd once been. I looked at the children born in the camp, the only world they had ever known, and felt overwhelmed because I had nothing to give but my music. Emma McCune and Mrs Mumo had taken me far away from a place like this, but would there be others like them to help these children? When would my people ever be able to return to their own lands?

When I got back to Nairobi, I started organising a big concert to launch the 'Gua' album with the rest of the USAID money. It was being held at Nairobi Cinema, and Mrs Mumo's son Michael was in charge of it for me. The video I'd shot at Kakuma was being played on *Stomp* and DJ Moz had also been playing 'Gua' on his show for several weeks now. My fans seemed to like it, really like it, and the song climbed the charts as hundreds of people bought tickets for the concert, which was being held in late February. We also gave free tickets to young people from the slums because I wanted as many people as possible to hear 'Gua' and feel its message.

I felt excited but afraid. 'Gua' was another hit, but I just wanted to know if people would feel my music in the way I hoped they would, to see an audience before me and know my new songs were speaking to their hearts as powerfully as the old ones did.

CHAPTER 25

I stared out at the sea of faces and started to sing.

'When I am broke . . .' I rapped.

'I just have to praise the Lord,' the audience screamed back.

Music boomed out of the speakers as people shouted louder and danced harder with each song. I was onstage and the crowd were cheering my Christian music. But I knew they really wanted 'Gua' – the song that had many people talking.

I felt a rush of nerves as I thought of rapping it. I was a better performer now but still wasn't the best. My voice pained me sometimes on the days when the the past rose up. I never knew when it would happen, but I'd sometimes wake from terrible dreams and know I wouldn't escape the darkness that day. But what I lacked in my voice, I made up for in the passion of my performance. It was the only time that emotions locked inside me came free, and now I felt light as I stood onstage. My fans were cheering, their hands in the air and bodies moving to the beats, their happiness washing through me like a drug and rubbing out everything else. Kenyans and Sudanese were in the audience, young people and old, and my friends such as Mrs Mumo, Andrew, Michael, and kids from Brookhouse.

The song finished and the crowd fell silent for a moment. It was time to perform 'Gua' and I turned to look at the Reborn Warriors. We knew people loved the song, but could they really feel it? Now I would find out.

'I will be so happy when there's peace in Sudan,' the backing singers started to chant.

I looked deep into the faces before me.

Oh, wait, wait, let's think
Think how it would be
If there was peace in Sudan
Let's sing, sing, 'O my Lord
Hear our prayer, hear our prayer'
It will be so good when there'll be peace
In my homeland Sudan.

Memories of the past were before me as I looked into the present. My chest tightened and I took a deep breath.

Not one sister will be forced into marriage
And not one cow will be taken by force
And not one person will starve from hunger again
I can't compare to anything
The time when people will understand each other
And there's peace in my homeland Sudan.

The crowd were dancing and jumping, drinking in each line as I dropped the words. People screamed and I could see cameras flashing. I felt strange inside, as if something were breaking within me as I sang. Pictures flooded through me – villages burning, my brothers and sisters running from war, the blackened bones of children lying amid a ruined village, the shadow of government planes overhead. I wanted a real end to this war. I wanted the world to hear.

. . . We shall rebuild our land
The whole world will respect us
And we shall rebuild our land
With one hand, one heart,

With one blood, one body
Because we are one.

My eyes burned as the song came to an end and I stood still. I could see people weeping and arms uplifted. The sound moved over me and the energy washed through me. These people had listened and heard. They understood what I was trying to say.

I reached up to wipe away the tears on my cheeks. They had been buried inside me for so long but would not be dammed up now. At last I was speaking – not about what I'd seen but what I hoped to see. I had a dream, and although I was just one voice in a chorus calling for an end to suffering, in this moment the audience were looking at me and waiting for my next words.

'Your story is a blow on the devil's face because God listened when you prayed,' Mrs Mumo had always told me.

I stared at the crowd. Should I tell them who I really was and why I was here? Should I hide myself any longer, or should I tell my story?

'The war in Sudan began long ago. And I was one of the many children caught up in it.'

People hushed as I spoke, and as I looked at their faces, I knew they were hearing me. I started to tell them about my life.

That night marked the release of the *Gua* album and it became a hit. My friends and I were kept busy taking CDs to the shops where they were being sold and collecting the money when they were. We were all pleased because it meant we could eat that day, but most of what I earned still went to CASSY. Within weeks of the concert, it wasn't just people in Kenya listening to what I was saying. Journalists from England and America wrote about me in *USA Today* and *The Observer* in London, and I told them a little about my life as a *jenajesh*. I was just glad that people were hearing my story because then they would learn that of my people. Nyaruach, Andrew Mumo, Philip, and all my friends were happy for me.

'People look up to you now,' my sister would tell me.

'This is just the beginning of your journey to great things,' Mrs Mumo would say.

She was right. In April I flew to England to record tracks for a second album I had agreed to make called *Ceasefire*. It was to be a collaboration with a famous Sudanese musician called Abdel Gadir Salim and the record would express our hope for peace – I a Christian and he a Muslim. Peter Moszynski had been right to believe that someone in the UK would want to record my music and I felt excited as I travelled over to London. When I was there, I took part in a demonstration about the war in Darfur and wondered how the world could believe there was peace in Sudan when people were still dying? During my trip I also heard about a huge event called Live 8, which was being staged in July. Bob Geldof was in charge – the man who'd once organised Live Aid, which had fed me and other refugees when I was a child. Live 8 concerts around the world were being staged in support of the UK's Make Poverty History campaign, a call to action for ordinary people, asking them to join together to tell world leaders that poverty in Africa had to be eliminated. It was an amazing thing and then Peter told me the charity Save the Children had asked me to return to London to be an African ambassador during the event. Did this mean I was going to perform? Would I be up onstage beside Madonna and U2? I felt scared at the thought because there wasn't going to be enough money to bring the Reborn Warriors with me and I would feel lost without them.

After going back to Kenya for a few weeks, I arrived back in London in June to be told I wouldn't be performing at Live 8 because few African musicians were. I didn't understand. I had a hit single in Kenya, and so many great African musicians weren't being given a chance. How could a party be thrown for our people if none of us was invited? Didn't music fans want to hear our message? If these people really cared enough to call for change in Africa, then surely they would want to hear from its artists as well as European and American stars?

But the answer to my questions was no and I tried to forget my anger and disappointment as I performed at events. This was the greatest opportunity I'd ever had to share my music and my message, but it wasn't being given to me. Many other people felt the same way too, and a new Live 8 concert had been announced. Africa Calling, organised by Peter Gabriel, was to be held at the Eden Project in Cornwall. African artists would be performing there, and although I wanted to as well, it still seemed like a thought that had come too late for the main event. So when I met Bob Geldof at a BBC event, I seized my chance to talk to him.

He was tall, like a Sudanese, with grey, wild hair. I looked at him and asked why I wasn't performing in his concert. Mr Geldof told me I hadn't sold four million CDs so I just wasn't big enough.

'But we're here to promote fair trade!' I exclaimed. I knew I must joke with Mr Geldof to make him laugh and relax. 'This is about making poverty history and giving African artists like me a chance to perform. If my music isn't enough, then I can tell my story, tell people about the problems we face in Africa, convince people that they must help.'

But Mr Geldof told me he needed people to watch the event and the Chinese would switch off their televisions if I came on.

I looked at him, but I knew I must be respectful to the man who'd once fed me.

'You are right,' I said eventually. 'But I'll work hard, and when I sell millions of CDs, I'll be on a big stage just like yours.'

Later that day I met the future British Prime Minister Gordon Brown and an artist called Rolf Harris, and I could see both were good men who cared about Africa. I wished everyone could be the same. I wanted the chance to perform, to see if *khawaja*s could feel my message just like the audience that night in Kenya. I wanted people to know about my country, which had been forgotten for so long.

And so, when I learned I was going to perform at Africa

Calling because Peter Gabriel wanted me to, I knew it would be the biggest night of my life.

The stage was tiny, hidden in a bush of flowers and plants. In the distance, I could hear thuds coming from the main event at Africa Calling, the huge stage where thousands of people were watching artists. But I was going to perform here, hidden away from them all. Just a few people were here to see me, only a handful to listen to my music. I thought of my friends and fans at home in Kenya watching the concert in London on TV and thinking I'd soon come on-screen.

I walked on to the stage and stood in front of the microphone. I was a no one once more here in England.

'Don't be surprised to see my face this way, but I'll try to give you what I can,' I said to the people standing in the almost empty space in front of me.

I fell quiet. I had to be humble and sing from the beginning, just as I'd learned in Kenya. I remembered for a moment – performing to a handful of children when no one turned up at shows, listening to the silence as I finished singing and no one clapped. Now I must do the best I could, and I talked to the audience a little, telling them who I was and what my songs were about before the backing track began and I started rapping. Dancing around the stage, I listened to the music of home and began to lose myself.

'Why are people being killed every day?' I sang in English as I performed a song I'd written for *Ceasefire* called 'Elengwen'. 'Why are people prevented from staying together?'

Just as on *Gua*, my songs for *Ceasefire* were a mixture of all the languages I knew, so the crowd could not understand every word. But music is a language everyone speaks, rhythm is not tribal or national, and they knew where I had been and where I was now as I sang for them. I hoped they would hear me.

'Please listen to my words / Peace is what we have to work for,' I rapped. I knew I had just three songs to perform – fifteen minutes to speak to these people's hearts – and I breathed deeply as the next one started. The audience was smiling, rocking to the music, and I told myself never to judge a crowd just because it's small. The fire inside me grew as I performed, and soon the audience were making a big noise. Hearing the applause, others came to see what was happening, and by the time I'd finished about fifty people were standing in front of me. My smile grew as the number of people in front of me did. They'd heard me, I could feel it, and that was why I'd come to England.

I came offstage and did more interviews with journalists. I knew they were interested in me – a *jenajesh* was unusual in a country where children are children until eighteen, many years more than in my village at home – and afterward I wandered into the main crowd to watch the big stage. I felt happy as I danced. The white people here were kind, the energy was good. Maybe they would hear what all of us were saying today and do something different tomorrow.

But as I walked out of the crowd, a woman grabbed me and said, 'Where have you been, Emmanuel? We've been looking for you. Peter Gabriel wants to meet you. You've caused quite a stir and he wants you to perform on the main stage. You've got ten minutes, two songs.'

I couldn't believe it. Peter Gabriel wanted to see me? He wanted me to sing in front of this huge crowd?

'I've never seen you perform,' he said when I met him backstage. 'But I believe you have something important to say, so the stage will be yours.'

The roar of the crowd fills my ears and blood leaps in my veins as I wait in the wings and look out at the audience. Far into the distance, faces are turned towards the stage, and beyond them I can see the hills of Cornwall.

'And now we are pleased to welcome Sudanese rap star Emmanuel Jal to the main stage at Live 8, Africa Calling,' a voice booms out.

I step on to the stage and my legs begin to shake as excitement fills me. I can see faces smiling and hands waving in expectation. The crowd is waiting for me.

I am here. I am speaking to all these people. I have come so far.

Suddenly time stands still. The lights, the noise, the colours, bleed into nothing and the faces melt away. I am a child again.

'God will look after us,' Mama whispers as we lie on the floor.

We are hiding from the war being waged outside our *tukul*, and I cling to Mama as the sounds of bullets and screams fill my ears.

'Hush, little *makuath*,' she says softly, and I breathe in the smell of milk, which clings to her skin. 'Hush, little darling.'

I pull closer to her and listen as she speaks again. Beside me, Miri and Marna, Nakouth and Nyaruach, move closer too.

'One day we will be in a better place,' Mama tells us, and we believe her.

Staring up, the stage lights blaze white into my eyes as I move towards the microphone. It is time for me to tell my story using the music and lyrics that are my weapons now I have laid down guns and machetes for ever.

The crowd calms as I stand still. I think of Mama and the songs we once sang in a village far away. For a moment I speak to her.

'Now we are in a better place,' I say silently.

I start to sing.

'What's up, Cornwall?' I shouted, and voices thundered back at me.

'I am Emmanuel Jal,' I shouted. 'And now I'm going to teach you some songs because, even though my band isn't here, I carry them with me on a CD, so can I hear you scream?'

The music blasted out as I looked at the crowd stretching into the distance and listening to my songs – people from another world who wanted to hear about Africa, learn our message, love our music. They roared and clapped, sang and shouted as I performed, and with each moment my heart filled fuller. I could feel that I was speaking to these people, knew that even if they could not understand every word of my songs, they could hear their message. I felt as if I were flying. There was no more pain inside me. My heart filled with happiness.

Pictures, pictures in my mind. Smiles flickering in firelight as villagers sang, soldiers chanting as they marched, faces upturned in church to praise the Lord. I had come so far – a child lost in a war people had forgotten standing onstage at the world's biggest music event.

For a moment I looked down and saw a shadow of the boy I'd once been standing beside me. He was small, his eyes full of pain and his gun heavy. I stared up into the lights and the sky above me, letting the sound of the crowd seep into my heart and soul. Once, before I had learned to transform the hate burning inside this boy into love, I had wanted to leave him behind. But now I knew I never wanted to forget the message the war child had taught me. We had travelled so far together to reach this place and I would carry him with me as I started a new journey.

EPILOGUE

It is strange how life can change in an instant – I met Emma and was rescued from war, I talked to Mrs Mumo and started conquering my hatred, and I performed at Africa Calling and people a world away from mine started listening. My life changed for ever after that day, and just as I had always done, I followed every road that opened up before me. My performance attracted a lot of interest and much was written about me. There was a big hype around my music and *Ceasefire* was released in September 2005 – the same month I recorded a song for the *War Child* charity album, which also featured such acts as Coldplay, Radiohead, and Gorillaz. Interest in my story spread far and I was profiled in *Time* magazine and *The New York Times*. In October I attended the first African Global Hip-Hop Summit in Johannesburg and the next month was nominated for a BBC World Music Award. I also won an American Gospel Music Award for international artist of the year. Most important, I continued to spread the message in my music through campaigning work with Amnesty International and Oxfam.

I could never have dreamed of such success as I rapped in Kileleshwa Church, and if I had, then I would surely have thought all my problems would have been solved. But of course there were new ones to face so far from home in a place I hardly knew. At times I felt more alone than I ever had before. I'd left friends and family behind in Kenya, and my relationship with Peter Moszynski broke down soon after I arrived in England. I was forced to learn hard lessons about life in a country where I didn't know the rules. Most of the money I earned from gigs was sent back to Nyaruach, CASSY, and to help Mrs Mumo's work in the slums, which meant that some nights I ended up sleeping on a park bench because I had nothing left. But I could not use my money when I knew others needed it so much. I told no one what was happening to me because I did not want people to know and pretended to those I met in England that I had somewhere to stay, until a Sudanese friend offered me a room. It was a hard time, but I told myself I had sown a seed and happy are those who sow in tears for they shall reap in joy.

Being in England, away from Africa and the people I knew, also freed me to hear music in a new way, and as I listened to Run-D.M.C., Public Enemy, Gospel Gangstaz, Nas, and Tupac, I realised they were talking about their situations and lives in their lyrics. It made me think deeply about what more I could do with my songs. I had rapped about God and peace, but was it now time to tell my whole story? Would it be the most powerful message I could give to people?

The first autobiographical song I wrote was called 'War Child' and said more about me than anything else I'd performed.

I believe I've survived for a reason
To tell my story, to touch lives

Lost my mother and father in this battle
My brothers too perished in this struggle
All my life I've been hiding in the jungle
The pain I carry
Is too much to handle
Who's there please to light my candle?
Is there anyone to hear my cry?
Here I am pale and dry
Born a leader and I wonder why

I'm a war child.

Soon a Sudanese R&B singer I'd met called Ayak introduced me to two men who would help me transform myself as an artist. One was a DJ and producer called Silvastone, who toured with Ayak and me; another was a songwriter and producer called Roachie. Both men were interested in me as a musician, and while they encouraged me to tell my story, they also helped me to grow as an artist. We started writing together, and song after song flooded out of me – the war in Sudan, the horrors I had seen, and the disappointment I felt when I heard rappers in the West boast about guns. My life's experiences poured into my music, and one song that meant a lot was called 'Emma'.

> *I got a reason for being on this earth 'cause I*
> *Know more than many what a life is worth*
> *Now that I got a chance to stand my ground*
> *I'm gonna run over mountains leaps and bounds*
> *I ain't an angel, hope I'll be one soon*
> *If I am I wanna be like Emma McCune.*

There was just one thing I could never speak or write about – the day of the raid in Juba. It tormented me and I could never imagine myself telling my secret. I would talk about my war but not that, and while American rappers seemed to wear violence like a badge of honour, I did not want people to know me for that.

As the months passed, I wrote more and more with Roachie. I'd written the words for 'War Child' and had an idea for the chorus, and he encouraged me to tell even more of my truth as we developed the song. He helped me transform the notes in my head into a tune, the words in my heart into a lyric, as my music moved away from gospel into rap mixed with the African beats and choruses of my childhood.

'Don't worry about the way you sound or try to be like anybody else,' he told me. 'Just be you.'

I knew I wanted to find another record deal. I'd had one for *Ceasefire*, but that had come to an end, and while some record labels were interested, I could only wait to see if anyone would have enough faith to sign me. As 2005 moved into 2006, I told myself I must keep telling my story and hope that a few of those who listened would really hear. A hundred miles begins with just one step.

Roachie and Silvastone were talking as we sat in the dressing room, but I was silent. We were about to perform at Joe's Pub in New York in October 2006, and I felt nervous because I had to sing well tonight. A lot of people from the music industry would be watching, and my old friend and sponsor Andrew Shand was also coming.

We'd arrived in America a couple of weeks before at the end of a big year. I'd done the African Soul Rebels tour around the UK, performed at the WOMAD festival of world music, and 'Gua' had been used on the hit TV show *ER*. Another of my songs, called 'Baai', was also going to be featured in the movie *Blood Diamond*, and now I was being filmed by a documentary maker as I toured with the National Geographic All Roads Film Festival.

I'd been so excited about coming to the USA. I was going to perform my music in front of people who knew it better than anyone else, the place where hip-hop and rap had been born, and I'd felt like a star when we were picked up in a huge car at Los Angeles airport. I soon discovered of course that everything in America was big – hotel rooms, beds, and plates of food – and I liked all of them. The only thing that confused me was that everyone smiled so much I didn't know who was real and who was not. The worst were the record-label people who wanted to talk about signing me. I might know my way in the jungle of Africa, but here a hyena, a snake, or a rat all looked the same. People said they liked my music, but then they'd tell me I had to change it.

'It's too gospel, too personal, too political, too niche,' they'd say.

The next place I performed was New Orleans. I knew it was a city of music with a history of slavery, but I was shocked to find parts of the city still torn apart after being devastated by floods the year before. Touring the area that had been worst hit reminded me of a war zone. Houses had been destroyed, communities torn apart, and thousands had fled their homes. I couldn't believe that something so terrible had happened in America and people were still suffering. So much money was being spent on wars, but none seemed to be left for the poor. I met many victims of the flooding, and their stories moved me as I looked at them and knew they felt despair just as I had once known.

Next we flew to Washington, DC, where I performed again and met many important people for the filming of the documentary about my life, including Andrew Natsios, the presidential special envoy to Sudan. I was lucky to meet him because I knew he would be talking to Mr Bush himself about my country, and even though some politicians are like men who play women, I could see Mr Natsios was serious about Sudan and the problems still affecting Darfur. I also performed for staff who worked for senators and congressmen on Capitol Hill, and for children at a school in a district of Washington where guns and drugs were common. I was a war child from Africa and they were the war children of America. I hoped my message of peace would speak to them.

But the most important job I had to do while I was here was still to come. I had become a spokesman for the Control Arms campaign, which was calling for an international arms-trade treaty, and three years of work by Oxfam, Amnesty International, and the International Action Network on Small Arms would soon end with a UN vote on a resolution to agree to start talks about introducing a treaty. My job was to perform at a reception for diplomats and lobby them to support it. I knew tighter arms controls could mean the difference between life and death for so many people. Government and rebel groups were killing citizens using guns and arms sold to them from all over the world, and I had seen what this meant – children loading guns before firing them, *jenajesh* screaming as they were hit by shells, and women and children lying dead after being hit by rockets. But who had supplied Sudan with the weapons we used to kill each other? How much blood money had been made?

Now, as I sat in Joe's Pub these thoughts lay heavy on me. Tonight I would perform in front of friends, but in a few days I'd have to move the hearts of UN diplomats. I was just a tiny part of the Control Arms campaign, but I wanted to do all I could. Would the politicians hear me? Was my music powerful enough to speak to them or even this audience?

'Emmanuel?' Roachie said as he stood up. 'We'd better get out there. The place is packed.'

I looked at him. Music people, friends from Oxfam, Andrew Shand, and fans were all waiting and each expected so much of me in different ways.

'If you don't make this audience forget their drinks and start to dance, then you're no good as an artist,' Roachie told me with a smile as we walked on to the stage. 'You've got to perform as if it's the last time, as if you're going to die.'

Once again I forgot everything as I walked onstage to perform and the beat lifted me up. It moved through me as the crowd started to dance. I stared at the faces, felt the music pound through me as I sang.

I am my music. My music is me.

My dreams are like torments
My every moment
Voices in my brain
Of friends that were slain
Friends like Lual
Who died by my side from starvation

In the barren jungle
And the desert plains
Next was I . . .
But Jesus heard my cry
As I was tempted to eat the rotten flesh of my comrade
He gave me comfort

We used to raid villages
Stealing chickens, goats, and sheep
Anything we could eat
I knew it was rude
But we needed food
And therefore I was

Forced to sin
Forced to sin to make a living.

When the show was finished, I stepped offstage to sign *Ceasefire* CDs, and as I talked and laughed with people, two white women I'd recognised in the audience earlier walked up to me. One was older with blonde hair, and the girl with her was dark. She looked about seventeen and was silent as the woman started to speak.

'We love the way you perform so much that we've followed your tour. I saw you in Los Angeles, flew to Washington, and now we're here. I thought it was important that my daughter heard your story.'

I was shocked. This woman had travelled thousands of miles to see me? A Lost Boy whom no one had wanted to find for so long?

'We admire your passion and your music is wonderful,' she continued. 'You have so much to say to the world and you do it in a way that everyone can hear.'

I had no words to speak back and the girl was silent too. But finally she lifted her eyes to mine.

'Your story has inspired me,' she said softly, and my heart felt full as I heard those words.

'Thank you,' I told her.

We smiled at each other.

AFTERWORD

Two million died during the war in Sudan – more than the casualties of Angola, Bosnia, Chechnya, Kosovo, Liberia, the Persian Gulf, Sierra Leone, Somalia, and Rwanda put together. I do not try to reduce the suffering in those countries by using this number, only to explain how high a price my people have paid in a war fought largely over oil. I am ashamed the world promised after the Second World War that genocide would never happen again, but then came Rwanda and now Darfur. It seems as if good things are signed on paper but the world turns its back when it comes to Africa.

Everyone in my country has a story to tell, but I am telling mine to speak for all those who can't. I'm still a soldier, fighting with my pen and paper, for peace till the day I cease. For now, the suffering in Sudan has not ended: the killing continues in Darfur, many of the four million refugees from Sudan wait to return home, and in May 2008 fighting broke out between northern and southern forces in the disputed oil-rich town of Abyei. The peace agreement between north and south still holds but is fragile.

It has been hard for me to tell my story – even physically painful at times as I've freed memories buried deep inside. Sometimes my nose bled uncontrollably or dreams would trap me until I woke up to see war still flashing before my eyes as I lay alone on a bed. After nights like those, I would sit silently for hours the next day, trying to ease the pain in my chest and calm the feelings inside.

The day of the raid in Juba was one of the hardest to remember because I had never spoken of it before. I feel no guilt about that day because I was a child who took part in killings as the hatred and sorrow built up over years was released in mob violence. I did not kill in cold blood, I killed in war. But that day has tormented me – just as the stories of others have.

It took many years for Nyaruach to tell me hers and that of my family, but I gradually learned that war drove them all in different directions. Nyakouth was forced into marriage at thirteen to a government commander to ensure safety for my family. Today she lives in Bantiu with her children, and I saw her when I returned to Sudan in January 2007 to film for the documentary. The happy big sister I remembered was dead; now I could only see a woman helpless to fight back and dying inside.

A warlord took Nyaruach to marry when she was a young girl, but she escaped to Khartoum, where she worked as a slave for an Arab family before fleeing to Ethiopia. Nyaruach was raped many times during the war and was around ten when it first happened. She is in Nairobi now at school, but I still find it hard to comfort her when she clings to me as she remembers.

Nyagai died during the war, and Marna became a soldier. He also now lives in Bantiu, and when I saw him on the trip home, I didn't recognise the man who'd been a small child when I left him. My little brother Miri found me with the help of a fan of my music and was smuggled out of Sudan to Kenya, where I put him into school. Baba is out of the army and in Bantiu, where Grandmother Nyapan Deng lives still.

It was sad to return to Sudan and know I didn't feel close to my family any more. But some bonds cannot be broken inside, and their stories are the ones that threaten to send me back to bitterness because we are tied together in blood. I no longer hate Arabs because my understanding has widened. I was young and blinded by rage, and now that I am older I know that if I ever fight again it will be for freedom, not hate. Not every Muslim is bad, just as not every Christian is good, and the colour of people's skins does not drive them to evil. But I still have to learn forgiveness each day, and I know I will keep doing it for the rest of my life. I hope that one day my family and I will reconnect.

I continue my activism with Oxfam. In December 2006, 153 governments voted at the United Nations to start work on developing an international arms-trade treaty, but now we must campaign to make sure it is effective. The community work I started in Nairobi with CASSY also carries on in the UK-registered charity GUA Africa, which supports seven survivors of war from Sudan and Rwanda, who are all in high school, and another who is studying medicine at university. These are the people who will rebuild their countries in the future. GUA Africa also sponsors eight children at a primary school in a Nairobi slum and hopes to find support for fifty pupils in total. My dream is to build a school in Leer, the place where Emma is buried, which will be called the Emma McCune Academy. Then I will be able to give the children from my home what Emma dreamed of for them and gave to me – education and freedom.

When I look back on my childhood, I know that communities are sometimes forced to give up their children to protect themselves. I would still like to see a world in which no child experiences what I did. In May 2008 a global report by the Coalition to Stop the Use of Child Soldiers stated that tens of thousands were still involved in conflicts worldwide. Children should be going to school, not fighting in battles, because they will still lose their life even if they survive.

I found a way to save mine through religion and music. My faith is something private, but I share my music with the world because I know it is the only thing that can speak to your mind, soul, heart, and spirit – enter into you without your permission and influence you. Music can make us happy or sad, calm or crazy, and it brings me peace and pleasure to share it. I kept my faith in it, continued believing, and in October 2007 I found someone else who did too, when I was signed to the UK record label Sonic360. My album *War Child* was released in May 2008 – three months after the documentary about my life premiered at the Berlin Film Festival. It was then shown at the Tribeca Film Festival in New York, where it won the Cadillac Award, which was voted for by festival audiences. In June 2008 I was privileged to perform at the concert to celebrate Nelson Mandela's ninetieth birthday in London.

Today poverty is what scares me – the poverty of my family, my people, and my country. I pray that one day we will not live on aid, because poverty is like a virus that torments you mentally and emotionally. It is a slow and painful death of hope, humiliating and degrading, a parasite that sucks life from everyone it touches. That is why the best investment is in human life – either spiritually or physically. Give people something to eat today and show them how to do it for themselves tomorrow; give them hope and their spiritual belief will sustain them. I am proof that one person can rise above any challenge, and if I can, then so will others if they are given the chance. Hope must never die.

FURTHER INFORMATION

• To learn about Emmanuel's music go to
www.emmanueljal.org or www.myspace.com/emmanueljal.
To hear more about the documentary on his life go to
www.warchildmovie.com.

• To find out more about GUA Africa, sponsoring a child,
or to donate, go to www.gua-africa.org.

• For further information on the life of Emma McCune
see *Till the Sun Grows Cold,* by Maggie McCune (Headline).
To learn more about the Lost Boys of Sudan see *The Journey
of the Lost Boys,* by Joan Hecht (Allswell Press).

ACKNOWLEDGEMENTS

I want to thank all the people without whom I would not have reached this far. There are so many that if I have forgotten you, then please forgive me.

Dr Kong Tut, who gave me biscuits in Pinyudu; Aliera Ayom, who cared for refugees in Pinyudu; Michael Elija Hon Top, who looked after me in prison, and his brother Khan Elija Hon Top; Lul, thank you for coming back in the desert to rescue us; Emma McCune, my guardian angel, God bless you and thank you for rescuing me; Sally Dudmesh, thank you for keeping me in your house; Peter Moszynski and Jill, I appreciate all your efforts; Mrs Jasper Mumo, thank you for opening your door to me; Mama Siongo, who prayed with me in church; Mamas Dona and Mukiama, thank you for allowing me to come into your house; Petrolina, for pushing me through my early days at school and opening your door; Andy MacDonald of Independiente, who saved me when I had nothing; Peter Gabriel, thank you for the doors you opened and believing in me; Clinton Outten (Roachie) for your studio, your music, and your inspiration; Silvastone (Davidson Lynch-Shyllon), you're a brother, man; all my bandmates from JAEEEM, the Reborn Warriors, and today; Alexis Grower, Angelina Machar, Uncle Taban, and Aunt Fathna; Dr Riek Machar, I caused you so much trouble but thank you for your patience; Maggie McCune, for giving me the most precious gift of all – education; Mr Mehta from Brookhouse, for the same; Andrew and Jennifer Shand, for supporting a stranger far away and believing in what he had to say; Sandra Laville, for making this book possible; Andrew Ray Allam, for all your kind help; Ivan Mulcahy, everyone at St Martin's Press and Little, Brown Book Group, for believing in my story; Ruth Gumm and family for making GUA Africa work; Andrew Mumo, we were destined to be brothers; Simon Alpin, Christopher Rushton Manase, Lam Tangwuar, Lisa Richards and Ayak Thikk, Pauline Barker, Yohannes Ajawin, Gonyi Ajawin, Deborah Ajawin, Philip Gitoni, Uncle John Bilia and John Paul; Ngor Deng, thank you for your support of Gua Africa and maintaining the website for the past two years; Nyagan Deng, you have loved through all the years; Dad, thank you for bringing me into this world; Mama – wherever you are, rest in peace, you planted faith inside me and it was a strong seed that helped me survive; my brothers and sisters, I thank God for you. I love you and, although the war separated us, I'm sure that one day we will all reconnect. Kemi Davies, you're a wonder girl. Megan Lloyd Davies – I don't want to thank you because you were a pain in the ass. I would also like to thank God for keeping me alive and helping me learn that my pain is a blessing to me.